T0355179

The Second
JIM CORBETT
Omnibus

OUP India's Omnibus collection offers readers
a comprehensive coverage of works of enduring
value, attractively packaged for easy reading.

THE SECOND
JIM
OMNIBUS
CORBETT

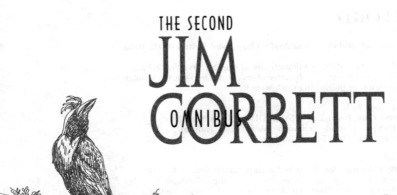

MY INDIA
JUNGLE LORE
TREE TOPS

OXFORD
UNIVERSITY PRESS

OXFORD
UNIVERSITY PRESS

22 Workspace, 2nd Floor, 1/22 Asaf Ali Road, New Delhi 110002, India

Oxford University Press is a department of the University of Oxford.
It furthers the University's objective of excellence in research, scholarship,
and education by publishing worldwide in

Oxford   New York
Auckland Cape Town Dar es Salaam Hong Kong Karachi
Kuala Lumpur Madrid Melbourne Mexico City Nairobi
New Delhi Shanghai Taipei Toronto

With offices in
Argentina Austria Brazil Chile Czech Republic France Greece
Guatemala Hungary Italy Japan Poland Portugal Singapore
South Korea Switzerland Thailand Turkey Ukraine Vietnam

Oxford is a registered trade mark of Oxford University Press
in the UK and in certain other countries.

Published in India
by Oxford University Press, New Delhi

Illustrated by Prashanto, Sanjib Singha, S.Das, Nilabho, and Dean Gasper

Typeset in Lapidary333BT, 12.5/15.3
by Eleven Arts, Keshav Puram, Delhi 110 035
Printed in India by Rakmo Press, New Delhi 110 020

CONTENTS

Tree Tops

MY INDIA

DEDICATION

If you are looking for a history of India, or for an account of the rise and fall of the British raj, or for the reason for the cleaving of the subcontinent into two mutually antagonistic parts and the effect this mutilation will have on the respective sections, and ultimately on Asia, you will not find it in these pages; for though I have spent a lifetime in the country, I lived too near the seat of events, and was too intimately associated with the actors, to get the perspective needed for the impartial recording of these matters.

In my India, the India I know, there are four hundred million people, ninety per cent of whom are simple, honest, brave, loyal, hard-working souls whose daily prayer to God, and to whatever Government is in power, is to give them security of life and of property to enable them to enjoy the fruits of their labours. It is of these people, who are admittedly poor, and who are often described as 'India's starving millions', among whom I have lived and whom I love, that I shall endeavour to tell in the pages of this book, which I humbly dedicate to my friends, the poor of India.

CONTENTS

INTRODUCTION

Having read my dedication you may ask: 'Who are these poor of India that you mention?' 'What do you mean by "My India"?' The questions are justified. The world has developed the habit of using the word 'Indian' to denote an inhabitant of the great peninsula that stretches upwards of two thousand miles from north to south, and as much from east to west. Geographically the term may pass muster, but when it comes to applying it to the people themselves one should not, without further explanation, use a description whose looseness has already led to infinite misunderstanding. The four hundred million people of India are divided horizontally by race, tribe, and caste into a far greater diversity than exists in Europe, and they are cleft vertically by religious differences fully as deep as those which sunder any one nation from another. It was religion, not race, that split the Indian Empire into Hindustan and Pakistan. Let me, therefore, explain what I mean by the title of this book.

'My India', about which these sketches of village life and work are written, refers to those portions of a vast land which I have known from my earliest days, and where I have worked; and the simple folk whose ways and characters I have tried to depict for you are those among whom I spent the greater part of seventy years. Look at a map of India. Pick out Cape Comorin, the most southerly point of the peninsula, and run your eye straight up to where the Gangetic Plain slopes up into the foothills of the Himalayas in the north of the United Provinces. There you will find the hill station of Naini Tal, the summer seat of the Government of the United Provinces, packed from April to November with Europeans and wealthier Indians seeking escape from the heat of the plains, and occupied during the winter only by few permanent residents, of whom most of my life I was one. Now leave this hill station and run your eye down the Ganges river on its way to the sea, past Allahabad, Benares, and Patna, till you reach Mokameh Ghat, where I laboured for twenty-one years. The scenes of my sketches centre round these two points in India: Naini Tal and Mokameh Ghat.

In addition to many footpaths, Naini Tal is accessible by a motor road of which we are justly proud, for it has the reputation of being the best-aligned and the best-maintained hill road in India. Starting at the railway terminus of Kathgodam the road, in its course of twenty-two miles, passes through forests where occasionally tiger and the dread hamadryad are to be seen, and climbs 4,500 feet by easy gradients to Naini Tal. Naini Tal can best be described as an open valley running east and west, surrounded on three sides by hills, the highest of which, Cheena, rises to a height of 8,569 feet. It is open at the end from which the motor road approaches it. Nestling in the valley is a lake a little more than two miles in circumference, fed at the upper end by a perennial spring and overflowing at the other end where the motor road terminates. At the upper and lower ends of the valley there are bazaars and the surrounding wooded hills are dotted with residential houses, churches, schools, clubs, and hotels. Near the margin of the lake are boat houses, a picturesque Hindu temple, and a very sacred rock shrine presided over by an old Brahmin priest who has been a lifelong friend of mine.

Geologists differ in their opinion as to the origin of the lake, some attributing it to glaciers and landslides, others to volcanic action. Hindu legends, however, give the credit for the lake to three ancient sages, Atri, Pulastya, and Pulaha. The sacred book *Skanda-Puran* tells how, while on a penitential pilgrimage, these three sages arrived at the crest of Cheena and, finding no water to quench their thirst, dug a hole at the foot of the hill and syphoned water into it from Manasarowar, the sacred lake in Tibet. After the departure of the sages the goddess Naini arrived and took up her abode in the waters of the lake. In course of time forests grew on the sides of the excavation and, attracted by the water and the vegetation, birds and animals in great numbers made their home in the valley. Within a radius of four miles of the goddess's temple I have, in addition to other animals, seen tiger, leopard, bear, and *sambhar*, and in the same area identified one hundred and twenty-eight varieties of birds.

Rumours of the existence of the lake reached the early administrators of this part of India, and as the hill people were unwilling to disclose the position of their sacred lake, one of these administrators, in the year 1839, hit on the ingenious plan of placing a large stone on the head of a hill man, telling him he would have to carry it until he arrived at goddess Naini's lake. After wandering over the hills for many days the man eventually got tired of carrying the stone, and led the party who were following him to the lake. The stone alleged to have been carried by the man was shown to me when I was a small boy, and when I remarked that it was a very big stone for a man to carry—it weighed about six hundred pounds—the hill man who showed it to me said, 'Yes, it is a big stone but you must remember that in those days our people were very strong'.

Provide yourself now with a good pair of field glasses and accompany me to the top of Cheena. From here you will get a bird's-eye view of the country surrounding Naini Tal. The road is steep, but if you are interested in birds, trees, and flowers you will not mind the three-mile climb and if you arrive at the top thirsty, as the three sages did, I will show you a crystal-clear spring of cold water to quench your thirst. Having rested and eaten your lunch, turn now to the north. Immediately below you is a deep well-wooded valley running down to the Kosi river. Beyond the river are a number of parallel ridges with villages dotted here and there; on one of these ridges is the town of Almora, and on another, the cantonment of Ranikhet. Beyond these again are more ridges, the highest of which, Dungar Buqual, rises to a height of 14,200 feet and is dwarfed into insignificance by the mighty mass of the snow-clad Himalayas. Sixty miles due north of you, as the crow flies, is Trisul, and to the east and to the west of this imposing 23,406-foot peak the snow mountains stretch in an unbroken line for many hundreds of miles. Where the snows fade out of sight to the west of Trisul are first the Gangotri group, then the glaciers and mountains above the sacred shrines of Kedarnath and Badrinath, and then Kamet made famous by Smythe. To the east of Trisul, and set farther back, you can just see the top of Nanda Devi (25,689 feet), the highest mountain in India. To your right front is Nanda Kot, the spotless pillow of the goddess Parvati, and a little farther east are the beautiful peaks of Panch Chuli, the 'five cooking-places' used by the Pandavas while on their way to Kailas in Tibet. At the first approach of dawn, while Cheena and the intervening hills are still shrouded in the mantle of night, the snowy range changes from indigo blue to rose pink, and as the sun touches the peaks nearest to heaven the pink gradually changes to dazzling white. During the day the mountains show up cold and white, each crest trailing a feather of powdered snow, and in the setting sun the scene may be painted pink, gold, or red according to the fancy of heaven's artist.

Turn your back now on the snows and face south. At the limit of your range of vision you will see three cities: Bareilly, Kashipur, and Moradabad. These three cities, the nearest of which, Kashipur, is some fifty miles as the crow flies, are on the main railway that runs between Calcutta and the Punjab. There are three belts of country between the railway and the foothills: first a cultivated belt some twenty miles wide, then a grass belt ten miles wide known as the Terai, and third a tree belt ten miles wide known as the Bhabar. In the Bhabar belt, which extends right up to the foothills, clearings have been made, and on this rich fertile soil, watered by many streams, villages of varying size have been established.

The nearest group of villages, Kaladhungi, is fifteen miles from Naini Tal by road, and at the upper end of this group you will see our village, Choti Haldwani, surrounded by a three-mile-long stone wall. Only the roof of our cottage, which is at the junction of the road running down from Naini Tal with the road skirting the foothills, is visible in a group of big trees. The foothills in this area are composed almost entirely of iron ore, and it was at Kaladhungi that iron was first smelted in northern India. The fuel used was wood, and as the King of Kumaon, General Sir Henry Ramsay, feared that the furnaces would consume all the forests in the Bhabar, he closed down the foundries. Between Kaladhungi and your seat on Cheena the low hills are densely wooded with sal, the trees which supply our railways with ties, or sleepers, and in the nearest fold of the ridge nestles the little lake of Khurpa Tal, surrounded by fields on which the best potatoes in India are grown. Away in the distance, to the right, you can see the sun glinting on the Ganges, and to the left you can see it glinting on the Sarda; the distance between these two rivers where they leave the foothills is roughly two hundred miles.

Now turn to the east, and before you in the near and middle distance you will see the country described in old gazetteers as 'the district of sixty lakes'. Many of these lakes have silted up, some in my lifetime, and the only ones of any size that now remain are Naini Tal, Sat Tal, Bhim Tal, and Nakuchia Tal. Beyond Nakuchia Tal is the cone-shaped hill, Choti Kailas. The gods do not favour the killing of bird or beast on this sacred hill, and the last man who disregarded their wishes—a soldier on leave during the war—unaccountably lost his footing after killing a mountain goat and, in full view of his two companions, fell a thousand feet into the valley below. Beyond Choti Kailas is the Kala Agar ridge on which I hunted the Chowgarh man-eating tiger for two years, and beyond this ridge the mountains of Nepal fade out of sight.

Turn now to the west. But first it will be necessary for you to descend a few hundred feet and take up a new position on Deopatta, a rocky peak 7,991 feet high adjoining Cheena. Immediately below you is a deep, wide, and densely wooded valley which starts on the saddle between Cheena and Deopatta and extends through Dachouri to Kaladhungi. It is richer in flora and fauna than any other in the Himalayas, and beyond this beautiful valley the hills extend in an unbroken line up to the Ganges, the waters of which you can see glinting in the sun over a hundred miles away. On the far side of the Ganges are the Siwalik range of hills—hills that were old before the mighty Himalayas were born.

THE QUEEN OF THE VILLAGE

Come with me now to one of the villages you saw in your bird's-eye view from the top of Cheena. The parallel lines you saw etched across the face of the hill are terraced fields. Some of these are no more than ten feet wide, and the stone walls supporting them are in some cases thirty feet high. The ploughing of these narrow fields, with a steep hill on one side and a big drop on the other, is a difficult and a dangerous job, and is only made possible by the use of a plough with a short shaft and of cattle that have been bred on the hills and that are in consequence small and stocky, and as sure-footed as goats. The stout-hearted people, who with

infinite labour have made these terraced fields, live in a row of
stone houses with slate roofs bordering the rough and narrow
road that runs from the Bhabar, and the plains beyond, to the
inner Himalayas. The people in this village know me, for in
response to an urgent telegram, which the whole village
subscribed to send me, and which was carried by runner to
Naini Tal for transmission, I once came hot-foot from Mokameh
Ghat, where I was working, to rid them of a man-eating tiger.

The incident which necessitated the sending of the telegram
took place at midday in a field just above the row of houses. A
woman and her twelve-year-old daughter were reaping wheat
when a tiger suddenly appeared. As the girl attempted to run to
her mother for protection the tiger struck at her, severed her
head from her body, and catching the body in mid-air bounded
away into the jungle adjoining the field, leaving the head near
the mother's feet.

Telegrams, even urgent ones, take long in transmission, and
as I had to do a journey of a thousand miles by rail and roads,
and the last twenty miles on foot, a week elapsed between the
sending of the telegram and my arrival at the village; and in the
meantime the tiger made another kill. The victim on this occasion
was a woman who, with her husband and children, had lived for
years in the compound of the house adjoining our home in Naini

Tal. This woman, in company with several others, was cutting grass on the hill above the village when she was attacked by the tiger, killed, and carried off in full view of her companions. The screams of the frightened women were heard in the village, and, while the women were running back to Naini Tal to report the tragedy, the men of the village assembled and with great gallantry drove away the tiger. Knowing—with an Indian's trust—that I would respond to the telegram they had sent me, they wrapped the body in a blanket and tied it to the topmost branch of a thirty-foot rhododendron tree. From the tiger's subsequent actions it was evident that he had been lying up close by and had watched these proceedings, for if he had not seen the body being put up in a tree he would never have found it, as tigers have no sense of smell.

When the women made their report in Naini Tal the husband of the dead woman came to my sister Maggie and told her of the killing of his wife, and at the crack of dawn next morning Maggie sent out some of our men to make a *machan* over the kill and to sit on the *machan* until I came, for I was expected to arrive that day. Materials for making the *machan* were procured at the village and, accompanied by the villagers, my men proceeded to the rhododendron tree, where it was found that the tiger had climbed the tree, torn a hole in the blanket, and carried away the body. Again with commendable courage—for they were unarmed— the villagers and my men followed up the drag for half a mile; and on finding the partly eaten body they started to put up a *machan* in an oak tree immediately above it. Just as the *machan* was completed, a sportsman from Naini Tal, who was out on an all-day shoot, arrived quite by accident at the spot and, saying he was a friend of mine, he told my men to go away, as he would sit up for the tiger himself.

So, while my men returned to Naini Tal to make their report

to me—for I had arrived in the meantime—the sportsman, his gunbearer, and a man carrying his lunch basket and a lantern, took up their positions on the *machan*. There was no moon, and an hour after dark the gunbearer asked the sportsman why he had allowed the tiger to carry away the kill, without firing at it. Refusing to believe that the tiger had been anywhere near the kill, the sportsman lit the lantern; and as he was letting it down on a length of string, to illuminate the ground, the string slipped through his fingers and the lantern crashed to the ground and caught fire. It was the month of May, when our forests are very dry, and within a minute the dead grass and brushwood at the foot of the tree were burning fiercely. With great courage the sportsman shinned down the tree and attempted to beat out the flames with his tweed coat, until he suddenly remembered the man-eater and hurriedly climbed back to the *machan*. He left his coat, which was on fire, behind him.

The illumination from the fire revealed the fact that the kill was indeed gone, but the sportsman at this stage had lost all interest in kills, and his anxiety now was for his own safety, and for the damage the fire would do to the Government forest. Fanned by a strong wind the fire receded from the vicinity of the tree and eight hours later a heavy downpour of rain and hail extinguished it, but not before it had burnt out several square miles of forest. It was the sportsman's first attempt to make contact with a man-eater and, after his experience of first nearly having been roasted and later having been frozen, it was also his last. Next morning, while he was making his weary way back to Naini Tal by one road, I was on my way out to the village by another, in ignorance of what had happened the previous night.

At my request the villagers took me to the rhododendron tree and I was amazed to see how determined the tiger had been to regain possession of his kill. The torn blanket was some twenty-five feet from the ground, and the claw marks on the tree, the condition of the soft ground, and the broken brushwood at the foot of it, showed that the tiger had climbed and fallen off the tree at least twenty times before he eventually succeeded in tearing a hole in the blanket and removing the body. From this spot the tiger had carried the body half a mile, to the tree on which the machan had been built. Beyond this point the fire had obliterated all trace of a drag but, following on the line I thought the tiger would have taken, a mile farther on I stumbled on the charred head of the woman. A hundred yards beyond this spot there was heavy cover which the fire had not reached and for hours I searched this cover, right down to the foot of the valley five miles away, without, however, finding any trace of the tiger. (Five people lost their lives between the accidental arrival of the sportsman at the machan, and the shooting of the tiger.)

I arrived back in the village, after my fruitless search of the cover, late in the evening, and the wife of the headman prepared for me a meal which her daughters placed before me on brass plates. After a very generous, and a very welcome meal—for I had eaten nothing that day—I picked up the plates with the intention of washing them in a nearby spring. Seeing my intention the three girls ran forward and relieved me of the plates, saying, with a toss of their heads and a laugh, that it would not break their caste—they were Brahmins—to wash the plates from which the White Sadhu had eaten.

The headman is dead now and his daughters have married and left the village, but his wife is alive, and you who are accompanying me to the village, after your bird's-eye view from Cheena, must be prepared to drink the tea, not made with water but with rich fresh milk sweetened with jaggery, which she will brew for us. Our approach down the steep hillside facing the village has been observed and a small square of frayed carpet and two wicker chairs, reinforced with *ghooral* skins, have been set ready for us. Standing near these chairs to welcome us is the wife of the headman; there is no purdah here and she will not be embarrassed if you take a good look at her, and she is worth looking at. Her hair, snow-white now was raven-black when I first knew her, and her cheeks, which in those far-off days had a bloom on them, are now ivory-white, without a single crease or wrinkle. Daughter of a hundred generations of Brahmins, her blood is as pure as that of the ancestors who founded her line. Pride of pure ancestry is inherent in all men, but nowhere is there greater *respect* for pure ancestry than there is in India. There are several different castes of people in the village this dear old lady administers, but her rule is never questioned and her word is law, not because of the strong arm of retainers, for of these she has none, but because she is a Brahmin, the salt of India's earth.

The high prices paid in recent years for field produce have brought prosperity—as it is known in India—to this hill village, and of this prosperity our hostess has had her full share. The string of fluted gold beads that she brought as part of her dowry are still round her neck, but the thin silver necklace has been deposited in the family bank, the hole in the ground under the cooking-place, and her neck is now encircled by a solid gold band. In the far-off days her ears were unadorned, but now she has a number of thin gold rings in the upper cartilage, and from her nose hangs a gold ring five inches in diameter, the weight of which is partly carried by a thin gold chain looped over her right ear. Her dress is the same as that worn by all high-caste hill women: a shawl, a tight-fitting bodice of warm material, and a voluminous print skirt. Her feet are bare, for even in these advanced days the wearing of shoes among our hill folk denotes that the wearer is unchaste.

The old lady has now retired to the inner recesses of her house to prepare tea, and while she is engaged on this pleasant task you can turn your attention to the *bania's* shop on the other side of the narrow road. The *bania*, too, is an old friend. Having greeted us and presented us with a packet of cigarettes he has gone back to squat cross-legged on the wooden platform on which his wares are exposed. These wares consist of the few articles that the village folk and wayfarers needed in the way of *atta*, rice, *dal*, ghee, salt, stale sweets purchased at a discount in the Naini Tal bazaar, hill potatoes fit for the table of a king, enormous turnips so fierce that when eaten in public they make the onlookers' eyes water, cigarettes and matches, a tin of kerosene oil, and near the platform and within reach of his hand an iron pan in which milk is kept simmering throughout the day .

As the *bania* takes his seat on the platform his few customers gather in front of him. First is a small boy, accompanied by an even smaller sister, who is the proud possessor of one pice,[1] all of which he is anxious to invest in sweets. Taking the pice from the small grubby hand the *bania* drops it into an open box. Then, waving his hand over the tray to drive away the wasps and files, he picks up a square sweet made of sugar and curds, breaks it in half and puts a piece into each eager outstretched hand. Next comes a woman of a depressed class who has two annas to spend on her shopping. One anna is invested in *atta*, the coarse ground wheat that is the staple food of our hill folk, and two pice in the coarsest of the three qualities of *dal* exposed on the stall. With

---

[1]A pice is worth about a farthing, but is itself made up of three smaller coins called pies. Four pice make an anna, sixteen annas a rupee.

the remaining two pice she purchases a little salt and one of the fierce turnips and then, with a respectful *salaam* to the *bania*, for he is a man who commands respect, she hurries off to prepare the midday meal for her family.

While the woman is being served the shrill whistles and shouts of men herald the approach of a string of pack mules, carrying cloth from the Moradabad hand looms to the markets in the interior of the hills. The sweating mules have had a stiff climb up the road from the foothills, and while they are having a breather the four men in charge have sat down on the bench provided by the *bania* for his customers and are treating themselves to a cigarette and a glass of milk. Milk is the strongest drink that has ever been served at this shop, or at any other of the hundreds of wayside shops throughout the hills, for, except for those few who have come in contact with what is called civilization, our hill men do not drink. Drinking among women, in my India, is unknown.

No daily paper has ever found its way into the village, and the only news the inhabitants get of the outside world is from an occasional trip into Naini Tal and from wayfarers, the best-informed of whom are the packmen. On their way into the hills they bring news of the distant plains of India and on their return journey a month or so later they have news from the trading centres where they sell their wares.

The tea the old lady has prepared for us is now ready. You must be careful how you handle the metal cup filled to the brim, for it is hot enough to take the skin off your hands. Interest has now shifted from the packmen to us, and whether or not you like the sweet, hot liquid you must drink every drop of it, for the eyes of the entire village, whose guest you are, are on you; and to leave any dregs in your cup would mean that you did not consider the drink good enough for you. Others have attempted to offer recompense for hospitality but we will not make this mistake, for these simple and hospitable people are intensely proud, and it would be as great an insult to offer to pay the dear old lady for her cup of tea as it would have been to have offered to pay the *bania* for his packet of cigarettes.

So, as we leave this village, which is only one of the many thousands of similar villages scattered over the vast area viewed through your good field glasses from the top of Cheena, where I have spent the best part of my life, you can be assured that the welcome we received on arrival, and the invitation to return soon, are genuine expressions of the affection and goodwill of the people in my India for all who know and understand them.

KUNWAR SINGH

Kunwar Singh was by caste a Thakur, and the headman of Chandni Chauk village. Whether he was a good or a bad headman I do not know. What endeared him to me was the fact that he was the best and the most successful poacher in Kaladhungi, and a devoted admirer of my eldest brother Tom, my boyhood's hero.

Kunwar Singh had many tales to tell of Tom, for he accompanied him on many of his *shikar* expeditions, and the tale I like best, and that never lost anything in repetition, concerned an impromptu competition between brother Tom and a man by the name of Ellis, whom Tom had beaten by one point the previous year to win the B.P. R.A. gold medal for the best rifle-shot in India.

Tom and Ellis, unknown to each other, were shooting in the same jungle near Garuppu, and early one morning, when the mist was just rising above the tree tops, they met on the approach to some high ground overlooking a wide depression in which, at that hour of the morning, deer and pig were always to be found. Tom was accompanied by Kunwar Singh, while Ellis was accompanied by a *shikari* from Naini Tal named Budhoo, whom

Kunwar Singh despised because of
his low caste and his ignorance
of all matters connected with the
jungles. After the usual greetings, Ellis
said that, though Tom had beaten him
by one miserable point on the rifle range,
he would show Tom that he was a better game
shot; and he suggested that they should each
fire two shots to prove the point. Lots were drawn
and Ellis, winning, decided to fire first. A careful approach
was then made to the low ground, Ellis carrying the ·450 Martini–
Henry rifle with which he had competed at the B.P. R.A.
meeting, while Tom carried a ·400 D.B. express by Westley-Richards
of which he was justly proud, for few of these weapons had up
to that date arrived in India.

The wind may have been wrong, or the approach careless.
Anyway, when the competitors topped the high ground, no animals
were in sight on the low ground. On the near side of the low
ground there was a strip of dry grass beyond which the grass had
been burnt, and it was on this burnt ground, now turning green
with sprouting new shoots, that animals were to be seen both
morning and evening. Kunwar Singh was of the opinion that some
animals might be lurking in the strip of dry grass, and at his
suggestion he and Budhoo set fire to it.

When the grass was well alight and the drongos, rollers, and
starlings were collecting from the four corners of the heavens
to feed on the swarms of grasshoppers that were taking flight to
escape from the flames, a movement was observed at the farther
edge of the grass, and presently two big boar came out and went
streaking across the burnt ground for the shelter of the tree jungle
three hundred yards away. Very deliberately Ellis, who weighed
fourteen stone, knelt down, raised his rifle and sent a bullet after

the hindmost pig, kicking up the dust between its hind legs. Lowering his rifle, Ellis adjusted the back sight to two hundred yards, ejected the spent cartridge, and rammed a fresh one into the breach. His second bullet sent up a cloud of dust immediately in front of the leading pig.

This second bullet deflected the pigs to the right, bringing them broadside on to the guns, and making them increase their speed. It was now Tom's turn to shoot, and to shoot in a hurry, for the pigs were fast approaching the tree jungle, and getting out of range. Standing four-square, Tom raised his rifle and, as the two shots rang out the pigs, both shot through the head, went over like rabbits. Kunwar Singh's recital of this event invariably ended up with: 'And then I turned to Budhoo, that city-bred son of a low-caste man, the smell of whose oiled hair offended me, and said, "Did you see that, you, who boasted that your *sahib* would teach mine how to shoot? Had my *sahib* wanted to blacken the face of yours he would not have used two bullets, but would have killed both pigs with one".' Just how this feat could have been accomplished, Kunwar Singh never told me, and I never asked, for my faith in my hero was so great that I never for one moment doubted that, if he had wished, he could have killed both pigs with one bullet.

Kunwar Singh was the first to visit me that day of days when I was given my first gun. He came early, and as with great pride I put the old double-barrelled muzzle-loader into his hands he never, even by the flicker of an eyelid, showed that he had seen the gaping split in the right barrel, or the lappings of brass wire that held the stock and the barrels together. Only the good qualities of the left barrel were commented on, and extolled; its length, thickness, and the years of service it would give. And then, laying the gun aside, he turned to me and gladdened my eight-year-old heart and made me doubly proud of my possession by saying: 'You are now no longer a boy, but a man; and with this good gun you can go anywhere you like in our jungles and never be afraid, provided you learn how to climb trees; and I will now tell you a story to show how necessary it is for us men who shoot in the jungles to know how to do so.

'Har Singh and I went out to shoot one day last April, and all would have been well if a fox had not crossed our path as we were leaving the village. Har Singh, as you know, is a poor *shikari* with little knowledge of the jungle folk, and when, after seeing the fox, I suggested we should turn round and go home he laughed at me and said it was child's talk to say that a fox would bring us bad luck. So we continued on our way. We had started when the stars were paling, and near Garuppu I fired at a *chital* stag and unaccountably missed it. Later Har Singh broke the wing of a pea fowl, but though we chased the wounded bird as hard as we could it got away in the long grass, where we lost it. Thereafter, though we combed the jungles we saw nothing to shoot, and towards the evening we turned our faces towards home.

'Having fired two shots, and being afraid that the forest guards would be looking for us, we avoided the road and took a sandy *nullah* that ran through dense scrub and thorn-bamboo jungle. As we went along talking of our bad luck, suddenly a tiger came out into the *nullah* and stood looking at us. For a long minute the tiger stared and then it turned and went back the way it had come.

'After waiting a suitable time we continued on our way, when the tiger again came out into the *nullah*; and this time, as it stood and looked at us, it was growling and twitching its tail. We again stood quite still, and after a time the tiger quietened down and left the *nullah*. A little later a number of jungle fowl rose cackling out of the dense scrub, evidently disturbed by the tiger, and one of them came and sat on a *haldu* tree right in front of us. As the bird alighted on a branch in full view of us, Har Singh said he would shoot it and so avoid going home empty handed. He added that the shot would frighten away the tiger, and before I could stop him he fired.

'Next second there was a terrifying roar as the tiger came crashing through the brushwood towards us. At this spot there were some *runi* trees growing on the edge of the *nullah*, and I dashed towards one while Har Singh dashed towards another. My tree was the nearer to the tiger, but before it arrived I had climbed out of reach. Har Singh had not learnt to climb trees when a boy, as I had, and he was still standing on the ground, reaching up and trying to grasp a branch, when the tiger, after leaving me, sprang at him. The tiger did not bite or scratch Har

Singh, but standing on its hind legs it clasped the tree, pinning Har Singh against it, and then started to claw big bits of bark and wood off the far side of the tree. While it was so engaged, Har Singh was screaming and the tiger was roaring. I had taken my gun up into the tree with me, so now, holding on with my bare feet, I cocked the hammer and fired the gun off into the air. On hearing the shot so close to it the tiger bounded away, and Har Singh collapsed at the foot of the tree.

'When the tiger had been gone some time, I climbed down very silently, and went to Har Singh. I found that one of the tiger's claws had entered his stomach and torn the lining from near his navel to within a few fingers' breadth of the backbone, and that all his insides had fallen out. Here was great trouble for me. I could not run away and leave Har Singh, and not having any experience in these matters, I did not know whether it would be best to try and put all that mass of insides back into Har Singh's stomach, or cut it off. I talked in whispers on this matter with Har Singh, for we were afraid that if the tiger heard us it would return and kill us, and Har Singh was of the opinion that his insides should be put back into his stomach. So, while he lay on his back on the ground, I stuffed it all back, including the dry leaves and grass and bits of sticks that were sticking to it. I then wound my pugree round him, knotting it tight to keep everything from falling out again, and we set out on the seven-mile walk to our village, myself in front, carrying the two guns, while Har Singh walked behind.

'We had to go slowly, for Har Singh was holding the pugree in position, and on the way night came on and Har Singh said he thought it would be better to go to the hospital at Kaladhungi than to our village; so I hid the guns, and we went the extra three miles to the hospital. The hospital was closed when we arrived, but the doctor babu who lives near by was awake, and when he heard our story he sent me to call Aladia the tobacco seller, who is also postmaster at Kaladhungi and who receives five rupees pay per month from Government, while he lit a lantern and went to the hospital hut with Har Singh. When I returned with Aladia, the doctor had laid Har Singh on a string bed and, while Aladia held the lantern and I held the two pieces of flesh together, the doctor sewed up the hole in Har Singh's stomach. Thereafter the doctor, who is a very kind man of raw years and who refused to take the two rupees I offered him, gave Har Singh a drink of very good medicine to make him forget the pain in his stomach and we went home and found our womenfolk crying, for they thought we had been killed in the jungle by dacoits, or by wild animals. So you see, Sahib, how necessary it is for us men who shoot in the jungles to know how to climb trees, for if Har Singh had had someone to advise him when he was a boy, he would not have brought all that trouble on us.'[1]

[1] The *runi* tree against which the tigress—who evidently had just given birth to cubs in that area, and who resented the presence of human beings—pinned Har Singh was about eighteen inches thick, and in her rage the tigress tore away a third of it. This tree became a landmark for all who shot or poached in the Garuppu jungles until, some twenty-five years later, it was destroyed by a forest fire.

I learnt many things from Kunwar Singh during the first few years that I carried the old muzzle-loader, one of the them being the making of mental maps. The jungles we hunted in, sometimes together, but more often alone—for Kunwar Singh had a horror of dacoits and there were times when for weeks on end he would not leave his village—were many hundreds of miles square with only one road running through them. Times without number when returning from a shoot I called in at Kunwar Singh's village, which was three miles nearer the forest than my house was, to tell him I had shot a *chital* or *sambhar* stag, or maybe a big pig, and to ask him to retrieve the bag. He never once failed to do so, no matter in how great a wilderness of tree or scrub or grass jungle I had carefully hidden the animal I had shot, to protect it from vultures. We had a name for every outstanding tree, and for every water hole, game track, and *nullah*. All our distances were measured by imaginary flight of a bullet fired from a muzzle-loader, and all our directions fixed by the four points of the compass. When I had hidden an animal, or Kunwar Singh had seen vultures collected on a tree and suspected that a leopard or a tiger had made a kill, either he or I would set out with absolute confidence that we would find the spot indicated, no matter what time of day or night it might be.

After I left school and started work in Bengal I was only able to visit Kaladhungi for about three weeks each year, and I was greatly distressed to find on one of these annual visits that my old friend Kunwar Singh had fallen a victim to the curse of our foothills, opium. With a constitution weakened by malaria the pernicious habit grew on him, and though he made me many

---

Har Singh, in spite of the rough and ready treatment he received at the hands of his three friends, and in spite of the vegetation that went inside him, suffered no ill effects from his wound, and lived to die of old age.

promises he had not the moral strength to keep them. I was therefore not surprised, on my visit to Kaladhungi one February, to be told by the men in our village that Kunwar Singh was very seriously ill. News of my arrival spread through Kaladhungi that night, and next day Kunwar Singh's youngest son, a lad of eighteen, came hot-foot to tell me that his father was at death's door, and that he wished to see me before he died.

As headman of Chandni Chauk, paying Government land revenue of four thousand rupees, Kunwar Singh was an important person, and lived in a big stone-built house with a slate roof in which I had often enjoyed his hospitality. Now as I approached the village in company with his son, I heard the wailing of women coming, not from the house, but from a small one-roomed hut Kunwar Singh had built for one of his servants. As the son led me towards this hut, he said his father had been moved to it because the grandchildren disturbed his sleep. Seeing us coming, Kunwar Singh's eldest son stepped out of the hut and informed me that his father was unconscious, and that he only had a few minutes to live.

I stopped at the door of the hut, and when my eyes had got accustomed to the dim light, made dimmer by a thick pall of smoke which filled the room, I saw Kunwar Singh lying on the bare mud floor, naked, and partly covered with a sheet. His nerveless right arm was supported by an old man sitting on the floor near him, and his fingers were being held round the tail of a cow. (This custom of a dying man being made to hold the tail of a cow—preferably that of a black heifer—has its origin in the Hindu belief that when the spirit leaves its earthly body it is confronted with a river of blood, on the far side of which sits the Judge before whom the spirit must appear to answer for its sins. The heifer's tail is the only way by which the departing spirit can cross the river, and if the spirit is not provided with

means of transit it is condemned to remain on earth, to be a
torment to those who failed to enable it to appear before the
judgment seat). Near Kunwar Singh's head was a brazier with
cow-dung cakes burning on it, and by the brazier a priest was
sitting, intoning prayers and ringing a bell. Every available inch
of floor space was packed with men, and with women who were
wailing and repeating over and over again, 'He has gone! He
has gone!'

I knew men died like this in India every day, but I was not
going to let my friend be one of them. In fact, if I could help
it he would not die at all, and anyway not at present. Striding
into the room, I picked up the iron brazier, which was hotter
than I expected it to be, and burnt my hands. This I carried to
the door and flung outside. Returning, I cut the bark rope by
which the cow was tethered to a peg driven into the mud floor,
and led it outside. As these acts, which I had performed in silence,
became evident to the people assembled in the room, the hubbub
began to die down, and it ceased altogether when I took the
priest's arm and conducted him from the room. Then, standing
at the door, I ordered everyone to go outside, the order was
obeyed without a murmur or a single protest. The number of
people, both old and young, who emerged from the hut was
incredible. When the last of them had crossed the doorstep, I
told Kunwar Singh's eldest son to warm two seers of fresh milk
and to bring it to me with as little delay as possible. The man
looked at me in blank surprise, but when I repeated the order
he hurried off to execute it.

I now re-entered the hut, pulled forward a string bed which
had been pushed against the wall, picked Kunwar Singh up and
laid him on it. Fresh air, and plenty of it, was urgently needed,
and as I looked round I saw a small window which had been
boarded up. It did not take long to tear down the boards and

let a stream of clean sweet air blow directly from the jungles into the overheated room which reeked with the smell of human beings, cow dung, burnt ghee, and acrid smoke.

When I picked up Kunwar Singh's wasted frame, I knew there was a little life in it, but only a very little. His eyes, which were sunk deep into his head, were closed, his lips were blue, and his breath was coming in short gasps. Soon, however, the fresh, clean air began to revive him and his breathing became less laboured and more regular, and presently, as I sat on his bed and watched through the door the commotion that was taking place among the mourners whom I had ejected from the death-chamber, I became aware that he had opened his eyes and was looking at me; and without turning my head, I began to speak.

'Times have changed, uncle, and you with them. There was a day when no man would have dared to remove you from your own house, and lay you on the ground in a servant's hut to die like an outcaste and a beggar. You would not listen to my words of warning and now the accursed drug has brought you to this. Had I delayed but a few minutes in answering your summons this day, you know you would by now have been on your way to the burning-ghat. As headman of Chandni Chauk and the best *shikari* in Kaladhungi, all men respected you. But now you have lost that respect, and you who were strong, and who ate of the best, are weak and empty of stomach, for as we came your son told me nothing has passed your lips for sixteen days. But you are not going to die, old friend, as they told you you were. You will live for many more years, and though we may never shoot together again in the Garuppu jungles, you will not want for game, for I will share all I shoot with you, as I have always done.

'And now, here in this hut, with the sacred thread round your fingers and a *pipal* leaf in your hands, you must swear an

oath on your eldest son's head that never again will you touch
the foul drug. And this time you will, and you *shall* keep your
oath. And now, while we wait for the milk your son is bringing,
we will smoke.'

Kunwar Singh had not taken his eyes off me while I was
speaking, and now for the first time he opened his lips and
said, 'How can a man who is dying smoke?'

'On the subject of dying', I said, 'we will say no more, for
as I have just told you, you are not going to die. And as to
how we will smoke, I will show you.'

Then, taking two cigarettes from my case, I lit one and placed
it between his lips. Slowly he took a pull at it, coughed, and
with a very feeble hand removed the cigarette. But when the
fit of coughing was over, he replaced it between his lips and
continued to draw on it. Before we had finished our smoke,
Kunwar Singh's son returned carrying a big brass vessel, which
he would have dropped at the door if I had not hurriedly
relieved him of it. His surprise was understandable, for the father
whom he had last seen lying on the ground dying, was now
lying on the bed, his head resting on my hat, smoking. There
was nothing in the hut to drink from, so I sent the son back to
the house for a cup; and when he had brought it I gave Kunwar
Singh a drink of warm milk.

I stayed in the hut till late into the night, and when I left
Kunwar Singh had drunk a seer of milk and was sleeping
peacefully on a warm and comfortable bed. Before I left I warned
the son that he was on no account to allow anyone to come
near the hut; that he was to sit by his father and give him a
drink of milk every time he awoke; and that if on my return in
the morning I found Kunwar Singh dead, I would burn down
the village.

The sun was just rising next morning when I returned to

Chandni Chauk to find both Kunwar Singh and his son fast asleep and the brass vessel empty.

Kunwar Singh kept his oath, and though he never regained sufficient strength to accompany me on my *shikar* expeditions, he visited me often and died peacefully four years later in his own house and on his own bed.

MOTHI

othi had the delicate, finely chiselled features that are the heritage of all high-caste people in India, but he was only a young stripling, all arms and legs, when his father and mother died and left him with the responsibilities of the family. Fortunately it was a small one, consisting only of his younger brother and sister.

Mothi was at that time fourteen years of age, and had been married for six years. One of his first acts on finding himself unexpectedly the head of the family was to fetch his twelve-year-old wife—whom he had not seen since the day of their wedding—from her father's house in the Kota Dun, some dozen miles from Kaladhungi.

As the cultivation of the six acres of land Mothi inherited entailed more work than the four young people could tackle, Mothi took on a partner, locally known as a *sagee*, who in return for his day-and-night services received free board and lodging and half of the crops produced. The building of the communal hut with bamboos and grass procured from the jungles, under permit, and carried long distances on shoulder and on head, and the constant repairs to the hut necessitated by the violent storms that sweep the foothills, threw a heavy burden on Mothi and his helpers, and to relieve them of this burden I built them a masonry house, with three rooms and a wide veranda, on a four-foot plinth. For, with the exception of Mothi's wife who had come from a higher altitude, all of them were steeped in malaria.

To protect their crops the tenants used to erect a thorn fence round the entire village, but though it entailed weeks of hard labour, this flimsy fence afforded little protection against stray cattle and wild animals, and when the crops were on the ground the tenants, or members of their families, had to keep watch in the fields all night. Firearms were strictly rationed, and for our forty tenants the Government allowed us one single-barrelled muzzle-loading gun. This gun enables one tenant in turn to protect his crops with a lethal weapon, while the others had to rely on tin cans which they beat throughout the night. Though the gun accounted for a certain number of pigs and porcupines, which were the worst offenders, the nightly damage was considerable, for the village was isolated and surrounded by forests. So, when my handling contract at Mokameh Ghat began paying a dividend, I started building a masonry wall round the village. When completed, the wall was six feet high and three miles long. It took ten years to build, for my share of the dividends was small. If today you motor from Haldwani to Ramnagar, through Kaladhungi, you will skirt the upper end of the wall before you cross the Boar Bridge and enter the forest.

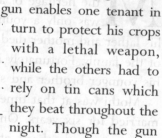

I was walking through the village one cold December morning, with Robin, my dog, running ahead and putting up covey after

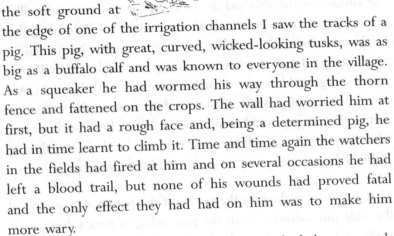

covey of grey partridge
which no one but Robin
ever disturbed—for all
who lived in the village
loved to hear them
calling at sunrise and
at sunset—when in
the soft ground at
the edge of one of the irrigation channels I saw the tracks of a
pig. This pig, with great, curved, wicked-looking tusks, was as
big as a buffalo calf and was known to everyone in the village.
As a squeaker he had wormed his way through the thorn
fence and fattened on the crops. The wall had worried him at
first, but it had a rough face and, being a determined pig, he
had in time learnt to climb it. Time and time again the watchers
in the fields had fired at him and on several occasions he had
left a blood trail, but none of his wounds had proved fatal
and the only effect they had had on him was to make him
more wary.

On this December morning the pig's tracks led me towards
Mothi's holding, and as I approached the house I saw Mothi's
wife standing in front of it, her hands on her hips, surveying the
ruin of their potato patch.

The pig had done a very thorough job, for the tubers were
not mature and he had been hungry, and while Robin cast round
to see in which direction the marauder had gone the woman
gave vent to her feelings. 'It is all Punwa's father's fault', she
said. 'It was his turn for the gun last night, and instead of staying
at home and looking after his own property he must needs go
and sit up in Kalu's wheat field because he thought there was a
chance of shooting a *sambhar* there. And while he was away, this
is what the *shaitan* has done.' No woman in our part of India

ever refers to her husband, or addresses him, by name. Before children are born he is referred to as the man of the house, and after children come is spoken of and addressed as the father of the firstborn. Mothi now had three children, of whom the eldest was Punwa, so to his wife he was 'Punwa's father', and his wife to everyone in the village was 'Punwa's mother'.

Punwa's mother was not only the hardest-working woman in our village but she also had the sharpest tongue, and after telling me in no uncertain terms what she thought of Punwa's father for having absented himself the previous night, she turned on me and said I had wasted my money in building a wall over which a pig could climb to eat her potatoes, and that if I could not shoot the pig myself it was my duty to raise the wall a few feet so that no pig could climb over it. Mothi fortunately arrived while the storm was still breaking over my head, so whistling to Robin I beat a hasty retreat and left him to weather it.

That evening I picked up the tracks of the pig on the far side of the wall and followed them for two miles, at times along game paths and at times along the bank of the Boar river, until they led me to a dense patch of thorn bushes interlaced with *lantana*. At the edge of this cover I took up position, as there was a fifty-fifty chance of the pig leaving the cover while there was still sufficient light for me to shoot by.

Shortly after I had taken up position behind a rock on the bank of the river, a *sambhar* hind started belling at the upper end of the jungle in which a few years later I was to shoot the Bachelor of Powalgarh.[1] The hind was warning the jungle folk of the presence of a tiger. A fortnight previously a party of three

[1] See *Man-eaters of Kumaon*.

guns, with eight elephants, had arrived in Kaladhungi with the express purpose of shooting a tiger which, at that time, had his headquarters in the forest block for which I had a shooting pass. The Boar river formed the boundary between my block and the block taken by the party of three guns, and they had enticed the tiger to kill in their block by tying up fourteen young buffaloes on their side of the river. Two of these buffaloes had been killed by the tiger, the other twelve had died of neglect, and at about nine o'clock the previous night I had heard the report of a heavy rifle.

I sat behind the rock for two hours, listening to the belling *sambhar* but without seeing anything of the pig, and when there was no longer any light to shoot by I crossed the river and, gaining the Kota road, loped down it, easing up and moving cautiously when passing the caves in which a big python lived, and where Bill Bailey of the Forest Department a month previously had shot a twelve-foot hamadryad. At the village gate I stopped and shouted to Mothi to be ready to accompany me at crack of dawn next morning.

Mothi had been my constant companion in the Kaladhungi jungles for many years. He was keen and intelligent, gifted with good eyesight and hearing, could move through the jungles silently, and was as brave as man could be. He was never late for an appointment, and as we walked through the dew-drenched jungle that morning, listening to the multitude of sounds of the awakening jungle folk, I told him of the belling of the *sambhar* hind and of my suspicion that she had witnessed the killing of her young one by the tiger, and that she had stayed to watch the tiger on his kill—a not uncommon occurrence—for in no other way could I account for her sustained belling. Mothi was delighted at the prospect of our finding a fresh kill, for his means only permitted of his buying meat for his family once a month, and a *sambhar*, *chital*, or pig, freshly killed by a tiger or by a leopard, was a godsend to him.

I had located the belling *sambhar* as being due north and some fifteen hundred yards from me the previous evening, and when we arrived at this spot and found no kill we started looking on the ground for blood, hair, or a drag mark that would lead us to the kill; for I was still convinced that there was a kill to be found and that the killer was a tiger. At this spot two shallow depressions, coming down from the foot of the hill a few hundred yards away, met. The depressions ran more or less parallel to each other at a distance of about thirty yards and Mothi suggested that he should go up the right-hand depression while I went up the other. As there were only low bushes between, and we should be close to, and within sight of, each other, I agreed to the suggestion.

We had proceeded a hundred yards examining every foot of the ground, and going dead slow, when Mothi, just as I turned my head to look at him started backwards, screaming as he did so. Then he whipped round and ran for dear life, beating the air with his hands as if warding off a swarm of bees and continuing to scream as he ran. The sudden and piercing scream of a human being in a jungle where a moment before all has been silent is terrifying to hear, and quite impossible to describe. Instinctively I knew what had happened. With his eyes fixed on the ground, looking for

blood or hair, Mothi had failed to see where he was going, and had walked on to the tiger. Whether he had been badly mauled or not I could not see, for only his head and shoulders were visible above the bushes. I kept the sights of my rifle a foot behind him as he ran, intending to press the trigger if I saw any movement, but to my intense relief there was no movement as I swung round, and after he had covered a hundred yards I considered he was safe. I yelled to him to stop, adding that I was coming to him. Then, backing away for a few yards, for I did not know whether the tiger had changed his position I hurried down the depression towards Mothi. He was standing with his back against a tree and I was greatly relieved to see that there was no blood on him or on the ground on which he was standing. As I reached him he asked what had happened, and when I told him that nothing had happened he expressed great surprise. He asked if the tiger had not sprung at him, or followed him; and when I replied that he had done everything possible to make the tiger do so, he said, 'I know, Sahib. I know I should not have screamed and run, but I—could—not—help—' As his voice tailed away and his head came forward I caught him by the throat, but he slipped through my hands and slumped to the ground. Every drop of blood had drained from his face, and as he lay minute after long minute without any movement, I feared the shock had killed him.

There is little one can do in the jungles in an emergency of this kind, and that little I did. I stretched Mothi on his back, loosened his clothes, and massaged the region of his heart. Just as I was giving up hope and preparing to carry him home, he opened his eyes.

When Mothi was comfortably seated on the ground with his back to the tree and a half-smoked cigarette between his lips I asked him to tell me exactly what had happened. 'I had gone a short distance up the depression after I left you', he said, 'closely examining the ground for traces of blood or hair, when I saw what looked like a spot of dry blood on a leaf. So I stooped down to have a closer look and, as I raised my head, I looked straight into the face of the tiger. The tiger was lying crouched down facing me at a distance of three or four paces. His head was a little raised off the ground; his mouth was wide open, and there was blood on his chin and on his chest. He looked as though he was on the point of springing at me, so I lost my head and screamed and ran away.' He had seen nothing of the *sambhar* kill. He said the ground was open and free of bushes and there was no kill where the tiger was lying.

Telling Mothi to stay where he was I stubbed out my cigarette and set off to investigate, for I could think of no reason why a tiger with its mouth open, and blood on its chin and on its chest, should allow Mothi to approach within a few feet, over open ground, and not kill him when he screamed in its face. Going with the utmost caution to the spot where Mothi was standing when he screamed, I saw in front of me a bare patch of ground from which the tiger had swept the carpet of dead leaves as he had rolled from side to side; at the nearer edge of this bare patch of ground there was a semicircle of clotted blood. Skirting round where the tiger had been lying, to avoid disturbing the ground, I picked up on the far side of it a light and fresh blood trail, which for no apparent reason zigzagged towards the hill, and then continued along the foot of the hill for a few hundred yards and entered a deep and narrow ravine in which there was a little stream. Up this ravine, which ran deep into the foothills, the tiger had gone. I made my way back to the bare patch of ground and examined the clotted blood. There were splinters of bone and teeth in it, and these splinters provided me with the explanation I was looking for. The rifle-shot I had heard two nights previously had shattered the tiger's lower jaw, and he had made for the jungle in which he had his home. He had gone as far as his sufferings and loss of blood permitted and had then lain down on the spot where first the *sambhar* had seen him tossing about, and where thirty hours later Mothi walked on to him. The most painful wound that can be inflicted on an animal, the shattering of the lower jaw, had quite evidently induced high fever and the poor beast had perhaps only been semi-conscious when he heard Mothi screaming in his face. He had got up quietly and staggered away, in a last effort to reach the ravine in which he knew there was water.

To make quite sure that my deductions were correct Mothi and I crossed the river into the adjoining shooting block to have a look at the ground where the fourteen buffaloes had been tied up. Here, high up in a tree, we found the *machan* the three guns had sat on, and the kill the tiger had been eating when fired at. From the kill a heavy blood trail led down to the river, with elephant tracks on each side of it. Leaving Mothi on the right bank I recrossed the river into my block, picked up the blood trail and the elephant tracks, and followed them for five or six hundred yards to where the blood trail led into heavy cover. At the edge of the cover the elephants had halted and, after standing about for some time, had turned to the right and gone away in the direction of Kaladhungi. I had met the returning elephants as I was starting out the previous evening to try and get a shot at the old pig, and one of the guns had asked me where I was going, and when I told him, had appeared to want to tell me something but was restrained from doing so by his companions. So, while the party of three guns went off on their elephants to the Forest Bungalow where they were staying, I had gone off on foot, without any warning, into the jungle in which they had left a wounded tiger.

The walk back to the village from where I had left Mothi was only about three miles, but it took us about as many hours to cover the distance, for Mothi was unaccountably weak and had to rest frequently. After leaving him at his house I went straight to the Forest Bungalow, where I found the party of three packed up and on the point of leaving to catch the evening train at Haldwani. We talked on the steps of the veranda for some little time, I doing most of the talking, and when I learnt that the only reason they could not spare the time to recover the tiger they had wounded was the keeping of a social engagement, I told them that if Mothi died as a result of shock or if the tiger killed any of my tenants, they would have to face a charge of manslaughter.

The party left after my talk with them, and next morning, armed with a heavy rifle, I entered the ravine up which the tiger had gone, not with the object of recovering a trophy for others, but with the object of putting the tiger out of his misery and burning his skin. The ravine, every foot of which I knew, was the last place I would have selected in which to look for a wounded tiger. However, I searched it from top to bottom, and also the hills on either side, for the whole of that day without finding any trace of the tiger, for the blood trail had stopped shortly after he entered the ravine.

Ten days later a forest guard on his rounds came on the remains of a tiger that had been eaten by vultures. In the summer of that year Government made a rule prohibiting sitting up for tigers between the hours of sunset and sunrise, and making it incumbent on sportsmen wounding tigers to make every effort to bring the wounded animal to bag, and to make an immediate report of the occurrence to the nearest Forest Officer and police outpost.

Mothi met with his experience in December, and when we left

Kaladhungi in April he appeared
to be little the worse for the
shock. But his luck was out, for
a month later he was badly
mauled by a leopard he wounded
one night in his field and followed
next morning into heavy cover; and
he had hardly recovered from his
wounds when he had the misfortune
of being responsible for the death of
a cow—the greatest crime a Hindu can
commit. The cow, an old and decrepit
animal that had strayed in from an adjoining
village, was grazing in Mothi's field, and as he
attempted to drive it out it put its hoof in a deep
rat-hole and broke its leg. For weeks Mothi attended
assiduously to the cow as it lay in his field, but it died eventually,
and the matter being too serious for the village priest to deal
with, he ordered Mothi to make a pilgrimage to Hardwar. So,
having borrowed money for the journey, to Hardwar Mothi went.
Here to the head priest at the main temple Mothi confessed
his crime, and after that dignitary had given the offence due
consideration he ordered Mothi to make a donation to the temple:
this would absolve him of his crime, but in order to show
repentance he would have also to do penance. The priest then
asked him from what acts he derived most pleasure and Mothi,
being without guile, made answer that he derived most pleasure
from shooting, and from eating meat. Mothi was then told by
the priest that in future he must refrain from these two pleasures.

Mothi returned from his pilgrimage cleared of his crime, but
burdened with a lifelong penance. His opportunities for shooting
had been few, for besides having to share the muzzle-loading

gun with others he had had to confine his shooting to the village boundaries, as no man in his position was permitted to shoot in Government forests; even so, Mothi had derived great pleasure from the old gun, and from the occasional shots I had permitted him—against all rules—to fire from my rifle. Hard as this half of his penance was the second half was even harder, and, moreover, it adversely affected his health. Though his means had only allowed him to buy a small meat ration once a month, pigs and porcupines were plentiful, and deer occasionally strayed into the fields at night. It was the custom in our village, a custom to which I also adhered, for an animal shot by one to be shared by all, so Mothi had not had to depend entirely on the meat he could buy.

It was during the winter following his pilgrimage to Hardwar that Mothi developed a hacking cough. As the remedies we tried failed to give relief, I got a doctor friend who was passing through Kaladhungi to examine him, and was horrified to learn that he was suffering from tuberculosis. On the doctor's recommendation I sent Mothi to the Bhowali Sanatorium, thirty miles away. Five days later he returned with a letter from the Superintendent of the Sanatorium saying that the case was hopeless, and that for this reason the Superintendent regretted he could not admit Mothi. A medical missionary who was staying with us at the time, and who had worked for years in a sanatorium, advised us to make Mothi sleep in the open and drink a quart of milk with a few drops of paraffin in it each morning. So for the rest of that winter Mothi slept in the open, and while sitting on our veranda, smoking a cigarette and talking to me, each morning drank a quart of milk fresh from our cows.

The poor of India are fatalists, and in addition have little stamina to fight disease. Deprived of our company, though not of our help, Mothi lost hope when we left for our summer home, and died a month later.

The women of our foothills are the hardest workers in India, and the hardest working of them all was Mothi's widow, Punwa's mother. A small compact woman, as hard as flint and a beaver for work—young enough to remarry but precluded from doing so by reasons of her caste—she bravely and resolutely faced the future, and right gallantly she fulfilled her task, ably assisted by her young children.

Of her three children, Punwa, the eldest, was now twelve, and with the assistance of neighbours was able to do the ploughing and other field jobs. Kunthi, a girl, was ten and married, and until she left the village five years later to join her husband she assisted her mother in all her thousand and one tasks, which included cooking the food and washing up the dishes; washing and mending the clothes—for Punwa's mother was very particular about her own and her children's dress, and no matter how old and patched the garments were, they always had to be clean; fetching water from the irrigation furrow or from the Boar river for domestic purposes; bringing firewood from the jungles, and grass and tender young leaves for the milch cows and their calves; weeding and cutting the crops; husking the paddy, in a hole cut in a slab of rock, with an ironshod staff that was heavy enough to tire the muscles of any man; winnowing the wheat for Punwa to take to the watermill to be ground into *atta*; and making frequent visits to the bazaar two miles away to drive hard bargains for the few articles of food and clothing the family could afford to buy. Sher Singh, the youngest child, was eight, and from the moment he opened his eyes at crack of dawn each morning until he closed them when the evening meal had been eaten he did everything that a boy could do. He even gave Punwa a hand with the ploughing, though he had to be helped at the end of each furrow as he was not strong enough to turn the plough.

Sher Singh, without a care in the world, was the happiest child in the village. When he could not be seen he could always be heard, for he loved to sing. The cattle—four bullocks, twelve cows, eight calves, and Lalu the bull—were his special charge, and each morning after milking the cows he released the herd from the stakes to which he had tethered them the evening before, drove them out of the shed and through a wicket in the boundary wall, and then set to clean up the shed. It would now be the time for the morning meal, and when he heard the call from his mother, or Kunthi, he would hurry home across the fields taking the milk can with him. The frugal morning meal consisted of fresh hot *chapattis* and *dal*, liberally seasoned with green chillies and salt and cooked in mustard oil. Having breakfasted, and finished any chores about the house that he was called upon to do, Sher Singh would begin his day's real work. This was to graze the cattle in the jungle, prevent them from straying, and guard them against leopards and tigers. Having collected the four bullocks and twelve cows from the open ground beyond the boundary wall, where they would be lying basking in the sun, and left Kunthi to keep an eye on the calves, this small tousle-headed boy, his axe over his shoulder and Lalu the bull following him, would drive his charges over the Boar

Bridge and into the dense jungle beyond, calling to each by name.

Lalu was a young scrub bull destined to be a plough-bullock when he had run his course but who, at the time I am writing about, was free of foot and the pride of Sher Singh his foster-brother, for Lalu had shared his mother's milk with Sher Singh. Sher Singh had christened his foster-brother *Lalu,* which means red. But Lalu was not red. He was of a light dun colour, with stronger markings on the shoulders and a dark, almost black line running down the length of his back. His horns were short, sharp, and strong, with the light and dark colourings associated with the shoehorns that adorned dressing tables of that period.

When human beings and animals live in close association with each other under conditions in which they are daily subjected to common dangers, each infuses the other with a measure of courage and confidence which the one possesses and the other lacks. Sher Singh, whose father and grandfather had been more at home in the jungles than in the walks of men, had no fear of anything that walked, and Lalu, young and vigorous, had unbounded confidence in himself. So while Sher Singh infused Lalu with courage, Lalu in turn infused Sher Singh with confidence. In consequence Sher Singh's cattle grazed where others feared to go, and he was justly proud of the fact that they were in better condition than any others in the village, and that no leopard or tiger had ever taken toll of them.

Four miles from our village there is a valley about five miles in length, running north and south, which has no equal in beauty or richness of wildlife in the five thousand square miles of forest land in the United Provinces. At the upper end of the valley a clear stream, which grows in volume as it progresses, gushes from a cave in which a python lives from under the roots of an old jamun tree. This crystal-clear stream with its pools and runs is alive with many kinds of small fish on which live no fewer than

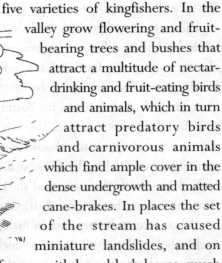

five varieties of kingfishers. In the valley grow flowering and fruit-bearing trees and bushes that attract a multitude of nectar-drinking and fruit-eating birds and animals, which in turn attract predatory birds and carnivorous animals which find ample cover in the dense undergrowth and matted cane-brakes. In places the set of the stream has caused miniature landslides, and on these grows a reedy kind of grass, with broad lush leaves, much fancied by *sambhar* and *kakar*.

The valley was a favourite haunt of mine. One winter evening, shortly after our descent to Kaladhungi from our summer home, I was standing at a point where there is a clear view into the valley when, in a clump of grass to the left, I saw a movement. After a long scrutiny the movement revealed itself as an animal feeding on the lush grass on a steep slope. The animal was too light for a *sambhar* and too big for a *kakar*, so I set out to stalk it, and as I did so a tiger started calling in the valley a few hundred yards lower down. My quarry also heard the tiger, and as it raised its head I saw to my surprise that it was Lalu. With head poised he stood perfectly still listening to the tiger, and when it stopped calling he unconcernedly resumed cropping the grass. This was forbidden ground for Lalu, for cattle are not permitted to graze in Government Reserved Forests, and moreover Lalu was in danger from the tiger; so I called to him by name and, after a little hesitation, he came up the steep bank and we returned to the village together. Sher Singh was tying up his cattle in the shed when we arrived, and when I told him where I had found Lalu he laughed and said, 'Don't fear for this one, Sahib. The forest guard is a friend of mine and would not impound my Lalu, and as for the tiger, Lalu is well able to take care of himself.'

Not long after this incident, the chief Conservator of Forests, Smythies, and his wife arrived on tour in Kaladhungi, and as the camels carrying their camp equipment were coming down the forest road towards the Boar Bridge, a tiger killed a cow on the road in front of them. On the approach of the camels, and the shouting of the men with them, the tiger left the cow on the road and bounded into the jungle. The Smythies were sitting on our veranda having morning coffee when the camel men brought word of the killing of the cow. Mrs Smythies was keen to shoot the tiger, so I went off with two of her men to put up a *machan* for her, and found that in the meantime the tiger had returned and dragged the cow twenty yards into the jungle. When the *machan* was ready I sent back for Mrs Smythies and, after putting her into the *machan* with a forest guard to keep her company, I climbed a tree on the edge of the road hoping to get a photograph of the tiger.

It was 4 p.m. We had been in position half an hour, and a *kakar* had just started barking in the direction in which we knew the tiger was lying up, when down the road came Lalu. On reaching the spot where the cow had been killed he very carefully smelt the ground and a big pool of blood, then turned to the edge of the road and with head held high and nose stretched out started to follow the drag. When he saw the cow he circled round her, tearing up the ground with his hoofs and snorting with rage. After tying my camera to a branch I slipped off the tree and conducted a very angry and protesting Lalu to the edge of the village. Hardly had I returned to my perch on the tree, however, when up the road came Lalu to make a second demonstration round the dead cow. Mrs Smythies now sent the forest guard to drive Lalu away, and as the man passed me I told him to take the bull across the Boar Bridge and to remain there with the elephant that was coming later for Mrs Smythies. The *kakar* had stopped barking some time previously and a covey of jungle fowl now started cackling a few yards behind the *machan*. Getting my camera ready I looked towards Mrs Smythies, and saw she had her rifle poised, and at that moment Lalu appeared for the third time. (We learnt later that, after being taken across the bridge, he had circled round, crossed the river bed lower down and disappeared into the jungle.) This time Lalu trotted up to the cow and, either seeing or smelling the tiger, lowered his head and charged into the bushes, bellowing loudly. Three times he did this, and after each charge he retreated backwards to his starting-point, slashing upwards with his horns as he did so.

I have seen buffaloes driving tigers away from their kills, and I have seen cattle doing the same with leopards but, with the exception of Himalayan bear, I had never before seen a solitary animal—and a scrub bull at that—drive a tiger away from his kill.

Courageous as Lalu was he was no match for the tiger, who was losing his temper and answering Lalu's bellows with angry growls. Remembering a small boy back in the village whose heart would break if anything happened to his beloved companion, I was on the point of going to Lalu's help when Mrs Smythies very sportingly gave up her chance of shooting the tiger, so I shouted to the mahout to bring up the elephant. Lalu was very subdued as he followed me to the shed where Sher Singh was waiting to tie him up, and I think he was as relieved as I was that the tiger had not accepted his challenge while he was defending the dead cow.

The tiger fed on the cow that night and next evening, and

while Mrs Smythies was having another unsuccessful try to get
a shot at him, I took a ciné picture which some who read this
story may remember having seen. In the picture the tiger is
seen coming down a steep bank, and drinking at a little pool.

The jungle was Sher Singh's playground, the only playground
he ever knew, just as it had been my playground as a boy, and
of all whom I have known he alone enjoyed the jungles as much
as I have done. Intelligent and observant, his knowledge of jungle
lore was incredible. Nothing escaped his attention, and he was
as fearless as the animal whose name he bore.

Our favourite evening walk was along one of the three roads
which met on the far side of the Boar Bridge—the abandoned
trunk road to Moradabad, the road to Kota, and the forest road
to Ramnagar. Most evenings at sundown we would hear Sher
Singh before we saw him, for he sang with abandon in a clear
treble voice that carried far as he drove his cattle home. Always
he would greet us with a smile and a *salaam*, and always he
would have something interesting to tell us. 'The big tiger's

tracks were on the road this morning coming from the direction of Kota and going towards Naya Gaon, and at midday I heard him calling at the lower end of the Dhunigad cane-brake'. 'Near Saryapani I heard the clattering of horns, so I climbed a tree and saw two *chital* stags fighting. One of them has very big horns, Sahib, and is very fat, and I have eaten no meat for many days.' 'What am I carrying?'——he had something wrapped in big green leaves and tied round with bark balanced on his tousled head. 'I am carrying a pig's leg. I saw some vultures on a tree, so I went to have a look and under a bush I found a pig killed by a leopard last night and partly eaten. If you want to shoot the leopard, Sahib, I will take you to the kill.' 'Today I found a beehive in a hollow *haldu* tree', he said one day, proudly exhibiting a large platter of leaves held together with long thorns on which the snow-white comb was resting. 'I have brought the honey for you.' Then, glancing at the rifle in my hands, he added, 'I will bring the honey to the house when I have finished my work for perchance you may meet a pig or a *kakar* and with the honey in your hands you would not be able to shoot.' The cutting of the hive out of the *haldu* tree with his small axe had probably taken him two hours or more, and he had got badly stung in the process, for his hands were swollen and one eye was nearly closed, but he said nothing about this and to have commented on it would have embarrassed him. Later that night, while we were having dinner, he slipped silently into the room and as he laid the brass tray, polished till it looked like gold, on our table, he touched the elbow of his right arm with the fingers of his left hand, an old hill custom denoting respect, which is fast dying out.

After depositing such a gift on the table, leaving the tray for Kunthi to call for in the morning, Sher Singh would pause at the door and, looking down and scratching the carpet with his toes, would say, 'If you are going bird shooting tomorrow I will send Kunthi out with the cattle and come with you, for I know where there are a lot of birds'. He was always shy in a house, and on these occasions spoke with a catch in his voice as though he had too many words in his mouth and was trying, with difficulty, to swallow the ones that were getting in his way.

Sher Singh was in his element on these bird shoots, which the boys of the village enjoyed as much as he and I did, for in addition to the excitement and the prospect of having a bird to take home at the end of the day, there was always a halt at midday at a prearranged spot to which the man sent out earlier would provide a meal for all.

When I had taken my position, Sher Singh would line up his companions and bear the selected cover towards me, shouting the loudest of them all and worming his way through the thickest cover. When a bird was put up he would yell, 'It's coming, Sahib! It's coming!' Or when a heavy animal went crashing through the undergrowth, as very frequently happened, he would call to his companions not to run away, assuring them that it was only a *sambhar*, or a *chital*, or maybe a sounder of pig. Ten to twelve patches of cover would be beaten in the course of the day, yielding as many pea fowl and jungle fowl, and two or three hares and possibly a small pig or a porcupine. At the end of the last beat the bag would be shared out among the beaters and the gun, or if the bag was small only among the beaters, and Sher Singh was never more happy than when, at the end of the day, he made for home with a peacock in full plumage proudly draped over his shoulders.

Punwa was now married, and the day was fast approaching when Sher Singh would have to leave the home, for there was not sufficient room on the small holding of six acres for the two brothers. Knowing that it would break Sher Singh's heart to leave the village and his beloved jungles, I decided to apprentice him to a friend who had a garage at Kathgodam, and who ran a fleet of cars on the Naini Tal motor road. After his training it was my intention to employ Sher Singh to drive our car and accompany me on my shooting trips during the winter, and to look after our cottage and garden at Kaladhungi while we were in Naini Tal during the summer. Sher Singh was speechless with delight when I told him of the plans I had made for him, plans which ensured his continued residence in the village, and within sight and calling distance of the home he had never left from the day of his birth.

Plans a-many we make in life, and I am not sure there is cause for regret when some go wrong. Sher Singh was to have started his apprenticeship when we returned to Kaladhungi in November. In October he contracted malignant malaria which led to pneumonia, and a few days before we arrived he died. During his boyhood's years he had sung through life happy as the day was long and, had he lived, who can say that his life in a changing world would have been as happy, and as carefree, as those first few years?

Before leaving our home for a spell, to regain in new climes the health we lost in Hitler's war, I called together our tenants and their families as I had done on two previous occasions, to tell them the time had come for them to take over their holdings and run the village for themselves. Punwa's mother was the spokesman for the tenants on this occasion, and after I had had my say she got to her feet and, in her practical way, spoke as follows: 'You have called us away from our work to no purpose.

We have told you before and we tell you again that we will not take your land from you, for to do so would imply that we were no longer your people. And now, Sahib, what about the pig, the son of the *shaitan* who climbed your wall and ate my potatoes? Punwa and these others cannot shoot it and I am tired of sitting up all night and beating a tin can.'

Maggie and I were walking along the fire-track that skirts the foothills with David at our heels when the pig—worthy son of the old *shaitan* who, full of years and pellets of buckshot, had been killed in an all-night fight with a tiger—trotted across the track. The sun had set and the range was long—all of three hundred yards—but a shot was justifiable for the pig was quite evidently on his way to the village. I adjusted the sights and, resting the rifle against a tree, waited until the pig paused at the edge of a deep depression. When I pressed the trigger, the pig jumped into the depression, scrambled out on the far side, and made off at top speed. 'Have you missed him?' asked Maggie, and with his eyes David put the same question. There was no reason, except miscalculation of the range, why I should not have hit the pig, for my silver foresight had shown up clearly on his back skin, and the tree had assisted me to take steady aim. Anyway, it was time to make for home, and as the cattle track down which the pig had been going would lead us to the Boar Bridge we set off to see the result of my shot. The pig's feet had bitten deeply into the ground where he had taken off, and on the far side of the depression, where he had scrambled out, there was blood. Two hundred yards in the direction in which the pig had gone there was a narrow strip of dense cover. I should probably find him dead in the morning in this cover, for the blood trail was heavy; but if he was not dead and there was trouble, Maggie would not be with me, and there would be more light to shoot by in the morning than there was now.

Punwa had heard my shot and was waiting on the bridge for us. 'Yes', I said, in reply to his eager inquiry, 'it was the old pig I fired at, and judging by the blood trail, he is hit hard.' I added that if he met me on the bridge next morning I would show him where the pig was, so that later he could take out a party of men to bring it in. 'May I bring the old *havildar* too?' said Punwa, and I agreed. The *havildar*, a kindly old man who had won the respect and affection of all, was a Gurkha who on leaving the army had joined the police, and having retired a year previously had settled down with his wife and two sons on a plot of land we had given him in our village. Like all Gurkhas the *havildar* had an insatiable appetite for pig's flesh, and when a pig was shot by any of us it was an understood thing that, no matter who went short, the ex-soldier-policeman must have his share.

Punwa and the *havildar* were waiting for me at the bridge next morning. Following the cattle track, we soon reached the spot where, the previous evening, I had seen the blood. From here we followed the well-defined blood trail which led us, as I had expected, to the dense cover. I left my companions at the edge of the cover, for a wounded pig is a dangerous animal, and with one exception—a bear—is the only animal in our jungles that has the unpleasant habit of savaging any human being who has the misfortune to be attacked and knocked down by him. For this reason wounded pigs, especially if they have big tusks, have to be treated with great respect. The pig had stopped where I had expected him to, but he had not died, and at daybreak he had got up from where he had been lying all night and left the cover. I whistled to Punwa and the *havildar* and when they rejoined me we set off to trail the animal.

The trail led us across the fire-track, and from the direction in which the wounded animal was going it was evident he was making for the heavy jungle on the far side of the hill, from

which I suspected he had come the previous evening. The
morning blood trail was light and continued to get lighter the
farther we went, until we lost it altogether in a belt of trees, the
fallen leaves of which a gust of wind had disturbed. In front of
us at this spot was a tinder-dry stretch of waist-high grass. Still
under the conviction that the pig was heading for the heavy jungle
on the far side of the hill, I entered the grass, hoping to pick up
the tracks again on the far side.

The *havildar* had lagged some distance behind, but Punwa
was immediately behind me when, after we had gone a few yards
into the grass, my woollen stockings caught on the thorns of a
low bush. While I was stooping to free myself Punwa, to avoid
the thorns, moved a few paces to the right and I just got free
and was straightening up when out of the grass shot the pig and
with an angry grunt went straight for Punwa, who was wearing
a white shirt. I then did what I have always asked companions
who have accompanied me into the jungles after dangerous game
to do if they saw me attacked by a wounded animal. I threw
the muzzle of my rifle into the air, and shouted at the top of my
voice as I pressed the trigger.

If the thorns had not caught in my stockings and lost me a
fraction of a second, all would have been well, for I should have
killed the pig before it got to Punwa; but once the pig had reached
him the only thing I could do to help him was to try to cause
a diversion, for to have fired in his direction would further have
endangered his life. As the bullet was leaving my rifle to the land
in the jungle a mile away, Punwa, with a despairing scream of
'Sahib', was falling backwards into the grass with the pig right
on top of him, but at my shout and the crack of the rifle the
pig turned like a whiplash straight for me, and before I was able
to eject the spent cartridge and ram a fresh one into the chamber
of the ·275 rifle, he was at me. Taking my right hand from the

rifle I stretched the arm out palm downwards, and as my hand came in contact with his forehead he stopped dead, for no other reason than that my time had not come, for he was big and angry enough to have knocked over and savaged a cart horse. The pig's body had stopped but his head was very active, and as he cut upwards with his great tusks, first on one side and then on the other, fortunately cutting only the air, he wore the skin off the palm of my hand with his rough forehead. Then, for no apparent reason, he turned away, and as he made off I put two bullets into him in quick succession and he pitched forward on his head.

After that one despairing scream Punwa had made no sound or movement, and with the awful thought of what I would say to his mother, and the still more awful thought of what she would say to me, I went with fear and trembling to where he was lying out of sight in the grass, expecting to find him ripped open from end to end. He was lying full stretch on his back, and his eyes were closed, but to my intense relief I saw no blood on his white clothes. I shook him by the shoulder and asked how he was, and where he had been hurt. In a very weak voice he said he was dead, and that his back was broken. I straddled his body and gently raised him to a sitting position, and was overjoyed to find that he was able to retain this position when I released my hold. Passing my hand down his back I assured him that it was not broken, and after he had verified this fact with his own hand, he turned his head and looked behind him to where a dry stump was projecting two or three inches above the ground. Evidently he had fainted when the pig knocked him over and, on coming to, feeling the stump boring into his back, had jumped to the conclusion that it was broken.

And so the old pig, son of the *shaitan*, died, and in dying nearly frightened the lives out of the two of us. But beyond rubbing a little skin off my hand he did us no harm, for Punwa escaped without a scratch and with a grand story to tell. The *havildar*, like the wise old soldier he was, had remained in the background. None the less he claimed a lion's share of the pig, for had he not stood foursquare in reserve to render assistance if assistance had been called for? And further, was it not the custom for those present at a killing to receive a double share, and what difference was there between seeing and hearing the shots that had killed the pig? So a double share was not denied him, and he too, in the course of time, had a grand story to tell of the part he took in that morning's exploit.

Punwa now reigns, and is raising a family, in the house I built for his father. Kunthi has left the village to join her husband, and Sher Singh waits in the Happy Hunting Grounds. Punwa's mother is still alive, and if you stop at the village gate and walk through the fields to Punwa's house you will find her keeping house for Punwa and his family and working as hard and as cheerfully at her thousand and one tasks as she worked when she first came to our village as Mothi's bride.

During the war years Maggie spent the winters alone in our cottage at Kaladhungi, without transport, and fourteen miles from the nearest settlement. Her safety gave me no anxiety, for I knew she was safe among my friends, the poor of India.

PRE-RED-TAPE DAYS

I WAS camping with Anderson one winter in the Terai, the low-lying stretch of country at the foot of the Himalayas, and having left Bindukhera after breakfast one morning in early January, we made a wide detour to Boksar, our next camping-place, to give our servants time to pack up and pitch our tents before our arrival.

There were two small unbridged rivers to cross between Bindukhera and Boksar, and at the second of these rivers one of the camels carrying our tents slipped on the clay bottom and deposited its load in the river. This accident resulted in a long delay, with the result that we arrived at Boksar, after a very successful day's black partridge shooting, while our kit was still being unloaded from the camels.

The camp site was only a few hundred yards from Boksar village, and as Anderson's arrival was a great event, the entire population had turned out to pay their respects to him and to render what assistance they could in setting up our camp.

Sir Frederick Anderson was at that time Superintendent of the Terai and Bhabar Government Estates, and by reason of the large amount of the milk of human kindness that he was endowed with he had endeared himself to the large population, embracing all castes and creeds living in the many thousands of square miles of country he ruled over. In addition to his kindly nature, Anderson was a great administrator and was gifted with a memory which I have only seen equalled in one other man, General Sir Henry Ramsay, who for twenty-eight years administered the same tract of country, and who throughout his service was known as the Uncrowned King of Kumaon. Both Ramsay and Anderson were Scotsmen, and it was said of them that once having heard a name or seen a face they never forgot it. It is only those who have had dealings with simple uneducated people who can realize the value of a good memory, for nothing appeals so much to a humble man as the remembering of his name, or the circumstances in which he has previously been met.

When the history of the rise and fall of British Imperialism is written, due consideration will have to be given to the important part red tape played in the fall of the British raj. Both Ramsay and Anderson served India at a time when red tape was unknown, and their popularity and the success of their administration was in great measure due to their hands' not being tied with it.

Ramsay, in addition to being Judge of Kumaon, was also magistrate, policeman, forest officer, and engineer, and as his duties were manifold and onerous he performed many of them while walking from one camp to another. It was his custom while on these long walks, and while accompanied by a crowd of people, to try all his civil and criminal cases. The complainant and his witnesses were first heard, and then the defendant and his witnesses, and after due deliberation, Ramsay would pronounce judgement, which might be either a fine or a sentence to imprisonment. In no case was his judgement known to be questioned, nor did any man whom he had sentenced to a fine or imprisonment fail to pay the fine into the Government Treasury or fail to report himself at the nearest jail to carry out the term of simple or rigorous imprisonment to which Ramsay had sentenced him.

As Superintendent of the Terai and Bhabar, Anderson had only to perform a part of the duties that had been performed by his predecessor Ramsay, but he had wide administrative powers, and that afternoon, while our tents were being pitched on the camping ground at Boksar, Anderson told the assembled people to sit down. Adding that he would listen to any complaints they had to make and receive any petitions they wished to present.

The first petition came from the headman of a village adjoining Boksar. It appeared that this village and Boksar had a joint irrigation channel that served both villages, and that ran through Boksar. Owing to the partial failure of the monsoon rains, the water in the channel had not been sufficient for both villages and Boksar village had used it all, with the result that the paddy crop of the lower village had been ruined. The headman of Boksar admitted that no water had been allowed to go down the channel to the lower village and justified his action by pointing out that, if the water had been shared, the paddy crops of both villages would have been ruined. The crop had been harvested and threshed a few days before our arrival, and after Anderson had heard what the two headmen had to say, he ordered that the paddy should be divided up according to the acreage of the two villages. The people of Boksar acknowledged the justice of this decision, but claimed they were entitled to payment of the labour that had been employed in harvesting and threshing the crop.

To this claim the lower village objected on the ground that no request had been made to them for help while the Boksar crop was being harvested and threshed. Anderson upheld the objection, and while the two headmen went off to divide the paddy the next petition was presented to him.

This was from Chadi, accusing Kalu of having abducted his wife Tilni. Chadi's complaint was that three weeks previously Kalu had made advances to Tilni; that in spite of his protests Kalu had persisted in his advances; and that ultimately Tilni had left his hut and taken up residence with Kalu. When Anderson asked if Kalu was present, a man sitting at the edge of the semicircle in front of us stood up and said he was Kalu.

While the case of the paddy had been under discussion the assembled women and girls had shown little interest, for that was a matter to be decided by their menfolk. But this abduction case, judging from the expression on their faces and the sharp intakes of breath, was one in which they were all intensely interested.

When Anderson asked Kalu if he admitted the charge that Chadi had brought against him, he admitted that Tilni was living in the hut he had provided for her but he stoutly denied that he had abducted her. When asked if he was prepared to return Tilni to her lawful husband, Kalu replied that Tilni had come to him of her own free will and that he was not prepared to force her to return to Chadi. 'Is Tilni present?' asked Anderson. A girl from among the group of women came forward and said, 'I am Tilni. What does Your Honour want with me?'

Tilni was a clean-limbed attractive young girl, some eighteen years of age. Her hair, done in a foot-high cone in the traditional manner of the women of the Terai, was draped with a white-bordered black sari, her upper person was encased in a tight-fitting red bodice, and a voluminous gaily coloured skirt completed her costume. When asked by Anderson why she had left her husband, she pointed to Chadi and said, 'Look at him. Not only is he dirty, as you can see, but he is also a miser; and during the two years I have been married to him he has not given me any clothes, nor has he given me any jewellery. These clothes that you are looking at and this jewellery', she said, touching some silver bangles on her wrists, and several strings of glass beads round her neck, 'were given to me by Kalu.' Asked if she was willing to go back to Chadi, Tilni tossed her head and said nothing would induce her to do so.

This aboriginal tribe, living in the unhealthy Terai, is renowned for two sterling qualities—cleanliness, and the independence of the women. In no other part of India are villages and the individual dwellings as spotlessly clean as they are in the Terai, and in no other part of India would a young girl have dared, or in fact been permitted, to stand before a mixed gathering including two white men to plead her own cause.

Chadi was now asked by Anderson if he had any suggestions to make, to which he replied: 'You are my mother and my father. I came to you for justice, and if Your Honour is not prepared to compel my wife to return to me, I claim compensation for her.' 'To what extent do you claim compensation for her?' asked Anderson, to which Chadi replied, 'I claim one hundred and fifty rupees'. From all sides of the semicircle there were now exclamations of 'He claims too much', 'Far too much', and 'She is not worth it'.

On being asked by Anderson if he was willing to pay one hundred and fifty rupees for Tilni, Kalu said the price demanded was excessive and added that he knew, as everyone in Boksar knew, that Chadi had only paid a hundred rupees for Tilni. This price, he argued, had been paid for Tilni when she was 'new', and as this was no longer the case the most he was willing to pay was fifty rupees.

The assembled people now took sides, some maintaining that the sum demanded was too great, while others as vigorously maintained that the sum offered was too small. Eventually, after giving due consideration to the arguments for and against— arguments that went into very minute and very personal details, and to which Tilni listened with an amused smile on her pretty face—Anderson fixed the price of Tilni at seventy-five rupees, and this sum Kalu was ordered to pay Chadi. Opening his waistband, Kalu produced a string purse, and emptied it on the carpet at Anderson's feet. The contents amounted to fifty-two silver rupees. When two of Kalu's friends had come to his assistance and added another twenty-three rupees, Chadi was told to count the money. When he had done so and stated that the sum was correct, a woman whom I had noticed coming very slowly and apparently very painfully from the direction of the village after all the others were seated and who had sat down a little apart from the rest, got with some difficulty to her feet and said, 'What about me, Your Honour?' 'Who are you?' asked Anderson. 'I am Kalu's wife', she replied.

She was a tall gaunt woman, every drop of blood drained from her ivory-white face, her body-line distorted with an enormous spleen, and her feet swollen—the result of malaria, the scourge of the Terai.

In a tired, toneless voice the woman said that now that Kalu had purchased another wife she would be homeless; and as she had no relatives in the village, and was too ill to work, she would die of neglect and starvation. Then she covered her face with her sari and began to cry silently, great sobs shaking her wasted frame and tears splashing down on her distorted body.

Here was an unexpected and an unfortunate complication, and one that was for Anderson difficult of solution, for while the case had been under discussion there had been no hint that Kalu already had a wife.

The uncomfortable silence following on the woman's pitiful outburst had lasted some time when Tilni, who had remained standing, ran across to the poor weeping woman, and flinging her strong young arms round her said, 'Don't cry, sister, don't cry; and don't say you are homeless, for I will share the new hut Kalu has built for me with you, and I will take care of you and nurse you and one half of all that Kalu gives me I will give you. So don't cry any more, sister, and now come with me and I will take you to our hut.'

As Tilni and the sick woman moved off, Anderson stood up and, blowing his nose violently, said the wind coming down from the hills had given him a damned cold, and that the proceedings were closed for the day. The wind coming down from the hills appeared to have affected others in the same way as it had affected Anderson, for his was not the only nose that was in urgent need of blowing. But the proceedings were not quite over, for Chadi now approached Anderson and asked for the return of his petition. Having torn his petition into small bits, Chadi took the piece of cloth in which he had tied up the seventy-five rupees from his pocket, opened it and said: 'Kalu and I be men of the same village, and as he has now two mouths to feed, one of which requires special food, he will need all his money. So permit me, Your Honour, to return this money to him.'

While touring his domain, Anderson and his predecessors in pre-red-tape days settled to the mutual satisfaction of all concerned hundreds, nay thousands, of cases similar to these, without the contestants being put to one pice of expense. Now, since the introduction of red tape, these cases are taken to courts of law where both the complainant and the defendant are bled white, and where seeds of dissension are sown that inevitably lead to more and more court cases, to the enrichment of the legal profession and the ruin of the poor, simple, honest hardworking peasantry.

THE LAW OF THE JUNGLES

Harkwar and Kunthi were married before their total ages had reached double figures. This was quite normal in the India of those days, and would possibly still have been so had Mahatma Gandhi and Miss Mayo never lived.

Harkwar and Kunthi lived in villages a few miles apart at the foot of the great Dunagiri mountain, and had never seen each other until the great day when, dressed in bright new clothes, they had for all too short a time been the centre of attraction of a vast crowd of relatives and friends. That day lived long in their memories as the wonderful occasion when they had been able to fill their small bellies to bursting-point with *halwa* and *puris*. The day also lived for long years in the memory of their respective fathers, for on it the village *bania*, who was their 'father and mother', realizing their great necessity had provided the few rupees that had enabled them to retain the respect of their community by marrying their children at the age that all children should be married, and on the propitious date selected by the priest of the village—and had made a fresh entry against their names in his register. True, the fifty per cent interest demanded for the accommodation was excessive, but, God willing,

a part of it would be paid, for there were other children yet to
be married, and who but the good *bania* was there to help them?

Kunthi returned to her father's home after her wedding and
for the next few years performed all the duties that children
are called upon to perform in the homes of the very poor. The
only difference her married state made in her life was that she
was no longer permitted to wear the one-piece dress that
unmarried girls wear. Her new costume now consisted of three
pieces, a *chaddar* a yard and a half long, one end of which was
tucked into her skirt and the other draped over her head, a
tiny sleeveless bodice, and a skirt a few inches long.

Several uneventful and carefree years went by for Kunthi
until the day came when she was judged old enough to join her
husband. Once again the *bania* came to the rescue and, arrayed
in her new clothes, a very tearful girl-bride set out for the home

of her boy-husband. The change from one home to another only meant for Kunthi the performing of chores for her mother-in-law which she had previously performed for her mother. There are no drones in a poor man's household in India; young and old have their allotted work to do and they do it cheerfully. Kunthi was now old enough to help with the cooking, and as soon as the morning meal had been eaten all who were capable of working for wages set to perform their respective tasks, which, no matter how minor they were, brought grist to the family mill. Harkwar's father was a mason and was engaged on building a chapel at the American Mission School. It was Harkwar's ambition to follow in his father's profession and, until he had the strength to do so, he helped the family exchequer by carrying the materials used by his father and the other masons, earning two annas a day for his ten hours' labour. The crops on the low irrigated lands were ripening, and after Kunthi had washed and polished the metal pots and pans used for the morning meal she accompanied her mother-in-law and her numerous sisters-in-law to the fields of the headman of the village, where with other women and girls she laboured as many hours as her husband for half the wage he received. When the day's work was done the family walked back in the twilight to the hut Harkwar's father had been permitted to build on the headman's land, and with the dry sticks the younger children had collected during their elders' absence, the evening meal was cooked and eaten. Except for the fire, there had never been any other form of illumination in the hut, and when the pots and pans had been cleaned and put away, each member of the family retired to his or her alloted place, Harkwar and his brothers sleeping with their father and Kunthi sleeping with the other female members of the family.

When Harkwar was eighteen and Kunthi sixteen, they left and, carrying their few possessions, set up home in a hut placed at their disposal by an uncle of Harkwar's in a village three miles from the cantonment of Ranikhet. A number of barracks were under construction in the cantonment and Harkwar had no difficulty in finding work as a mason; nor had Kunthi any difficulty in finding work as a labourer, carrying stones from a quarry to the site of the building.

For four years the young couple worked on the barracks at Ranikhet, and during this period Kunthi had two children. In November of the fourth year the buildings were completed and Harkwar and Kunthi had to find new work, for their savings were small and would only keep them in food for a few days.

Winter set in early that year and promised to be unusually severe. The family had no warm clothes, and after a week's unsuccessful search for work Harkwar suggested that they should migrate to the foothills where he heard a canal headworks was being constructed. So, early in December, the family set out in high spirits on their long walk to the foothills. The distance between the village in which they had made their home for four years and the canal headworks at Kaladhungi, where they hoped to procure work, was roughly fifty miles. Sleeping under trees at night, toiling up and down steep and rough roads during the day, and carrying all their worldly possessions and the children by turns, Harkwar and Kunthi, tired and footsore, accomplished the journey to Kaladhungi in six days.

Other landless members of the depressed class had migrated earlier in the winter from the high hills to the foothills and built themselves communal huts capable of housing as many as thirty families. In these huts Harkwar and Kunthi were unable to find accommodation, so they had to build a hut for themselves. They chose a site at the edge of the forest where there was an abundant supply of fuel, within easy reach of the bazaar, and laboured early and late on a small hut of branches and leaves, for their

supply of hard cash had dwindled to a few rupees and there was
no friendly *bania* here to whom they could turn for help.

The forest at the edge of which Harkwar and Kunthi built
their hut was a favourite hunting-ground of mine. I had first
entered it carrying my old muzzle-loader to shoot red jungle
fowl and pea fowl for the family larder, and later I had penetrated
to every corner, armed with a modern rifle, in search of big
game. At the time Harkwar and Kunthi and their two children,
Punwa, a boy aged three, and Putali, a girl aged two, took up
their residence in the hut, there were in that forest, to my certain
knowledge, five tigers; eight leopards; a family of four sloth bears;
two Himalayan black bears, which had come down from the
high hills to feed on wild plums and honey; a number of hyenas
who had their burrows in the grasslands five miles away and
who visited the forest nightly to feed on the discarded portions
of the tigers' and leopards' kills; a pair of wild dogs; numerous
jackals and foxes and pine martens; and a variety of civet and
other cats. There were also two pythons, many kinds of snakes,
crested and tawny eagles, and hundreds of vultures in the forest.
I have not mentioned animals such as deer, antelope, pigs, and
monkeys, which are harmless to human beings, for they have no
part in my story.

The day after the flimsy hut was completed, Harkwar found
work as a qualified mason on a daily wage of eight annas with
the contractor who was building the canal headworks, and Kunthi
purchased for two rupees a permit from the Forest Department
which entitled her to cut grass on the foothills, which she sold
as fodder for the cattle of the shopkeepers in the bazaar. For
her bundle of green grass weighing anything up to eighty pounds
and which necessitated a walk of from ten to fourteen miles,
mostly up and down steep hills, Kunthi received four annas, one
anna of which was taken by the man who held the Government

contract for sale of grass in the bazaar. On the eight annas earned by Harkwar, plus the three annas earned by Kunthi, the family of four lived in comparative comfort, for food was plentiful and cheap and for the first time in their lives they were able to afford one meat meal a month.

Two of the three months that Harkwar and Kunthi intended spending in Kaladhungi passed very peacefully. The hours of work were long, and admitted of no relaxation, but to that they had been accustomed from childhood. The weather was perfect, the children kept in good health, and except during the first few days while the hut was being built they had never gone hungry.

The children had in the beginning been an anxiety, for they were too young to accompany Harkwar to the canal headworks, or Kunthi on her long journeys in search of grass. Then a kindly old crippled woman living in the communal hut a few hundred yards away came to the rescue by offering to keep a general

eye on the children while the parents were away at work. This arrangement worked satisfactorily for two months, and each evening when Harkwar returned from the canal headworks four miles away, and Kunthi returned a little later after selling her grass in the bazaar, they found Punwa and Putali eagerly awaiting their return.

Friday was fair day in Kaladhungi and on that day everyone in the surrounding villages made it a point to visit the bazaar, where open booths were erected for the display of cheap food, fruit, and vegetables. On these fair days Harkwar and Kunthi returned from work half an hour before their usual time, for if any vegetables had been left over it was possible to buy them at a reduced price before the booths closed down for the night.

One particular Friday, when Harkwar and Kunthi returned to the hut after making their modest purchases of vegetables and a pound of goat's meat, Punwa and Putali were not at the hut to welcome them. On making inquiries from the crippled woman at the communal hut, they learned that she had not seen the children since midday. The woman suggested that they had probably gone to the bazaar to see a merry-go-round that had attracted all the children from the communal hut, and as this seemed a reasonable explanation Harkwar set off to search the bazaar while Kunthi returned to the hut to prepare the evening meal. An hour later Harkwar returned with several men who had assisted him in his search to report that no trace of the children could be found, and that of all the people he had questioned, none admitted having seen them.

At that time a rumour was running through the length and breadth of India of the kidnapping of Hindu children by *fakirs*, for sale on the north-west frontier for immoral purposes. What truth there was in this rumour I am unable to say, but I had frequently read in the daily press of *fakirs* being manhandled, and on several occasions being rescued by the police from crowds intent on lynching them. It is safe to say that every parent in India had heard these rumours, and when Harkwar and the friends who had helped him in his search returned to the hut, they communicated their fears to Kunthi that the children had been kidnapped by the *fakirs*, who had probably come to the fair for that purpose.

At the lower end of the village there was a police station in charge of a head constable and two constables. To this police station Harkwar and Kunthi repaired, with a growing crowd of well-wishers. The head constable was a kindly old man who had children of his own, and after he had listened sympathetically to the distracted parents' story, and recorded their statements in his diary, he said that nothing could be done that night, but that next morning he would send the town crier round to all the fifteen villages in Kaladhungi to announce the loss of the children.

He then suggested that if the town crier could announce a reward of fifty rupees, it would greatly assist in the safe return of the children. Fifty rupees! Harkwar and Kunthi were aghast at the suggestion, for they did not know there was so much money in all the world. However, when the town crier set out on his round the following morning, he was able to announce the reward, for a man in Kaladhungi who had heard of the head constable's suggestion had offered the money.

The evening meal was eaten late that night. The childrens' portion was laid aside, and throughout the night a small fire was kept burning, for it was bitterly cold, and at short intervals Harkwar and Kunthi went out into the night to call to their children, though they knew there was no hope of receiving an answer.

At Kaladhungi two roads cross each other at right angles, one running along the foot of the hills from Haldwani to Ramnagar, and the other running from Naini Tal to Bazpur. During that Friday night, sitting close to the small fire to keep themselves warm, Harkwar and Kunthi decided that if the children did not turn up by morning, they would go along the former road and make inquiries, as this was the most likely route for the kidnapper to have taken. At daybreak on Saturday morning they went to the police station to tell the head constable of their decision, and were instructed to lodge a report at the Haldwani and Ramnagar police stations. They were greatly heartened when the head constable told them that he was sending a letter by mail runner to no less a person than the Inspector of Police at Haldwani, requesting him to telegraph to all railway junctions to keep a look-out for the children, a description of whom he was sending with his letter.

Near sunset that evening Kunthi returned from her twenty-eight-mile walk to Haldwani and went straight to the police station to inquire about her children and to tell the head constable that, though her quest had been fruitless, she had lodged a report as instructed at the Haldwani police station. Shortly afterwards

Harkwar returned from his thirty-six-mile walk to
Ramnagar, and he too went straight to the
police station to make inquiries and to
report that he had found no trace of
the children, but had carried out the
head constable's instructions.
Many friends, including a
number of mothers who
feared for the safety of their
own children, were waiting at
the hut to express their
sympathy for Harkwar and for
Punwa's mother—for, as is the
custom in India, Kunthi when she

married lost the name she had been given at birth and until
Punwa was born had been addressed and referred to as
'Harkwar's wife', and after Punwa's birth as 'Punwa's mother'.

Sunday was a repetition of Saturday, with the difference that
instead of going east and west Kunthi went north to Naini Tal
while Harkwar went south to Bazpur. The former covered thirty
miles, and the latter thirty-two. Starting early and returning at
nightfall, the distracted parents traversed many miles of rough
roads through dense forests, where people do not usually go
except in large parties, and where Harkwar and Kunthi would
not have dreamed of going alone had not anxiety for their children
overcome their fear of dacoits and of wild animals.

On that Sunday evening, weary and hungry, they returned
to their hut from their fruitless visit to Naini Tal and to Bazpur,
to be met by the news that the town crier's visit to the villages
and the police inquiries had failed to find any trace of the children.
Then they lost heart and gave up all hope of ever seeing Punwa
and Putali again. The anger of the gods, that had resulted in a
fakir being able to steal their children in broad daylight, was not

to be explained. Before starting on their long walk from the hills they had consulted the village priest, and he had selected the propitious day for them to set out on their journey. At every shrine they had passed they had made the requisite offering; at one place, a dry bit of wood, in another a small strip of cloth torn from the hem of Kunthi's *chaddar*, and in yet another a pice, which they could ill afford. And here, at Kaladhungi, every time they passed the temple that their low caste did not permit them to enter, they had never failed to raise their clasped hands in supplication. Why then had this great misfortune befallen them, who had done all that the gods demanded of them and who had never wronged any man?

Monday found the pair too dispirited and too tired to leave their hut. There was no food, and would be none until they resumed work. But of what use was it to work now, when the children for whom they had ungrudgingly laboured from morn to night were gone? So, while friends came and went, offering what sympathy they could. Harkwar sat at the door of the hut staring into a bleak and hopeless future, while Kunthi, her tears all gone, sat in a corner, hour after hour, rocking herself to and fro, to and fro.

On that Monday a man of my acquaintance was herding buffaloes in the jungle in which lived the wild animals and birds I have mentioned. He was a simple soul who had spent the greater part of his life in the jungles herding the buffaloes of the headman at Patabpur village. He knew the danger from the tigers, and near sundown he collected the buffaloes and started to drive them to the village, along a cattle track that ran through the densest part of the jungle. Presently he noticed that as each buffalo got to a certain spot in the track it turned its head to the right and stopped, until urged on by the horns of the animal following. When he got to this spot he also turned his head to the right, and in a little depression a few feet from the track saw two small children lying.

He had been in the jungle with his buffaloes when the town crier had made his round of the villages on Saturday, but that night, and the following night also, the kidnapping of Harkwar's children had been the topic of conversation round the village fire, as in fact it had been round every village fire in the whole of Kaladhungi. Here then were the missing children for whom a reward of fifty rupees had been offered. But why had they been murdered and brought to this remote spot? The children were naked, and were clasped in each other's arms. The herdsman descended into the depression and squatted down on his hunkers to determine, if he could, how the children had met their death. That the children were dead he was convinced, yet now as he sat closely scrutinizing them he suddenly saw that they were breathing; that in fact they were not dead, but sound asleep. He was a father himself, and very gently he touched the children and roused them. To touch them was a crime against his caste, for he was a Brahmin and they were low-caste children, but what mattered caste in an emergency like this? So, leaving his buffaloes to find their own way home, he picked up the children, who were too weak to walk, and set out for the Kaladhungi bazaar with one on each shoulder. The man was not too strong himself, for like all who live in the foothills he had suffered much from malaria. The children were an awkward load and had to be held in position. Moreover, as all the cattle tracks and game paths in this jungle run from north to south, and his way lay from east to west, he had to make frequent detours to avoid impenetrable thickets and deep ravines. But he carried on manfully, resting every now and then in the course of his six-mile walk. Putali was beyond speech, but Punwa was able to talk a little and all the explanation he could give for their being in the jungle was that they had been playing and had got lost.

Harkwar was sitting at the door of his hut staring into the darkening night, in which points of light were beginning to appear as a lantern or cooking-fire was lit here and there, when he saw a small crowd of people appearing from the direction of the bazaar. At the head of the procession a man was walking, carrying something on his shoulders. From all sides people were converging on the procession and he could hear an excited murmur of 'Harkwar's children'. Harkwar's children! He could not believe his ears, and yet there appeared to be no mistake, for the procession was coming straight towards his hut.

Kunthi, having reached the limit of her misery and of her physical endurance, had fallen asleep curled up in a corner of the hut. Harkwar shook her awake and got her to the door just as the herdsman carrying Punwa and Putali reached it.

When the tearful greetings, and blessings and thanks for the rescuer, and the congratulations of friends had partly subsided, the question of the reward the herdsman had earned was mooted. To a poor man fifty rupees was wealth untold, and with it the herdsman could buy three buffaloes, or ten cows, and be independent for life. But the rescuer was a better man than the crowd gave him credit for. The blessings and thanks that had been showered on his head that night, he said, was reward enough for him, and he stoutly refused to touch one pice of the fifty rupees. Nor would Harkwar or Kunthi accept the reward either as a gift or a loan. They had got back the children they had lost all hope of ever seeing again, and would resume work as their strength returned. In the meantime the milk and sweets and *puris* that one and another of the assembled people, out of the goodness of their hearts, had run to the bazaar to fetch would be amply sufficient to sustain them.

Two-year-old Putali and three-year-old Punwa were lost at

midday on Friday, and were found by the herdsman at about 5 p.m. on Monday, a matter of seventy-seven hours. I have given a description of the wild life which to my knowledge was in the forest in which the children spent those seventy-seven hours, and it would be unreasonable to assume that none of the animals or birds saw, heard, or smelt the children. And yet, when the herdsman put Putali and Punwa into their parents' arms, there was not a single mark of tooth or claw on them.

I once saw a tigress stalking a month-old kid. The ground was very open and the kid saw the tigress while she was still some distance away and started bleating, whereon the tigress gave up her stalk and walked straight up to it. When the tigress had approached to within a few yards, the kid went forward to meet her, and on reaching the tigress stretched out its neck and put up its head to smell her. For the duration of a few heart beats the month-old kid and the Queen of the Forest stood nose to nose, and then the queen turned and walked off in the direction from which she had come.

When Hitler's war was nearing its end, in one week I read extracts from speeches of three of the greatest men in the British Empire, condemning war atrocities, and accusing the enemy of attempting to introduce the 'law of the jungle' into the dealings of warring man and man. Had the Creator made the same law for man as He has made for the jungle folk, there would be no wars, for the strong in man would have the same consideration for the weak as is the established law of the jungles.

THE BROTHERS

The long years of training boys for jungle warfare were over, and we were sitting one morning after breakfast on the veranda of our cottage at Kaladhungi. My sister Maggie was knitting a khaki pullover for me, and I was putting the finishing touches to a favourite fly-rod that suffered from years of disuse, when a man wearing a clean but much-patched cotton suit walked up the steps of the veranda with a broad grin on his face, *salaamed*, and asked if we remembered him.

Many people, clean and not so clean, old and young, rich and poor (but mostly poor), Hindus, Mohammedans, and Christians, walked up those steps, for our cottage was at a cross-roads at the foot of the hills and on the border line between the cultivated land and the forest. All who were sick or sorry, in want of a helping hand, or in need of a little human companionship and a cup of tea, whether living on the cultivated land or working in the forest or just passing on their way from one place to another, found their way to our cottage. Had a record been maintained over the years of only the sick and injured treated, it would have had thousands of names in it. And the cases dealt with would have covered every ailment that human flesh is heir to—and subject to, when living in an unhealthy area, working in forests on dangerous jobs among animals who occasionally lose their tempers.

There was the case of the woman who came one morning and complained that her son had great difficulty in eating the linseed poultice that had been given to her the previous evening to apply on a boil: as the poultice did not appear to have done the boy any good, she asked to have the medicine changed. And the case of the old Mohammedan woman who came late one evening, with tears streaming down her face, and begged Maggie to save her husband who was dying of pneumonia. She looked askance at the tablets of M. & B. 693 and asked if that was all that was to be given to a dying man to make him well; but next day she returned with a beaming countenance to report that her husband had recovered, and begged for the same kind of medicine for the four friends she had brought with her, each of whom had husbands as old as hers who might at any time get pneumonia. And there was the case of the girl about eight years old, who, after some difficulty in reaching the latch of the gate, marched up to the veranda firmly holding the hand of a boy some two years younger, and asked for medicine for the boy's sore eyes. She sat herself down on the ground, made the boy lie on his back, and having got his head between her knees said, 'Now, Miss Sahib, you can do anything you like to him.' This girl was the daughter of the headman of a village six miles away. Seeing her class mate suffering from sore eyes, she had taken it upon herself to bring him to Maggie for treatment, and for a whole week, until his eyes were quite well, the young Samaritan brought the boy to the cottage, though in order to do so she had to walk an additional four miles each day.

Then there was the case of the sawyer from Delhi, who limped into the compound one day with his right leg ripped open by the tusk of a pig from his heel to the back of his knee. All the time his leg was being attended to he swore at the unclean beast that had done this terrible thing to him, for he was a follower of the Prophet. His story was that when that morning he had approached the tree he had felled the previous day, to saw it up, a pig which had been sheltering among the branches ran against him and cut his leg. When I suggested that it was his own fault for having got in the way of the pig, he indignantly exclaimed: 'With the whole jungle to run about in, what need was there for it to have run against me when I had done nothing to offend it, and in fact before I had even seen it?'

There was another sawyer too. While turning over a log he had been stung on the palm of his hand by a scorpion 'as big as this'. After treatment, he rolled on the ground loudly lamenting his fate and asserting that the medicine was doing him no good, but not long after he was observed to be holding his sides and choking with laughter. It was the day of the children's annual fête, and when the races had been run and the two hundred children and their mothers had been fed on sweets and fruit, a circle had been formed. A blindfolded boy had been set to break a paper bag containing nuts of all kinds, which was slung between two bamboos held upright by two men; and it was when the boy brought his stick down on the head of one of these men that the scorpion patient was found to be laughing the loudest of all the assembly. When asked how the pain now was the man replied that it had gone, and that in any case he would not mind how many scorpions stung him provided he could take part in a *tamasha* like this.

The members of our family have been amateur physicians for

more years than I can remember, and as Indians, especially the poorer ones, have long memories, and never forget a kindness no matter how trivial it may have been, not all the people who walked up the steps of our cottage at Kaladhungi were patients. Many there were who had marched for days over rough tracks in all weathers to thank us for small kindnesses shown to them, maybe the previous year, or maybe many years previously. One of these was a sixteen-year-old boy, who with his mother had been housed for some days in our village while Maggie treated his mother for influenza and badly inflamed eyes; now he had done a march of many days to bring Maggie his mother's thanks and a present of a few pomegranates which his mother had picked for her 'with her own hand'. And only that day, an hour before the man wearing the patched suit had arrived, an old man had walked up the steps and seated himself on the veranda with his back to one of the pillars and, after looking at me for some time, had shaken his head in a disapproving manner and said, 'You are looking much older, Sahib, than you were when I last saw you.' 'Yes', I replied, 'all of us are apt to look older after ten years.' 'Not all of us, Sahib,' he rejoined, 'for I look and feel no older than when I last sat in your veranda not ten, but twelve years ago. On that occasion I was returning on foot from a pilgrimage to Badrinath, and seeing your gate open, and being tired and in urgent need of ten rupees, I asked you to let me rest for a while, and appealed to you for help. I am now returning from another pilgrimage, this time to the sacred city of Benares. I am in no need of money and have only come to thank you for the help you gave me before and to tell you that I got home safely. After this smoke, and a little rest, I shall return to rejoin my family, whom I left at Haldwani.' A fourteen-mile walk each way. And in spite of his assertion that twelve years had not made him look or feel any older, he was a frail old man.

Though the face of the man in the patched cotton suit who now stood before us on the veranda was vaguely familiar, we could not remember his name or the circumstances in which we had last seen him. Seeing that he was not recognized, the man removed his coat, opened his shirt, and exposed his chest and right shoulder. That shoulder brought him to instant memory. He was Narwa. Narwa the basket-maker, and there was some excuse for our not having recognized him, for when we had last seen him, six years previously, he was mere skin and bone; only with great difficulty had he been able to put one foot before another, and he had needed a stick to support himself. Looking now at his misshapen shoulder, the crushed and broken bones of which had calloused without being set, the puckered and discoloured skin of his chest and back, and his partially withered right arm, we who for three months had watched his gallant fight for life marvelled how well he had survived his ordeal. Moving his arm up and down, and closing and opening his hand, Narwa said that his arm was getting stronger every day. His fingers had not got stiff, as we feared they would, so he had been able to resume his trade. His object now, he said, was to show us that he was quite well and to thank Maggie—which he proceeded to do by putting his head on her feet—for having supplied all his wants, and the wants of his wife and child, during the months he had lain between life and death.

Narwa's Ordeal

Narwa and Haria were not blood brothers, though they so described themselves. They had been born and had grown up in the same village near Almora, and when old enough to work had adopted the same profession, basket-making—which means that they were untouchables, for in the United Provinces baskets are only made by untouchables. During the summer months Narwa and Haria worked at their trade in their village near Almora, and in the winter months they came down to Kaladhungi where there was a great demand for the huge baskets, measuring up to fifteen feet in diameter, which they made for our villagers for the storage of grain. In their hill village near Almora they made their baskets of ringals—thin bamboo an inch thick and up to twenty feet long, which grows at an altitude of four to ten thousand feet, and which incidentally makes the most perfect of fly-rods—and in Kaladhungi they made them of bamboos.

The bamboos in Kaladhungi grow in the Government Reserved Forests, and we who cultivate land near the Reserved Forests are permitted to cut a certain number each year for our personal use. But people who use the bamboos for commercial purposes have to take out a licence from the forest guard of the area, paying two annas per headload, and a small consideration to the forest guard for his trouble in filling in the licence. As the licence is a personal one and covers an individual headload it is safe to assume that as many lengths of two-year-old bamboos—the age when a bamboo is best for basket-making—were included in the load as a man could carry.

At daybreak on the morning of 26 December 1939 Narwa and Haria set out from their communal hut near the bazaar at Kaladhungi to walk eight miles to Nalni village, obtain a licence from the forest guard, cut two headloads of bamboos in the Nalni

Reserved Forests, and return to Kaladhungi the same evening. It was bitterly cold when they started, so the two men wrapped coarse cotton sheets round their shoulders to keep out the cold. For a mile their way ran along the canal bank. Then, after negotiating the series of high walls which form the headworks of the canal, they took a footpath which runs alternately through patches of dense scrub jungle and over long stretches of the boulder-strewn bank of the Boar river, stretches where a pair of otters are usually to be seen in the early morning, and where, when the sun is on the water, *mahseer* up to three or four pounds can be taken on a fly-rod. Two miles up they crossed by a shallow ford from the right to the left bank of the river and entered a tree and grass jungle, where morning and evening are to be seen several small herds of *chital* and *sambhar*, and an occasional *kakar*, leopard, or tiger. A mile through this jungle, they came to where the hills converge, and where some years previously Robin picked up the tracks of the Bachelor of Powalgarh. From this point onwards the valley opens out and is known to all who graze cattle,

or who poach or shoot in the area, as Samal Chour. In this valley one has to walk warily, for the footpath is used almost as much by tigers as it is by human beings.

At the upper end of the valley the footpath, before going steeply up the hill for two miles to Nalni village, passes through a strip of grass. This strip of eight-foot grass is thirty yards wide and extends for about fifty yards on either side of the path. In anticipation of the stiff climb up the Nalni hill, shortly before reaching the grass Narwa divested himself of his cotton sheet, folded it small and placed it on his right shoulder. Haria was leading, with Narwa following a few steps behind, and he had only gone three or four yards into the grass when he heard the angry roar of a tiger, and simultaneously a shriek from Narwa. Haria turned and dashed back, and on the open ground at the edge of the grass he saw Narwa on his back with a tiger lying diagonally across him. Narwa's feet were nearest to him, and grasping an ankle in each hand he started to pull him away from under the tiger. As he did this the tiger stood up, turned towards him and started to growl. After dragging Narwa along on his back for a short distance Haria got his arms round him and set him on his feet. But Narwa was too badly injured and shaken to stand or walk, so Haria put his arms round him, and alternately dragged and carried him—while the tiger continued to growl— through the open ground skirting the grass, and so regained the path to Nalni village. By superhuman efforts Haria eventually got Narwa to Nalni, where it was found that in spite of the folded sheet which he had been carrying on his right shoulder, and which Haria had retrieved while pulling him away, the tiger had crushed the bones of the shoulder, lacerated the flesh, and exposed the bones on the right side of the chest and back. All four of the tiger's canine teeth had penetrated some eight folds of the sheet, and but for this obstruction they would have met in Narwa's chest and inflicted a fatal wound.

The forest guard and the people in Nalni were unable to do anything for Narwa, so Haria hired a pack pony for two rupees, mounted Narwa on it, and set out for Kaladhungi. The distance, as I have already said, was eight miles, but Haria was unwilling to face the tiger a second time so he made a wide detour through Musabanga village, adding ten miles to Narwa's agonizing journey. There were no saddles at Nalni and he had been mounted on a hard pack used for carrying grain, and the first nine miles of his ride was over incredibly steep and rough ground.

Maggie was having tea on the veranda of our cottage when Narwa, soaked in blood and being held on the pony by Haria, arrived at the steps. A glance was enough to show that the case was one she could not deal with, so she quickly gave Narwa a stiff dose of sal volatile—for he was on the point of fainting— and made a sling for his arm. Then she tore up a bed sheet to be used for bandages and wrote a note to the Assistant Surgeon in charge of the Kaladhungi hospital, begging him to attend to Narwa immediately, and do all he could for him. She gave the note to our head boy and sent him to the hospital with the two men.

I was out bird shooting that day with a party of friends who were spending their Christmas holiday at Kaladhungi, and when I returned in the late evening Maggie told me about Narwa. Early next morning I was at the hospital, where I was informed by a very young and very inexperienced doctor that he had done all he could for Narwa, but as he had little hope of his recovery, and no arrangements for in-patients, he had sent Narwa home after treating him. In the large communal hut, which housed about twenty families, each of which appeared to have a record number of small children, I found Narwa lying in a corner on a bed of straw and leaves. It was the last place for a man in his terrible condition to be in, for his wounds were showing signs of getting septic. For a week Narwa lay in the corner of the noisy and insanitary hut, at times raving in high fever, at times in a state of coma, watched over by his weeping wife, and his devoted 'brother' Haria, and by other friends. It was now apparent, even to my inexperienced eyes, that if Narwa's septic wounds were not opened up, drained, and cleaned, there was a certainty of the doctor's predictions being fulfilled, so, after making arrangements for his care while under treatment, I removed him to the hospital. To give the young doctor credit, when he undertook to do a job he did it thoroughly, and many of the long scars on his chest and back that Narwa will carry to the burning-ghat were made not by the tiger but by the doctor's lancet, which he used very freely.

With the exception of professional beggars, the poor in India can only eat when they work, and as Narwa's wife's days were fully occupied in visiting him at the hospital, and later in nursing him when he returned to the communal hut, and in caring for her three-year-old girl and her young baby, Maggie supplied all Narwa's wants,[1] and the wants of his family. Three months later, reduced to skin and bone and with a right arm that looked as though it could never be used again, Narwa crawled from the hut to our cottage to bid us goodbye and the next day he and Haria and their families set out for their village near Almora.

After visiting Narwa in the communal hut that first morning, and getting a firsthand account of the incident from Haria, I was convinced that the tiger's encounter with Narwa was accidental. However, to satisfy myself that my reconstruction of the event was right—and to shoot the tiger if I was wrong—I followed, foot by foot, the track the brothers had taken the previous day

---

[1]Small hospitals in India do not provide either attendants or food for patients.

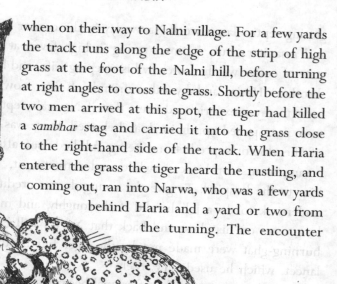

when on their way to Nalni village. For a few yards the track runs along the edge of the strip of high grass at the foot of the Nalni hill, before turning at right angles to cross the grass. Shortly before the two men arrived at this spot, the tiger had killed a *sambhar* stag and carried it into the grass close to the right-hand side of the track. When Haria entered the grass the tiger heard the rustling, and coming out, ran into Narwa, who was a few yards behind Haria and a yard or two from the turning. The encounter was accidental, for the grass was too thick and too high for the tiger to have seen Narwa before he bumped into him. Furthermore it had made no attempt to savage Narwa, and had even allowed Haria to drag the man on whom it was lying away from under it. So the tiger was allowed to live, and was later induced to join the party of tigers that are mentioned in the chapter 'Just Tigers' in *Man-eaters of Kumaon*.

Of all the brave deeds that I have witnessed, or that I have read or heard about, I count Haria's rescue of Narwa the greatest. Unarmed and alone in a great expanse of jungle, to respond to the cry of a companion in distress and to pull that companion away from an angry tiger that was lying on him, and then to drag and carry that companion for two miles up a steep hill to a place of safety, not knowing but that the tiger was following, needed a degree of courage that is given to few, and that any man could envy. When I took down Haria's statement—which was later corroborated in every detail by Narwa—with the object, unknown to him, of his act receiving recognition, so far from thinking that he had done anything deserving of commendation, after I had finished questioning him he said: 'I have not done anything, Sahib, have I, that is likely to bring trouble on me or on my brother Narwa?' And Narwa, a few days later, when I took down what I feared would be his dying declaration, said in a voice racked with pain and little above a whisper, 'Don't let my brother get into any trouble, Sahib, for it was not his fault that the tiger attacked me, and he risked his life to save mine'.

I should have liked to have been able to end my story by telling you that Haria's brave act, and Narwa's heroic fight for life against great odds, had been acknowledged by a certificate of merit, or some other small token of award, for both were poor men. Unfortunately red tape proved too much for me, for the Government were not willing to make any award in a case of which the truth could not be sworn to by independent and unbiased witnesses.

So one of the bravest deeds ever performed has gone unrecognized because there were no 'independent and unbiased witnesses'; and of the brothers Haria is the poorer of the two, for he has nothing to show for the part he played, while Narwa has his scars and the sheet with many holes, stained with his blood.

For many days I toyed with the idea of appealing to His Majesty the King, but with a world war starting and all it implied I very reluctantly abandoned the idea.

SULTANA: INDIA'S ROBIN HOOD

In a country as vast as India, with its great areas of forest land and bad communications, and with its teeming population chronically on the verge of starvation, it is easy to understand the temptations to embark on a life of crime, and the difficulty the Government have in rounding up criminals. In addition to the ordinary criminals to be found in all countries, there are in India whole tribes classed as criminals who are segregated in settlements set apart for them by the Government and subjected to a greater or lesser degree of restraint according to the crimes they specialize in.

While I was engaged on welfare work during a part of the last war, I frequently visited one of these criminal settlements. The inmates were not kept under close restraint, and I had many interesting talks with them and with the Government representative in charge of the settlement. In an effort to wean this tribe from a life of crime the Government had given them, free of rent, a large tract of alluvial land on the left bank of the Jumna river in the Meerut District. This rich land produced bumper crops of sugarcane, wheat, barley, rape seed, and other cereals, but crime persisted. The Government representative blamed the girls, who, he said, refused to marry any but successful criminals. The tribe specialized in robbery, and there were old men in the settlement who trained the younger generation on a profit-sharing basis. Men were allowed to leave the settlement on ticket of leave for stated periods, but women were not permitted to leave. The elders of the tribe strictly enforced three rules: first, that all robberies were to be carried out single-handed; second, that the scene of the crime was to be as distant from the settlement as possible; and third, that violence while committing the crime was not to be resorted to in any circumstances.

The method invariably adopted by a young man, after he had completed his training, was to secure employment as a house servant with a rich man in Calcutta, Bombay, or some other distant city, and when opportunity offered to rob his master of articles which could be easily secreted, such as gold, jewellery, or precious stones. On one occasion while I was paying a number of young men who had been driving black partridge out of a sugarcane field for me, the Government representative informed me that the young man into whose hands I had just dropped his wage of eight annas, plus two annas for a runner he had retrieved, had returned to the settlement a few days previously, after an absence of a year, with a diamond worth thirty thousand rupees. After valuation by the experts of the tribe the diamond had been hidden, and the most sought-after girl in the settlement had promised to marry the successful criminal during the next marriage season. Another of the men standing near by, who had not taken part in the partridge drive, had conceived the novel plan of impressing the girl of his choice by driving up to the settlement, along a most appalling cart-track, in a new motor-car he had stolen in Calcutta. In order to carry out his plan he had first had to pay for driving lessons.

Some members of criminal tribes who are not subjected to

strict control find employment as night watchmen in private houses, and I know of instances where it was a sufficient guarantee against theft for the watchman to place a pair of his shoes on the doorstep of the house in which he was employed. This may savour of blackmail, but it was cheap blackmail, for the wages paid varied from three to five rupees a month, according to the standing of the criminal, and the money was easily earned as all the watchman had to do was to place his shoes in position at night, and remove them again the next morning.

Owing to their preference for violent crime the Bhantus were one of the criminal tribes in the United Provinces that were kept under strict restraint, and Sultana, the famous dacoit who for three years defied all the Government's efforts to capture him, was a member of this tribe. It is about Sultana that this story is written.

When I first knew it, Naya Gaon was one of the most flourishing villages in the Terai and Bhabar—the tract of land running along the foothills of the Himalayas. Every yard of the rich soil, carved out of virgin forest, was under intensive cultivation, and the hundred or more tenants were prosperous, contented, and happy. Sir Henry Ramsay, the King of Kumaon, had brought these hardy people down from the Himalayas, and for a generation they retained their vigour and flourished exceedingly.

Malaria at that time was known as 'Bhabar fever', and the few doctors, scattered over a wide area, who were responsible for the health of the people, had neither the ability nor the means to cope with this scourge of the foothills. Naya Gaon, situated in the heart of the forest, was one of the first villages in the Bhabar to be decimated by the disease. Field after field went out of cultivation as the tenants died, until only a handful of the sturdy pioneers were left, and when these survivors were given land in our village Naya Gaon reverted to jungle. Only once in later years was an attempt made to recultivate the land, the intrepid pioneer on this occasion being a doctor from the Punjab; but when first his daughter, then his wife, and finally he himself died of malaria, Naya Gaon for the second time went back to the jungle.

On the land which had been cleared with great labour, on which bumper crops of sugarcane, wheat, mustard, and rice had been grown, luxuriant grass sprang up. Attracted by this rich feed, the cattle from our village three miles away adopted the deserted fields of Naya Gaon as their regular feeding ground. When cattle graze for long periods over open ground surrounded by jungle they invariably attract carnivora, and I was not surprised to hear one year, on our descent from our summer home in Naini Tal to our winter home in Kaladhungi, that a leopard had taken up residence in the jungles adjoining the grazing-ground and that he was taking heavy toll of our cattle. There were no trees on the grassland in which I could sit over a kill, so I determined to shoot the leopard either in the early morning, when he was on his way to lie up in thick cover for the day, or in the evening, when he was returning to a kill or intent on making a fresh one. For either of these plans to be effective it was necessary to discover in what part of the surrounding jungles the leopard had made his home, so early one morning Robin and I set out to glean this information.

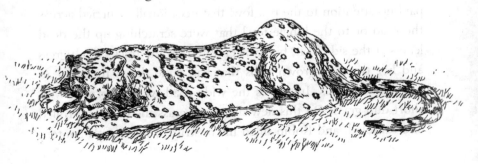

Naya Gaon—for though the land has been out of cultivation for many years it retains its name to this day—is bounded on the north by the road known as the Kandi Sarak, and on the east by the old Trunk Road which before the advent of railways connected the plains of the United Provinces with the interior of Kumaon. To the south and west, Naya Gaon is bounded by dense jungle.

Both the Kandi Sarak and the Trunk Road are little used in these days and I decided to try them first before trying the more difficult ground to the south and west. At the junction of the roads, where in the days gone by a police guard was posted for the protection of wayfarers against dacoits, Robin and I found the tracks of a female leopard. This leopard was well known to Robin and me, for she had lived for several years in a heavy patch of lantana at the lower end of our village. Apart from never molesting our cattle, she had kept pigs and monkeys from damaging our crops, so we ignored her tracks and carried on along the Trunk Road in the direction of Garuppu. There had been no traffic on the road since the previous evening, and the tracks of animals who had used or crossed it were registered on the dusty surface.

From the rifle in my hands Robin, who was a wise dog and my constant companion, knew we were not after birds so he paid no attention to the pea fowl that occasionally scurried across the road or to the jungle fowl that were scratching up the dead leaves at the side of it, but concentrated on the tracks of a tigress and her two half-grown cubs that had gone down the road an hour ahead of us. In places the wide road was overgrown with short dub grass. On this dew-drenched grass the cubs had rolled and tumbled, and Robin filled his nostrils to his heart's content with the sweet and terrifying smell of tiger. The family had kept to the road for a mile and had then gone east along a game track. Three miles from the junction and two miles above Garuppu, a well-used game track coming from the direction of Naya Gaon crosses the road diagonally, and on this track we saw the fresh pug marks of a big male leopard. We had found what we were looking for. This leopard had come from the grazing ground and crossed the road. It was capable of killing a full-grown cow and there were not likely to be two leopards of this size in the same area. Robin was keen on following up the tracks, but the dense scrub jungle the leopard was making for—the same jungle in which Kunwar Singh and Har Singh had nearly lost their lives some years previously—was not suitable for stalking an animal with the sight and hearing of a leopard. Moreover, I had a better and simpler plan of making contact with the leopard, so we turned about and made for home and breakfast.

After lunch Robin and I, accompanied by Maggie, retraced our steps down the Garuppu road. The leopard had not killed any of our cattle the previous day but he might have killed a *chital* or a pig which shared the grazing ground with the cattle; and even if he had no kill to return to there was a very good chance of his visiting his regular hunting ground. So Maggie and I, with Robin lying between us, took up position behind a bush on the side of the road, a hundred yards from the game track along which the leopard had gone that morning. We had been in position about an hour, listening to the multitude of bird calls, when a peacock in full plumage majestically crossed the road and went down the game path. A little later, ten or a dozen *chital*, in the direction of the heavy jungle in which we expected the leopard to be lying up, warned the jungle folk of the presence of a leopard. Ten minutes thereafter, and a little nearer to us, a single *chital* repeated the warning. The leopard was on the move and coming in our direction, and as he was making no attempt to conceal himself he was probably on his way to a kill.

Robin had lain with chin on outstretched paws without movement, listening as we were to what the jungle folk had to say, and when he saw me draw up my leg and rest the rifle on my knee, his body, which was against my left leg, started to tremble. The spotted killer whom he feared more than any other beast in the jungle would presently put its head out of the bushes and, after looking up and down the road, would come towards us. Whether it died in its tracks, or roared and tumbled about with a mortal wound, he would remain perfectly still and silent, for he was taking part in a game with every move of which he was familiar, and which was as fascinating as it was terrifying.

After going a short distance down the game path the peacock had climbed into the branches of a plum tree and was busily engaged in eating ripe fruit. Suddenly it sprang into the air with a harsh scream and alighted on the limb of a dead tree, adding its warning to that already given by the *chital*. A few minutes now, five at the most, for the leopard would approach the road very cautiously, and then out of the corner of my eye I caught sight of a movement far down the road. It was a man running, and every now and then, without slackening his pace, he looked over his shoulder behind him. To see a man on that road at this hour of the evening—the sun was near setting—was very unusual, and to see him alone was even more unusual. Every stride the man took lessened our chances of bagging the leopard. However, that could not be helped, for the runner was evidently in great distress, and possibly in need of help. I recognized him while he was still some distance from us; he was a tenant in a village adjoining ours who during the winter months was engaged as herdsman at a cattle station three miles east of Garuppu. On catching sight of us the runner started violently, but when he recognized me he came towards us and in a very agitated voice said, 'Run, Sahib, run for your life! Sultana's men are after me.'

He was winded and in great distress. Taking no notice of my invitation to sit down and rest, he turned his leg and said, 'See what they have done to me! If they catch me they will surely kill me, and you also, if you do not run.' The leg he turned for our inspection was slashed from the back of the knee to the heel, and dust-clotted blood was flowing from the ugly wound. Telling the man that if he would not rest there was at least no need for him to run any more, I moved out of the bushes to where I could get a clear view down the road, while the man limped off in the direction of his village. Neither the leopard nor Sultana's men showed up, and when there was no longer light for accurate shooting, Maggie and I, with a very disgusted Robin at our heels, returned to our home at Kaladhungi.

Next morning I got the man's story. He was grazing his buffaloes between Garuppu and the cattle station when he heard a gunshot. The nephew of the headman of his village had arrived at the cattle station at dawn that morning with the object of poaching a *chital*, and while he had been sitting in the shade of a tree, speculating as to whether the shot had been effective or not and, if effective, whether a portion of the venison would be left at the cattle station for his evening meal, he heard a rustle behind him. Looking round, he saw five men standing over him. He was told to get up and take the party to where the gun had been fired. When he said he had been asleep and had not heard the shot he was ordered to lead the way to the cattle station, to which they thought the gunman would probably go. The party had no firearms, but the man who appeared to be their leader had a naked sword in his hand and said he would cut the herdsman's head off with it if he attempted to run away or shout a warning.

As they made their way through the jungle the swordsman informed the herdsman that they were members of Sultana's gang and that Sultana was camped near by. When he heard the shot Sultana had ordered them to bring him the gun. Therefore if they met with any opposition at the cattle station they would burn it down and kill their guide. This threat presented my friend with a dilemma. His companions at the cattle station were a tough lot, and if they offered resistance he would undoubtedly be killed; on the other hand, if they did not resist, his crime in leading the dread Sultana's men to the station would never be forgotten or forgiven. While these unpleasant thoughts were running through his head a *chital* stag pursued by a pack of wild dogs came dashing through the jungle and passed within a few yards of them. Seeing that his escort had stopped and were watching the chase the herdsman dived into the high grass on the side of the path and, despite the wound he received on his leg as the swordsman tried to cut him down, he had managed to shake his pursuers off and gain the Trunk Road, where in due course he ran into us while we were waiting for the leopard.

Sultana was a member of the Bhantu criminal tribe. With the rights and wrongs of classing a tribe as 'criminal' and confining it within the four walls of the Najibabad Fort I am not concerned. It suffices to say that Sultana, with his young wife and infant son and some hundreds of other Bhantus, was confined in the fort under the charge of the Salvation Army. Chafing at his confinement, he scaled the mud walls of the fort one night and escaped, as any young and high-spirited man would have done. This escape had been effected a year previous to the opening of my story and during that year Sultana had collected a hundred kindred spirits, all armed with guns, around him. This imposing gang, whose declared object was dacoity, led a roving life in the jungles of the Terai and Bhabar, their activities extending from Gonda in the east to Saharanpur in the west, a distance of several hundred miles, with occasional raids into the adjoining province of the Punjab.

There are many fat files in Government offices on the activities of Sultana and his gang of dacoits. I have not had access to these files, and if my story, which only deals with events in which I took part or events which came to my personal notice, differs or conflicts in any respects with government reports I can only express my regret. At the same time I do not retract one word of my story.

I first heard of Sultana when he was camping in the Garuppu jungles a few miles from our winter home at Kaladhungi. Percy Wyndham was at that time Commissioner of Kumaon, and as the Terai and Bhabar forests in which Sultana had apparently established himself were in Wyndham's charge he asked Government for the services of Freddy Young, a keen young police officer with a few years' service in the United Provinces to his credit. The Government granted Wyndham's request, and sanctioned the creation of a Special Dacoity Police Force of three hundred picked men. Freddy was put in supreme command of this force and given a free hand in the selection of his men. He earned a lot of unpopularity by building up his force with the best men from adjoining districts, for Sultana was a coveted prize and their own officers resented having to surrender men who might have helped them to acquire the prize.

While Freddy was mustering his force, Sultana was getting his hand in by raiding small townships in the Terai and Bhabar. Freddy's first attempt to capture Sultana was made in the forests west of Ramnagar. The Forest Department were felling a portion of these forests, employing a large labour force, and one of the contractors in charge of the labour was induced to invite Sultana, who was known to be camping in the vicinity, to a dance to be followed by a feast. Sultana and his merry men accepted the invitation, but just before the festivities began they prevailed on their host to make a slight alteration in the programme and have the feast first and the dance later. Sultana said his men would enjoy the dance more on full stomachs than on empty ones.

Here it is necessary to interrupt my story to explain for the benefit of those who have never been in the East that guests at a dance, or a 'nautch' as it is called here, do not take any part in the proceedings. The dancing is confined to a troop of professional dancing-girls and their male orchestra.

Funds in plenty were available on both sides and, as money goes as far in the East towards buying information as it does in the West, one of the first moves of the two contestants in the game that was to be played was the organization of efficient secret services. Here Sultana had the advantage, for whereas Freddy could only reward for services rendered, Sultana could not only reward but could also punish for information withheld, or for information about his movements to the police, and when his method of dealing with offenders became known none were willing to court his displeasure.

Having known what it was to be poor, really poor, during his long years of confinement in the Najibabad Fort, Sultana had a warm corner in his heart for all poor people. It was said of him that, throughout his career as a dacoit, he never robbed a pice from a poor man, never refused an appeal for charity, and paid twice the price asked for all he purchased from small shopkeepers. Little wonder then that his intelligence staff numbered hundreds and that he knew the invitation he had received to the dance and feast had been issued at Freddy's instigation.

Meanwhile plans were on foot for the great night. The contractor, reputed to be a rich man, extended invitations to his friends in Ramnagar and in Kashipur; the best dancing-girls and their orchestras were engaged, and large quantities of eatables and drink—the latter specially for the benefit of the dacoits—were purchased and transported by bullock cart to the camp.

At the appointed time on the night that was to see the undoing of Sultana, the contractor's guests assembled and the feast began. It is possible that the contractor's friends did not know who their fellow guests were, for on these occasions the different castes sit in groups by themselves and the illumination provided by firelight and a few lanterns was of the poorest. Sultana and his men ate and drank wisely and well, and when the feast was nearing its end the dacoit leader led his host aside, thanked him for his hospitality, and said that as he and his men had a long way to go he regretted they could not stay for the dance. Before leaving, however, he requested—and Sultana's requests were never disregarded—that the festivities should continue as had been arranged.

The principal instrument of music at a nautch is a drum, and the sound of the drums was to be Freddy's signal to leave the position he had taken up and deploy his force to surround the camp. One section of this force was led

by a forest guard, and the night being dark the forest guard lost his way. This section, which was to have blocked Sultana's line of retreat, remained lost for the remainder of the night. As a matter of fact the forest guard, who had to live in the forest with Sultana and was a wise man, need not have given himself the trouble of getting lost, for by his request for a slight alteration in the programme Sultana had given himself ample time to get clear of the net before the signal was given. So all that the attacking force found when they arrived at the camp, after a long and a difficult march through dense forest, was a troop of frightened girls, their even more frightened orchestra, and the mystified friends of the contractor.

After his escape from the Ramnagar forests Sultana paid a visit to the Punjab. Here, with no forests in which to shelter, he was out of his element and after a brief stay, which yielded a hundred thousand rupees' worth of gold ornaments, he returned to the dense jungles of the United Provinces. On his way back from the Punjab he had to cross the Ganges canal, the bridges over which are spaced at intervals of four miles, and as his movements were known, the bridges he was likely to cross were heavily guarded. Avoiding these, Sultana made for a bridge which his intelligence staff informed him was not guarded, and on his way passed close to a large village in which a band was playing Indian music. On learning from his guides that a rich man's son was being married, he ordered them to take him to the village.

The wedding party and some thousand guests were assembled on a wide open space in the centre of the village. As he entered the glare of the high-powered lamps Sultana's appearance caused a stir, but he requested the assembly to remain seated and added that if they complied with his request they had nothing to fear. He then summoned the headman of the village and the father of the bridegroom and made it known that, as this was a propitious time for the giving and receiving of gifts, he would like the headman's recently purchased gun for himself, and ten thousand rupees in cash for his men. The gun and the money were produced in the shortest time possible, and having wished the assembly good night Sultana led his men out of the village. Not till the following day did he learn that his lieutenant, Pailwan, had abducted the bride. Sultana did not approve of women being molested by his gang, so Pailwan was severely reprimanded and the girl was sent back, with a suitable present to compensate her for the inconvenience to which she had been put.

After the incident of the herdsman's slashed leg Sultana remained in our vicinity for some time. He moved camp frequently and I came upon several old sites while out shooting. It was at this time that I had a very exciting experience. One evening I shot a fine leopard on a fire-track five miles from home, and as there was not sufficient time to collect carriers to bring it in, I skinned it on the spot and carried the skin home; but on arrival I found that I had left my favourite hunting-knife behind. Early next morning I set out to retrieve the knife and as I approached the spot where I had left it I saw the glimmer of a fire through a forest glade, some distance from the track. Reports of Sultana's presence in this forest had been coming in for some days, and on the spur of the moment I decided to investigate the fire. Heavy dew on the dead leaves made it possible to move without sound, so taking what cover was available I stalked the fire, which was burning in a little hollow, and found some twenty to twenty-five men sitting round it. Stacked upright against a nearby tree, the fire glinting on their barrels, were a number of guns. Sultana was not present, for, though I had not seen him up to that time, he had been described to me as a young man, small and trim, who invariably dressed in semi-military khaki uniform. This was evidently part of his gang, however, and what was I going to do about it? The old head constable and his equally elderly force of two constables at Kaladhungi would be of little help, and Haldwani, where there was a big concentration of police, was fifteen miles away.

While I was considering my next move, I heard one of the men say it was time to be going. Fearing that if I now tried to retreat I should be seen, and trouble might follow, I took a few rapid steps forward and got between the men and their guns. As I did so a ring of surprised faces looked up at me, for I was on slightly higher ground. When I asked them what they were doing here the men looked at each other,  and the first to recover from his surprise said, 'Nothing'. In reply to further questions I was told that they were charcoal burners who had come from Bareilly and had lost their way. I then turned and looked towards the tree, and found that what I had taken to be gun barrels were stacked axes, the handles of which, polished by long and hard use, had reflected the firelight. Telling the men that my feet were wet and cold I joined their circle, and after we had smoked my cigarettes and talked of many things, I directed them to the charcoal-burners' camp they were looking for, recovered my knife, and returned home.

In times of sustained excitement imagination is apt to play queer tricks. Sitting on the ground near a *sambhar* killed by the tiger I have heard the tiger coming and coming, and getting no nearer, and when the tension had become unbearable have turned round with finger on trigger to find a caterpillar biting minute bits out of a crisp leaf near my head. Again, when the light was fading and the time had come for the tiger to return to his kill, out of the corner of my eye I had seen a large animal appear; and as I was gripping my rifle and preparing for a shot an ant had crawled

out on a dry twig a few inches from my face. With my thoughts
on Sultana the glint of firelight on the polished axe-handles had
converted them into gun barrels, and I never looked at them
again until the men had convinced me they were charcoal burners.

With his efficient organization and better means of transport,
Freddy was beginning to exert pressure on Sultana, and to ease
the strain the dacoit leader took his gang, by this time considerably
reduced by desertion and capture, to Pilibhit on the eastern
border of the district. Here he remained for a few months, raiding
as far afield as Gorakhpur and building up his store of gold.
On his return to the forests in our vicinity he learned that a very
rich dancing-girl from the State of Rampur had recently taken
up residence with the headman of Lamachour, a village seven
miles from our home. Anticipating a raid, the headman provided
himself with a guard of thirty of his tenants. The guard was not
armed, and when Sultana arrived, before his men were able to
surround the house the dancing-girl slipped through a back door
and escaped into the night with all her jewellery. The headman
and his tenants were rounded up in the courtyard, and when
they denied all knowledge of the girl orders were given to tie
them up and beat them to refresh their memories. To this order
one of the tenants raised an objection. He said Sultana could
do what he liked to him and his fellow tenants, but that he had
no right to disgrace the headman by having him tied up and
beaten. He was ordered to keep his mouth shut, but as one of
the dacoits advanced towards the headman with a length of rope
this intrepid man pulled a length of bamboo out of a lean-to and
dashed at the dacoit. He was shot through the chest by one of
the gang, but fearing the shot would arouse armed men in
neighbouring villages Sultana beat a hasty retreat, taking with
him a horse which the headman had recently purchased.

I heard of the murder of the brave tenant next morning and sent one of my men to Lamachour to inquire what family the dead man had left, and I sent another man with an open letter to all the headmen of the surrounding villages to ask if they would join in raising a fund for the support of his family. The response to my appeal was as generous as I expected it to be, for the poor are always generous, but the fund was never raised, for the man who had given his life for his master came from Nepal twenty years previously, and neither his friends nor the inquiries I made in Nepal revealed that he had a wife or children.

It was after the incident just related that I accepted Freddy's invitation to take a hand in rounding up Sultana, and a month later I joined him at his headquarters at Hardwar. During his eighteen years as Collector of Mirzapur Wyndham had employed ten Koles and ten Bhunyas from the tribes living in the Mirzapur forests to assist him in tiger shooting, and the four best of these men, who were old friends of mine, were now placed by Wyndham at Freddy's disposal and I found them waiting for me at Hardwar. Freddy's plan was for my four friends and myself to track down Sultana, and when we had done this, to lead his force to a convenient place from which to launch his attack. Both these operations, for reasons already given, were to be carried out at night. But Sultana was restless. Perhaps it was just nervousness, or he may have had forewarning of Freddy's plans; anyway he never stayed for more than a day in any one place, and he moved his force long distances at night.

The weather was intensely hot and eventually, tired of inaction, the four men and I held a council of war the result of which was that after dinner that night, when Freddy was comfortably seated in a cool part of the veranda where there was no possibility of our being overheard, I put the following proposal before him. He was to let it be known that Wyndham had recalled his men for a tiger shoot, to which I had been invited, and was to have tickets to Haldwani purchased for us and see us off from the Hardwar station by the night train. At the first stop the train made, however, the four men, armed with guns provided by Freddy, and I with my own rifle were to leave the train. Thereafter we were to have a free hand to bring in Sultana, dead or alive, as opportunity offered.

Freddy sat for a long time with his eyes closed after hearing my proposal—he weighed 20 stone 4 pounds and was apt to doze after dinner—but he was not asleep, for he suddenly sat up and in a very decided voice said, 'No. I am responsible for your lives, and I won't sanction this mad scheme'. Arguing with him was of no avail, so the next morning the four men and I left for our respective homes. I was wrong to have made the proposal, and Freddy was right in turning it down. The four men and I had no official standing, and had trouble resulted from our attempt to capture Sultana our action could not have been justified. For the rest, neither Sultana's life nor ours was in any danger, for we had agreed that if Sultana could not be taken alive he would not be taken at all, and we were quite capable of looking after ourselves.

Three months later, when the monsoon was in full blast, Freddy asked Herbert of the Forest Department, Fred Anderson, Superintendent of the Terai and Bhabar, and myself, to join him at Hardwar. On arrival we learnt that Freddy had located Sultana's permanent camp in the heart of the Najibabad jungles, and he wanted us to assist him in surrounding the camp, and to cut off Sultana's retreat if he slipped out of the ring. Herbert, a famous polo player, was to be put in command of the fifty mounted men who were to prevent Sultana's escape, while Anderson and I were to accompany Freddy and help him to form the ring.

By this time Freddy had no illusions about the efficiency of

Sultana's intelligence service, and with the exception of Freddy's two assistants, and the three of us, no one knew of the contemplated raid. Each evening the police force, fully armed, were sent out on a long route march, while the four of us went out for an equally long walk, returning after dark to the Dam Bungalow in which we were staying. On the appointed night, instead of marching over the level crossing as they had been wont to do, the route marchers went through the Hardwar goods yard to a siding in which a rake of wagons, with engine and brake-van attached, was standing with the doors open on the side away from the station buildings. The last of the doors was being shut as we arrived, and the moment we had climbed into the guard's van the train, without any warning whistles, started. Everything that could be done to allay suspicion had been done, even to the cooking of the men's food in their lines and to the laying of our table for dinner. We had started an hour after dark. At 9 p.m. the train drew up between two stations in the heart of the jungle and the order was passed from wagon to wagon for the force to detrain, and as soon as this order had been carried out the train steamed on.

Of Freddy's force of three hundred men, the fifty to be led by Herbert—who served in France in the First World War with the Indian cavalry—had been sent out the previous night with instructions to make a wide detour to where their mounts were waiting for them, while the main force of two hundred and

fifty men with Freddy and Anderson in the lead, and myself
bringing up the rear, set off for a destination which was said to
be some twenty miles away. Heavy clouds had been banking up
all day and when we left the train it was raining in torrents.
Our direction was north for a mile, then east for two miles,
again north for a mile, then west for two miles, and finally again
north. I knew the changes in direction were being made to avoid
villages in which there were men in Sultana's pay, and the fact
that not a village pye, the best watchdog in the world, barked
at us testifies to the skill with which the manoeuvre was carried
out. Hour after hour I plodded on, in drenching rain, in the
wake of two hundred and fifty heavy men who had left potholes
in the soft ground into which I floundered up to my knees at
every second step. For miles we went through elephant grass
higher than my head, and balancing on the pitted and slippery
ground became more difficult from the necessity of using one
hand to shield my eyes from the stiff razor-edged grass. I had
often marvelled at Freddy's 20 stone 4 pounds of energy, but
never as I did that night. True, he was walking on comparatively
firm ground while I was walking in a bog; yet even so he was
carrying nine stone more than I, and the line moved on with
never a halt.

We had started at 9 p.m. At 2 a.m. I sent a verbal message
up the line to ask Freddy if we were going in the right direction.
I sent this message because for an hour we had left our original
direction northwards, and had been going east. After a long
interval word came back that the Captain Sahib said it was all
right. After another two hours, through thick tree and scrub
jungle or across patches of high grass, I sent a second message
to Freddy asking him to halt the line as I was coming up to
speak to him. Silence had been enjoined before starting, and as
I made my way to the front I passed a very quiet and weary

line of men, some of them sitting on the wet ground and others leaning against trees.

I found Freddy and Anderson with their four guides at the head of the column. When Freddy asked if anything was wrong—this I knew referred to stragglers—I said all was well with the men but otherwise everything was wrong, for we were walking in circles. Having lived so much of my life in jungles in which it is very easy to get lost I have acquired a sense of direction which functions as well by night as it does by day. Our change of direction when we first started had been as evident to me as it had been two hours back when we changed direction from north to east. In addition, an hour previously I had noted that we passed under a *simul* tree with a vulture's nest in it, and when I sent my message to Freddy to halt the line I was again under the same tree.

Of the four guides, two were Bhantus of Sultana's gang who had been captured a few days previously in the Hardwar bazaar, and on whose information the present raid had been organized. These two men had lived off and on for two years in Sultana's camp and had been promised their freedom for this night's work. The other two were cattle men who had grazed their cattle in these jungles all their lives, and who daily supplied Sultana with milk. All four men stoutly denied having lost their way, but on being pressed, they hesitated, and finally admitted that they would feel happier about the direction in which they were leading the force if they could see the hills. To see the hills, possibly thirty miles away, on a dark night with thick fog descending down to tree-top level, was impossible, so here was a check which threatened to ruin all Freddy's well-laid plans and, what was even worse, to give Sultana the laugh on us.

Our intention had been a surprise attack on the camp, and in order to accomplish this it was necessary to get within striking

distance while it was still dark. The guides had informed us
that it was not possible to approach the camp in daylight from
the side we had chosen without being seen by two guards who
were constantly on watch from a *machan* in a high tree which
overlooked a wide stretch of grass to the south of the camp.

With our guides now freely admitting they had lost their
way, only another hour of darkness left and, worst of all, without
knowing how far we were from the camp or in which direction
it lay, our chance of a surprise attack was receding with every
minute that passed. Then a way out of the dilemma occurred
to me. I asked the four men if there was any feature, such as a
stream or a well-defined cattletrack, in the direction in which
we had originally started, by which they could regain direction,
and when they replied that there was an old and well-defined
cart-track a mile to the south of the camp, I obtained Freddy's
permission to take the lead. I set off at a fast pace in a direction
which all who were following me were, I am sure, convinced
would lead back to the railway line we had left seven hours earlier.

The rain had stopped, a fresh breeze had cleared the sky of
clouds, and it was just getting light in the east when I stumbled
into a deep cart-rut. Here was the disused track the guides
had mentioned, and their joy on seeing it confirmed the opinion
I had formed earlier, that losing themselves in the jungle had
not been intentional. Taking over the lead again, the men led
us along the track for a mile to where a well-used game-track
crossed it. Half a mile up the game-track we came to a deep and
sluggish stream some thirty feet wide which I was glad to see the
track did not cross, for I am terrified of these Terai streams, on
the banks and in the depths of which I have seen huge pythons
lurking. The track skirted the right bank of the stream, through
shoulder-high grass, and after going along it for a few hundred
yards the men slowed down. From the way they kept looking

to the left I concluded we were getting within sight of the *machan*, for it was now full daylight with the sun touching the tops of the trees. Presently the leading man crouched down, and when his companions had done the same, he beckoned us to approach.

After signalling to the line to halt and sit down, Freddy, Anderson, and I crept up to the leading guide. Lying beside him and looking through the grass in the direction in which he was pointing we saw a *machan*, built in the upper branches of a big tree, between thirty and forty feet above ground. On the *machan*, with the level sun shining on them, were two men, one sitting with his right shoulder towards us smoking a hookah, and the other lying on his back with his knees drawn up. The tree in which the *machan* was built was growing on the border of the tree and grass jungle and overlooked a wide expanse of open ground. Sultana's camp, the guides said, was three hundred yards inside the tree jungle.

A few feet from where we were lying was a strip of short grass twenty yards wide, running from the stream on our right far out on to the open ground. To retreat a little, cross the stream, and recross it opposite Sultana's camp was the obvious thing to do, but the guides said this would not be possible; not only was the stream too deep to wade, but there was quicksand along the far bank. There remained the doubtful possibility of getting the whole force across the strip of short grass without being seen by the two guards, either of whom might at any moment look in our direction.

Freddy had a service revolver, Anderson was unarmed, and I was the only one in the whole force who was carrying a rifle—the police were armed with 12-bore muskets using buckshot, with an effective range of from sixty to eighty yards. I was therefore the only one of the party who could deal with the two guards from our present position. The rifle shots would, of course, be heard in the camp, but the two Bhantus with us were of the opinion that when the guards did not return to the camp to report, men would be sent out to make inquiries. They thought that while this was being done it would be possible for us to encircle the camp.

The two men on the machan were outlaws, and quite possibly murderers to boot, and with the rifle in my hands I could have shot the hookah out of the smoker's hands and the heel off the other man's shoe without injury to either. But to shoot the men in cold, or in any other temperature of blood, was beyond my powers. So I made the following alternative suggestion: that Freddy give me permission to stalk the men—which would be quite easy, for the tall grass and tree jungle extended right up to the tree in which the machan was built and was soaking wet after the all-night rain—and occupy the machan with them while Freddy and his men carried on with their job. At first Freddy demurred, for there were two guns on the machan within easy reach of the men's hands, but eventually he consented and without further ado I slipped across the open ground and set off, for the Bhantus said the time was approaching for the guards to be changed.

I had covered about a third of the way to the tree when I heard a noise behind and saw Anderson hurrying after me. What

Anderson had said to Freddy, or Freddy had said to Anderson I do not know—both were my very good friends. Anyway, Anderson was determined to accompany me. He admitted he could not get through the jungle silently; that there was a good chance of the men on the *machan* hearing and seeing us; that we might run into the relief guard or find additional guards at the foot of the tree; that being unarmed he would not be able to defend himself, nevertheless and notwithstanding, *he was not going to let me go alone.* When a man from across the Clyde digs his toes in he is more stubborn than a mule. In desperation I started to retrace my steps to solicit Freddy's help. But Freddy in the meantime had had time to regret his sanction (I learnt later the Bhantus had informed him the men on the *machan* were very good shots), and when he saw us returning he gave the signal for the line to advance.

Fifty or more men had crossed the open strip of ground and we who were in advance were within two hundred yards of the camp when a zealous young constable, catching sight of the *machan*, fired off his musket. The two men on the *machan* were down the ladder in a flash. They mounted the horses that were tethered at the foot of the tree and raced for the camp. There was now no longer any necessity for silence, and in a voice that did not need the aid of a megaphone, Freddy gave the order to charge. In a solid line we swept down on the camp, to find it deserted.

The camp was on a little knoll and consisted of three tents and a grass hut used as a kitchen. One of the tents was a store and was stacked with sacks of *atta*, *rice*, dal, sugar, tins of *ghee*, two pyramids of boxes containing some thousands of rounds of 12-bore ammunition, and eleven guns in gun cases. The other two tents were sleeping-places and were strewn with blankets and a medley of articles of clothing. Hanging from branches near the kitchen were three flayed goats.

In the confusion following the arrival in camp of the two guards it was possible that some of the partly clothed gang had taken shelter in the high grass surrounding the camp, so orders were given to our men to make a long line, our intention being to beat a wide strip of jungle in the direction in which Herbert and his mounted men were on guard. While the line was being formed I made a cast round the knoll. Having found the tracks of ten or a dozen barefooted men in a *nullah* close to the camp, I suggested to Freddy that we should follow them and see where they led to. The *nullah* was fifteen feet wide and five feet deep, and Freddy, Anderson, and I had proceeded along it for about two hundred yards when we came on an outcrop of gravel, where I lost the tracks. Beyond the gravel the *nullah* opened out and on the left bank, near where we were standing, was a giant banyan tree with multiple stems. With its forest of stems, and branches sweeping down to the ground, this tree appeared to me to be an ideal place for anyone to hide in, so going to the bank, which at this point was as high as my chin, I attempted to climb up. There was no handhold on the bank and each time I kicked a hole in the soft earth the foothold gave way, and I was just contemplating going forward and getting on to the bank where the *nullah* flattened out, when a fusillade of shots followed by shouting broke out in the direction of the camp. We dashed back the way we had come and near the camp found a *havildar* shot through the chest, and near him a dacoit, with a wisp of cloth round his loins, shot through both legs. The *havildar* was sitting on the ground with his back to a tree; his shirt was open, and on the nipple of his left breast there was a spot of blood. Freddy produced a flask and put it to the *havildar*'s lips, but the man shook his head and put the flask aside, saying, 'It is wine. I cannot drink it'. When pressed he added, 'All my life I have been an abstainer, and I cannot go to my Creator with wine on my lips. I am thirsty and crave a little water'. His brother was standing near by. Someone gave him a hat and he dashed off to the stream that had hampered our movements, and returned in a few minutes with some dirty water which the wounded man drank eagerly. The wound had been made by a pellet of shot and when I could not feel it under the skin I said, 'Keep a strong heart, Havildar Sahib, and the doctor at Najibabad will make you well'. Smiling up at me he replied, 'I will keep a strong heart, Sahib; but no doctor can make me well'.

The dacoit had no inhibitions about 'wine,' and in a few gulps he emptied the contents of the flask of which he was in great need, for he had been shot with a 12-bore musket at very short range.

Two stretchers were improvised from material taken from Sultana's camp, and willing hands—for no distinction was made between the high-caste member of the police force and the low-caste dacoit—took them up. With spare runners running alongside, the stretchers set off through the jungle for the Najibabad hospital twelve miles away. The dacoit died of loss of blood and of shock on the way, and the *havildar* died a few minutes after being admitted to the hospital.

The beat was abandoned. Herbert did not come into the picture, for Sultana had been warned of the concentration of horse and none of the dacoits tried to cross the line he was guarding. So the sum total of our carefully planned raid, which had miscarried through no one's fault, was Sultana's entire camp less a few guns, and two dead men. One a poor man, who, chafing at confinement, had sought liberty and adopted the only means of livelihood open to him and who would be mourned by a widow in the Najibabad fort. And the other a man respected by his superiors and loved by his men, whose widow would be cared for, and who had bravely died for a principle—for the 'wine' with which he refused to defile his lips would have sustained him until he had been laid on the operating table.

Three days after the raid Freddy received a letter from the dacoit leader in which Sultana regretted that a shortage of arms and ammunition in the police force had necessitated a raid on his camp, and stating that if in future Freddy would let him know his requirements he, Sultana, would be very glad to supply him.

The supply of arms and ammunition to Sultana was a very sore point with Freddy. Stringent orders on the subject had been issued, but it was not surprising that every licensed dealer and every licensed gun-holder in the area in which Sultana was operating was willing to risk the Government's displeasure when the alternative was the certainty of having his house raided, and the possibility of having his throat cut, if he refused Sultana's demands. So the offer of arms and ammunition was no idle one and it was the most unkind cut the dacoit leader could have delivered to the head of the Special Dacoity Police Force.

With his hide-out gone, harried from end to end of the Terai and Bhabar, and with his gang reduced to forty—all well armed, for the dacoits had soon replaced the arms and ammunition taken from them—Freddy thought the time had now come for Sultana to surrender. So, after obtaining Government sanction—which was given on the understanding that he personally accepted full responsibility—he invited Sultana to a meeting, whenever and wherever convenient. Sultana accepted the invitation, named the time, date, and place, and stipulated that both should attend the meeting alone and unarmed. On the appointed day, as Freddy stepped out on one side of a wide open glade, in the centre of which a solitary tree was growing, Sultana stepped out on the other side. Their meeting was friendly, as all who have lived in the East would have expected it to be, and when they had seated themselves in the shade of the tree—one a mountain of energy and good humour with the authority of the Government behind him, and the other a dapper little man with a price on his head—Sultana produced a water melon which he smilingly said Freddy could partake of without reservation. The meeting ended in a deadlock, however, for Sultana refused to accept Freddy's terms of unconditional surrender. It was at this meeting that Sultana begged Freddy not to take undue risks. On the day of the raid, he said, he with ten of his men, all fully armed, had taken cover under a banyan tree and had watched Freddy and two other sahibs coming down the *nullah* towards the tree. 'Had the sahib who was trying to climb the bank succeeded in doing so', Sultana added, 'It would have been necessary to shoot the three of you.'

The final round of the heavy-light-weight contest was now to be staged, and Freddy invited Wyndham and myself to Hardwar to witness and take part in it. Sultana and the remnants of his gang, now weary of movement, had taken up residence at a cattle station in the heart of the Najibabad jungles, and Freddy's plan was to convey his entire force down the Ganges in boats, land at a convenient spot, and surround the cattle station. This raid, like the one already described, was to take place at night. But on this occasion the raid had been timed for the full moon.

On the day chosen, the entire force of three hundred men, with the addition of Freddy's cousin, Wyndham, and myself, embarked as night was falling in ten country boats which had been assembled at a secluded spot on the right bank of the

Ganges, a few miles below Hardwar. I was in the leading boat, and all went well until we crossed to the left bank and entered a side channel. The passage down this channel was one of the most terrifying experiences, off dry land, that I have ever had. For a few hundred yards the boat glided over a wide expanse of moonlit water without a ripple on its surface to distort the reflection of the trees on the margin. Gradually the channel narrowed and the speed of the boat increased, and at the same time we heard the distant sound of rushing water. I have often fished in these side channels of the Ganges, for they are preferred to the main stream by fish, and I marvelled at the courage of the boatmen who were willing to risk their lives and their craft in the rapids we were fast approaching. The boat, like the other nine, was an open cargo freighter eminently suitable for work on the open Ganges, but here in this narrow swift-flowing channel she was just an unmanageable hulk, which threatened to become a wreck every time her bottom planks came in violent contact with submerged boulders. The urgent call of the captain to his crew to fend the boat off the rocky banks and keep her in the middle of the stream, or she would founder, did nothing to allay my fears, for at the time the warning was given the boat was drifting sideways and threatening to break up or capsize every time she struck the bottom. But nightmares cannot last for ever. Though the one that night was long-drawn-out, for we had twenty miles to go, mostly through broken water, it ended when one of the boatmen sprang ashore on the left bank with one end of a long rope and made it fast to a tree. Boat after boat passed us and tied up lower down, until all ten had been accounted for.

The force was disembarked on a sandy beach and when cuts and abrasions resulting from contact with the rough timbers of the boats had been attended to, and the boatmen had been instructed to take their craft five miles farther down stream and await orders, we set off in single file to battle our way through half a mile of the heaviest elephant grass I have ever tried to penetrate on foot. The grass was ten to twelve feet high and was weighted down with river fog and dew, and before we had gone a hundred yards we were wet to the skin. When we eventually arrived on the far side we were faced with a wide expanse of water which we took to be an old bed of the Ganges, and scouting parties were sent right and left to find the shortest way round the obstruction. The party that had gone to the right returned first and reported that a quarter of a mile from where we were standing the 'lake' narrowed, and that from this point to the junction of channel down which we had come there was a swift-flowing river. Soon after the other party returned and reported that there was an unfordable river flowing into the upper end of the lake. It was now quite evident that our boatmen, intentionally or accidentally, had marooned us on an island.

With our boats gone and daylight not far off it was necessary to do something, so we moved down to the lower end of the

wide expanse of water to see if we could effect a crossing between it and the junction of the two channels. Where the water narrowed and the toe or draw of the stream started, there appeared to be a possible crossing; above this point the water was twenty feet deep, and below it was a raging torrent. While the rest of us were looking at the fast-flowing water and speculating as to whether anyone would be able to cross it, Wyndham was divesting himself of his clothes. When I remarked that this was an unnecessary proceeding in view of the fact that he was already wet to the skin, he replied that he was not thinking of his clothes, but of his life. When he had taken off every stitch of clothing he tied it into a bundle, using his shirt for the purpose, and placed the bundle firmly on his head, caught the arm of a strapping young constable standing near by and said, 'Come with me'. The young man was so taken aback at being selected to have the honour of drowning with the Commissioner Sahib that he said nothing, and together, with linked arms, the two stepped into the water.

I do not think any of us breathed while we watched that crossing. With the water at times round their waists, and at times up to their armpits, it seemed impossible for them to avoid being carried off their feet and swept into the raging torrent below where no man, no matter how good a swimmer he was, could have lived. Steadily the two brave men, one the oldest in the party and the other possibly the youngest, fought their way on and when at last they struggled out on the far bank a sigh of relief went up from the spectators, which would have been a cheer audible in Hardwar, twenty miles away, had silence not been imposed on us. Where two men could go three hundred could follow, so a chain was made; and though individual links were at times swept off their feet, the chain held, and the whole force landed safely on the far side. Here we were met by one of Freddy's most trusted informers who, pointing to the rising sun, said we had come too late; that it would not be possible for such a large force to cross the open ground between us and the forest without being seen by the herdsmen in the area, and that therefore the only thing for us to do was to go back to the island. So back to the island we went, the crossing from this side not being as bad as it had been from the other.

Back in the elephant grass our first concern was to dry our clothes. This was soon accomplished, for the sun was by now hot, and when we were once again dry and warm Freddy, from his capacious haversack, produced a chicken and a loaf of bread which were no less welcome for having been immersed in the cold waters of the Ganges. I have the ability to sleep anywhere and at any time, and, having found a sandy hollow, most of the day had passed when I was awakened by violent sneezing. On joining my companions I found that all three of them were suffering from varying degrees of hay fever. The grass we were in was of the plumed variety and when we had passed through it in the early morning the plume had been wet. But now, in the hot sun, the plumes had fluffed out and while moving about and trying to find cool places to rest in my companions had shaken the pollen down, with the result that they had given themselves hay fever. Indians do not get hay fever and I myself have never had it. This was the first time I had ever seen anyone suffering from it, and what I saw alarmed me. Freddy's cousin—a planter on holiday from Bengal—was the worst of the three; his eyes were streaming and swollen

to the extent that he could not see, and his nose was running. Freddy could see a little but he could not stop sneezing, and when Freddy sneezed the earth shook. Wyndham, tough old campaigner that he was, while protesting that he was quite all right, was unable to keep his handkerchief away from his nose and eyes. It was bad enough being thrown about in an open boat, marooned on a desert island, and fording raging torrents; but here was the climax. To lead three men who threatened to go blind back to Hardwar at the head of the three hundred policemen was a prospect that made me feel colder than I had felt when crossing the ice-cold waters of the Ganges. As evening closed in the condition of the sufferers improved, much to my relief, and by the time we had crossed the ford for the third time Freddy and Wyndham were all right and the cousin had regained his sight to the extent that it was no longer necessary to tell him when to raise his foot to avoid a stone.

Freddy's informer and a guide were waiting for us and led us over the open ground to the mouth of a dry watercourse about a hundred yards wide. The moon had just risen and visibility was nearly as good as in sunlight when, rounding a bend, we came face to face with an elephant. We had heard there was a rogue elephant in this area, and here he was, tusks flashing in the moonlight, ears spread out, and emitting loud squeals. The guide did nothing to improve the situation by stating that the elephant was very bad tempered, that he had killed many people, and that he was sure to kill a number of us. At first it appeared that the rogue was going to make good the guide's predictions, for with trunk raised high he advanced a few yards. Then he swung round and dashed up the bank, trumpeting defiance as he gained the shelter of the jungle. Another mile up the watercourse and we came on what the guide said was a fire-track. Here the going was very pleasant, for with short green

grass underfoot, and the moonlight glinting on every leaf and blade, it was possible to forget our errand and revel in the beauty of the jungle. As we approached a stretch of burnt grass where an old peacock, perched high on a leafless tree, was sending his warning cry into the night, two leopards stepped out on the track, saw us, and gracefully bounded away and faded out of sight in the shadows.

I had been out of my element during the long passage down the side channel, but now, what with the elephant—who was, I knew, only curious and intended us no harm—and the peacock warning the jungle folk of the presence of danger, and finally the leopards merging into the shadows, I was back on familiar ground, ground that I loved and understood.

Leaving the track, which ran from east to west, the guide led us north for a mile or more through scrub and tree jungle to the bank of a tiny stream overhung by a giant banyan tree. Here we were told to sit down and wait, while the guide went forward to confer with his brother at the cattle station. A long and weary wait it was, which was in no way relieved by pangs of hunger, for we had eaten nothing since our meal off the chicken and loaf of bread, and it was now past midnight; and to make matters worse I, the only one who smoked, had exhausted my supply of cigarettes. The guide returned towards the early hours of the morning and reported that Sultana and the remnants of his gang, now reduced to nine, had left the cattle station the previous evening to raid a village in the direction of Hardwar and that they were expected back that night, or the following day. Before leaving to try to get us a little food, of which we were in urgent need, the guide and the informer warned us that we were in Sultana's territory and that it would be unwise for any of us to leave the shelter of the banyan tree.

Another weary day passed, the last Wyndham could spend with us, for in addition to being Commissioner of Kumaon he was Political Agent of Tehri State and was due to meet the ruler at Narindra Nagar in two days' time. After nightfall a cart loaded with grass arrived, and when the grass had been removed a few sacks of parched gram and forty pounds of gur were revealed. This scanty but welcome ration was distributed among the men. The guide had not forgotten the sahibs, and before driving away he handed Freddy a few *chapattis* tied up in a piece of cloth that had seen hard times and better days. As we lay on our backs with all topics of conversation exhausted, thinking of hot meals and soft beds in far-off Hardwar, I heard the welcome sounds of a leopard killing a *chital* a few hundred yards from our tree. Here was an opportunity of getting a square meal, for my portion of *chapatti*, far from allaying my hunger, had only added to it; so I jumped up and asked Freddy for his *kukri*. When he asked what on earth I wanted for, I told him it was to cut off the hind legs of the *chital* the leopard had just killed. 'What leopard and what *chital*', he asked, 'are you talking about?' Yea, he could hear the *chital* calling, but how was he to know that they were not alarmed by some of Sultana's men who were scouting round to spy on us? And anyway, if I was right in thinking a leopard had made a kill, which he doubted, how was I going to take the *chital* away from it when I could not use a musket (I had not brought my rifle with me on this occasion for I did not know to what use I might be asked to put it) so close to the cattle station? No, he concluded, the whole idea was absurd. So very regretfully I again lay down with my hunger. How could I convince anyone who did not know the jungle folk

and their language that I *knew* the deer had not been alarmed by human beings; that they were watching one of their number being killed by a leopard; and that there was no danger in taking the kill, or as much of it as I wanted, away from the leopard?

The night passed without further incident and at crack of dawn Wyndham and I set out on our long walk to Hardwar. We crossed the Ganges by the Bhimgoda Dam and after a quick meal at the Dam Bungalow had an evening's fishing on the wide expanse of water above the dam that will long be remembered.

Next morning, just as Wyndham was leaving to keep his appointment at Narindra Nagar, and I was collecting some eatables to take back to my hungry companions, word was brought to us by runner that Freddy had captured Sultana.

Sultana had returned to the cattle station the previous evening. After his men had surrounded the station, Freddy crept up to the large hut used by the cattle men, and, seeing a sheeted figure asleep on the only *charpoy* the hut contained, sat down on it. Pinned down by 20 stone 4 pounds Sultana was unable to offer any resistance, nor was he able to carry out his resolve of not being taken alive. Of the six dacoits in the hut at the time of the raid, four, including Sultana, were captured and the other two, Babu and Pailwan, Sultana's lieutenants, broke through the police cordon and escaped, after being fired at.

I do not know how many murders Sultana was responsible for, but when brought to trial the main charge against him was the murder, by one of his gang, of the tenant of the headman of Lamachour. While in the condemned cell Sultana sent for Freddy and bequeathed to him his wife and son in the Najibabad Fort, and his dog, of whom he was very fond. Freddy adopted the dog, and those who know Freddy will not need to be told that he faithfully carried out his promise to care for Sultana's family.

Some months later Freddy, now promoted and the youngest man in the Indian Police service ever to be honoured by His Majesty the King with a C.I.E., was attending the annual Police Week at Moradabad. One of the functions at this week was a dinner to which all the police officers in the province were invited. During the dinner one of the waiters whispered to Freddy that his orderly wanted to speak to him. This orderly had been with Freddy during the years Freddy had been in pursuit of Sultana. Now, having an evening off, he had strolled down to the Moradabad railway station. While he was there, a train came in,

and as he idly watched the passengers alighting two men came out of a compartment near him. One of these men spoke to the other, who hastily put a handkerchief up to his face, but not before the orderly had seen that he had a piece of cotton wool sticking to his nose. The orderly kept his eye on the men, who had a considerable amount of luggage, and when they had made themselves comfortable in a corner of the waiting room he commandeered an *ekka* and hastened to inform Freddy.

When Sultana's two lieutenants, Babu and Pailwan, broke through the cordon surrounding the cattle station, they had been fired at, and shortly thereafter a man had visited a small dispensary near Najibabad to have an injury to his nose, which he said had been caused by a dog bite, attended to. When reporting the case to the police, the compounder who dressed the wound said he suspected it had been caused by a pellet of buckshot. So the entire police force of the province were on the lookout for a man with an injured nose, all the more so because Babu and Pailwan were credited with having committed most of the murders for which Sultana's gang were responsible.

When he heard the orderly's story Freddy jumped into his car and dashed to the station—dashed is the right word, for when Freddy is in a hurry the road is before him and traffic and corners do not exist. At the station he placed guards at all the exits to the waiting room and then went up to the two men and asked them who they were. Merchants, they answered, on their way from Bareilly to the Punjab. Why then, asked Freddy, had they taken a train that terminated at Moradabad? He was told that there had been two trains at the Bareilly platform and they had been directed to the wrong one. When Freddy learnt the men had not had any food, and that they would have to wait until next morning for a connecting train, he invited them to accompany him and be his guests. For a moment the men hesitated, and then said, 'As you wish, Sahib'.

With the two men in the back of the car Freddy drove slowly, closely questioning them, and to all his questions he received prompt answers. The men then asked Freddy if it was customary for sahibs to visit railway stations at night and carry off passengers, leaving their luggage to be plundered by any who cared to do so. Freddy knew that his action, without a duly executed warrant, could be described as high-handed and might land him in serious trouble if the members of Sultana's gang serving sentences in the Moradabad jail failed to identify their late companions. While these unpleasant thoughts were chasing each other through his mind, the car arrived at the bungalow in which he was putting up for the Police Week.

All dogs love Freddy, and Sultana's dog was no exception. In the months that had passed this pye with a dash of terrier blood had given Freddy all his affection, and now, when the car stopped and the three men got out, the dog came dashing out of the bungalow, stopped in surprise, and then hurled himself at the two travellers with every manifestation of delight that a dog can exhibit. For a tense minute Freddy and the two men looked at each other in silence and then Pailwan, who knew the fate that awaited him, 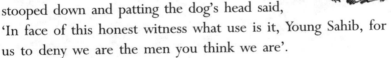 stooped down and patting the dog's head said, 'In face of this honest witness what use is it, Young Sahib, for us to deny we are the men you think we are'.

Society demands protection against criminals, and Sultana was a criminal. He was tried under the law of the land, found guilty, and executed. Nevertheless, I cannot withhold a great measure of admiration for the little man who set at nought the might of

the Government for three long years, and who by his brave demeanour won the respect of those who guarded him in the condemned cell.

I could have wished that justice had not demanded that Sultana be exhibited in manacles and leg-irons, and exposed to ridicule from those who trembled at the mere mention of his name while he was at liberty. I could also have wished that he had been given a more lenient sentence, for no other reasons than that he had been branded a criminal at birth, and had not had a fair chance; that when power was in his hands he had not oppressed the poor; that when I tracked him to the banyan tree he spared my life and the lives of my friends. And finally, that he went to his meeting with Freddy, not armed with a knife or a revolver, but with a water melon in his hands.

LOYALTY

The mail train was running at its maximum speed of thirty miles per hour through country that was familiar. For mile upon mile the newly risen sun had been shining on fields where people were reaping the golden wheat, for it was the month of April and the train was passing through the Gangetic valley, the most fertile land in India. During the previous year India had witnessed one of her worst famines. I had seen whole villages existing on the bark of trees; on minute grass seeds swept up with infinite labour from scorching plains; and on the wild plums that grow on waste lands too poor for the raising of crops. Mercifully the weather had changed, good winter rains had brought back fertility to the land, and the people who had starved for a year were now eagerly reaping a good harvest. Early though the hour was, the scene was one of intense activity in which every individual of the community had his, or her, allotted part. The reaping was being done by women, most of them landless labourers who move from area to area, as the crop ripens, and who for their labour—which starts at dawn and ends when there is no longer light to work by—receive one-twelfth to one-sixteenth of the crop they cut in the course of the day.

There were no hedges to obstruct the view, and from the carriage window no mechanical device of any kind was to be seen. The ploughing had been done by oxen, two to a plough; the reaping was being done by sickles with a curved blade eighteen inches long; the sheaves, tied with twisted stalks of wheat straw, were being carted to the threshing floor on ox-carts with wooden wheels; and on the threshing floor, plastered over with cow dung, oxen were treading out the corn; they were tied to a long rope, one end of which was made fast to a pole firmly fixed in the ground. As a field was cleared of the sheaves children drove cattle on to it to graze on

the stubble, and amongst the cattle old and infirm women were sweeping the ground to recover any seed that had fallen from the ears when the wheat was being cut. Half of what these toilers collected would be taken by the owner of the field and the other half—which might amount to as much as a pound or two, if the ground was not too sun cracked—they would be permitted to retain.

My journey was to last for thirty-six hours. I had the carriage to myself, and the train would stop for breakfast, lunch, and dinner. Every mile of the country through which the train was running was interesting; and yet I was not happy, for in the steel trunk under my seat was a string bag containing two hundred rupees which did not belong to me.

Eighteen months previously I had taken employment as a Fuel Inspector with the railway on which I was now travelling. I had gone straight from school to this job, and for those eighteen months I had lived in the forest cutting five hundred thousand cubic feet of timber, to be used as fuel in locomotives. After the trees had been felled and billeted, each billet not more and not less than thirty-six inches long, the fuel was carted ten miles to the nearest point of the railway, where it was stacked and measured and then loaded into fuel trains and taken to the stations where it was needed. Those eighteen months alone in the forest had been strenuous, but I had kept fit and enjoyed the work. There was plenty of game in the forest in the way of chital, four-horned antelope, pig, and pea fowl, and in the river that formed one boundary of the forest there were several varieties of fish and many alligators and pythons. My work did not permit of my indulging in sport during daylight hours so I had to do all my shooting for the pot, and fishing, at night. Shooting by moonlight is very different from shooting in daylight, for though it is easier to stalk a deer or a rooting pig at night it is difficult to shoot accurately unless the moon can be got to shine on the foresight. The pea fowl had to be shot while they were roosting, and I am not ashamed to say that I occasionally indulged in this form of murder, for the only meat I ate during that year and a half was what I shot on moonlight nights; during the dark period of the moon I had perforce to be a vegetarian.

The felling of the forest disarranged the normal life of the jungle folk and left me with the care of many waifs and orphans, all of whom had to share my small tent with me. It was when I was a bit crowded with two broods of partridges—one black and the other grey, four pea fowl chicks, two leverets, and two baby four-horned antelope that could only just stand upright on their spindle legs, that Rex the python took up his quarters in the tent. I returned an hour after nightfall that day, and while I was feeding the four-footed inmates with milk I saw the lantern light glinting on something in a corner of the tent and on investigation found Rex coiled up on the straw used as a bed by the baby antelope. A hurried count revealed that none of the young inmates of the tent were missing, so I left Rex in the corner he had selected. For two months thereafter Rex left the tent each day to bask in the sun, returning to his corner at sundown, and during the whole of that period he never harmed any of the young life he shared the tent with.

Of all the waifs and orphans who were brought up in the tent, and who were returned to the forest as soon as they were able to fend for themselves, Tiddley-de-winks, a four-horned antelope, was the only one who refused to leave me. She followed me when I moved camp to be nearer to the railway line to supervise the loading of the fuel, and in doing so nearly lost her life. Having been brought up by hand she had no fear of human beings and the day after our move she approached a man who, thinking she was a wild animal, tried to kill her. When I returned to the tent that evening I found her lying near my camp bed and on picking her up saw that both her forelegs had been broken, and that the broken ends of the bones had worked through the skin. While I was getting a little milk down her throat, and trying to summon sufficient courage to do what I knew should be done, my servant came into the tent with a man who admitted to having tried to kill the poor beast. It appeared that this man had been working in his field when Tiddley-de-winks went up to him, and thinking she had strayed in from the nearby forest, he struck her with a stick and then chased her; and it was only when she entered my tent that he realized she was a tame animal. My servant had advised him to leave before I returned, but this the man had refused to do. When he had told his story he said he would return early next morning with a bone-setter from his village. There was nothing I could do for the injured animal, beyond making a soft bed for her and giving her milk at short intervals, and at daybreak next morning the man returned with the bone-setter.

It is unwise in India to judge from appearances. The bone-setter was a feeble old man, exhibiting in his person and tattered dress every sign of poverty, but he was none the less a specialist, and a man of few words. He asked me to lift up the injured animal, stood looking at her for a few minutes, and then turned and left the tent, saying over his shoulder that he would be back in two hours. I had worked week in week out for months on end so I considered I was justified in taking a morning off, and before the old man returned I had cut a number of stakes in the nearby jungle and constructed a small pen in a corner of the tent. The man brought back with him a number of dry jute stalks from which the bark had been removed, a quantity of green paste, several young castor-oil plant leaves as big as plates, and a roll of thin jute twine. When I had seated myself on the edge of the camp bed with Tiddley-de-winks across my knees, her weight partly supported by her hind legs and partly by my knees, the old man sat down on the ground in front of her with his materials within reach.

The bones of both forelegs had been splintered midway between the knees and the tiny hooves, and the dangling portion of the legs had twisted round and round. Very gently the old man untwisted the legs, covered them from knee to hoof with a thick layer of green paste, laid strips of the castor-oil leaves over the paste to keep it in position, and over the leaves laid the jute stalks, binding them to the legs with jute twine. Next morning he returned with splints made of jute stalks strung together, and when they had been fitted to her legs Tiddley-de-winks was able to bend her knees and place her hooves, which extended an inch beyond the splints, on the ground.

The bone-setter's fee was one rupee, plus two annas for the ingredients he had put in the paste and the twine he had purchased in the bazaar, and not until the splints had been removed and the little antelope was able to skip about again would he accept either his fee or the little present I gratefully offered him.

My work, every day of which I had enjoyed, was over now and I was on my way to headquarters to render an account of the money I had spent and, I feared, to look for another job; for the locomotives had been converted to coal-burning and no more wood fuel would be needed. My books were all in perfect order and I had the feeling that I had rendered good service, for I had done in eighteen months what had been estimated to take two years. Yet I was uneasy, and the reason for my being so was the bag of money in my steel trunk.

I reached my destination, Samastipur, at 9 a.m. and after depositing my luggage in the waiting-room set out for the office of the head of the department I had been working for, with my account books and the bag containing the two hundred rupees. At the office I was told by a very imposing doorkeeper that the master was engaged, and that I would have to wait. It was hot in the open veranda, and as the minutes dragged by my nervousness increased, for an old railway hand who had helped me to make up my books had warned me that to submit balanced accounts and then admit, as I had every intention of doing, that I had two hundred rupees in excess would land me in very great trouble. Eventually the door opened and a very harassed-looking man emerged; and before the doorkeeper could close it, a voice from inside the room bellowed at me to come in. Ryles, the head of the Locomotive Department of the Bengal and North Western Railway, was a man weighing sixteen stone, with a voice that struck terror into all who served under him, and with a heart of gold. Bidding me sit down he drew my books towards him, summoned a clerk and very carefully checked my figures with those received from the stations to which the fuel had been sent. Then he told me he regretted my services would no longer be needed, said that discharge orders would be sent to me later in the day, and indicated that the interview was over. Having picked my hat off the floor I started to leave, but was called back and told I had forgotten to remove what appeared to be a bag of money that I had placed on the table. It was foolish of me to have thought I could just leave the two hundred rupees and walk away, but that was what I was trying to do when Ryles called me; so I went back to the table and told him that the money belonged to the Railway, and as I did not know how to account for it in my books, I had brought it to him. 'Your books are balanced', Ryles said, 'and if you have not faked your accounts I should like an explanation.' Tewari, the head clerk, had come into the room with a tray of papers and he stood behind Ryles's chair, with encouragement in his kindly old eyes, as I gave Ryles the following explanation.

When my work was nearing completion, fifteen cartmen, who had been engaged to cart fuel from the forest to the railway line, came to me one night and stated they had received an urgent summons to return to their village, to harvest the crops. The fuel they had carted was scattered over a wide area, and as it would take several days to stack and measure it they wanted me to make a rough calculation of the amount due to them, as it was essential for them to start on their journey that night. It was a dark night and quite impossible for me to calculate the cubic contents of the fuel, so I told them I would accept their figures. Two hours later they returned, and within a few minutes of paying them, I heard their carts creaking away into the night.

They left no address with me, and several weeks later, when the fuel was staked and measured, I found they had underestimated the amount due to them by two hundred rupees.

When I had told my story Ryles informed me that the Agent, Izat, was expected in Samastipur next day, and that he would leave him to deal with me.

Izat, Agent of three of the most flourishing railways in India, arrived next morning and at midday I received a summons to attend Ryles' office. Izat, a small dapper man with piercing eyes, was alone in the office when I entered it, and after complimenting me on having finished my job six months ahead of time, he said Ryles had shown him my books and given him a report and that he wanted to ask one question! Why had I not pocketed the two hundred rupees, and said nothing about it? My answer to this question was evidently satisfactory, for that evening, while waiting at the station in a state of uncertainty, I received two letters, one from Tewari thanking me for my contribution of two hundred rupees to the Railwaymen's Widows' and Orphans' Fund, of which he was Honorary Secretary, and the other from Izat informing me that my services were being retained, and instructing me to report to Ryles for duty.

For a year thereafter I worked up and down the railway on a variety of jobs, at times on the footplates of locomotives reporting on consumption of coal—a job I liked for I was permitted to drive the engines; at times as guard of goods trains, a tedious job, for the railway was short-handed and on many occasions I was on duty for forty-eight hours at a stretch; and at times as assistant storekeeper, or assistant station-master. And then one day I received orders to go to Mokameh Ghat and see Storrar, the Ferry Superintendent. The Bengal and North Western Railway runs through the Gangetic valley at varying

distances from the Ganges river, and at several places branch
lines take off from the main line and run down to the river
and, by means of ferries, connect up with the broad-gauge
railways on the right bank. Mokameh Ghat on the right bank
of the Ganges is the most important of these connexions.

I left Samastipur in the early hours of the morning and at
the branch-line terminus, Samaria Ghat, boarded the S.S.
Gorakhpur. Storrar had been apprised of my visit but no reason
had been given, and as I had not been told why I was to go to
Mokameh Ghat, we spent the day partly in his house and partly
in walking about the extensive sheds, in which there appeared
to be a considerable congestion of goods. Two days later I was
summoned to Gorakhpur, the headquarters of the railway, and
informed that I had been posted to Mokameh Ghat as Trans-
shipment Inspector, that my pay had been increased from one
hundred to one hundred and fifty rupees per month, and that
I was to take over the contract for handling goods a week later.

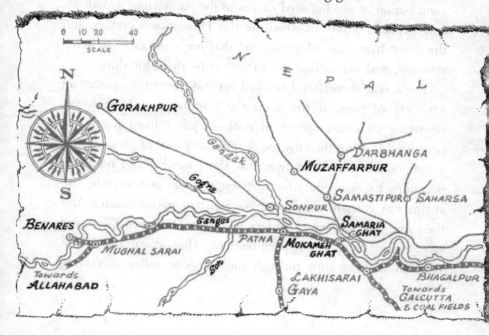

So back to Mokameh Ghat I went, arriving on this occasion at night, to take up a job about which I knew nothing, and to take on a contract without knowing where to get a single labourer, and, most important of all, with a capital of only one hundred and fifty rupees, saved during my two and a half years' service.

Storrar was not expecting me on this occasion, but he gave me dinner, and when I told him why I had returned we took our chairs on to the veranda, where a cool wind was blowing off the river, and talked late into the night. Storrar was twice my age and had been at Mokameh Ghat for several years. He was employed as Ferry Superintendent by the Bengal and North Western (metre-gauge) Railway, and was in charge of a fleet of steamers and barges that ferried passengers and metre-gauge wagons between Samaria Ghat and Mokameh Ghat. I learnt from him that eighty per cent of the long-distance traffic on the Bengal and North Western Railway passed through Mokameh Ghat; and that each year, from March to September, congestion of goods traffic took place at Mokameh Ghat and caused serious loss to the Railway.

The transfer of goods between the two railways at Mokameh Ghat, necessitated by a break of gauge, was done by a Labour Company which held the contract for handling goods throughout the length of the broad-gauge railway. In Storrar's opinion the indifference of this company to the interests of the metre-gauge railway, and the seasonal shortage of labour due to the harvesting of crops in the Gangetic valley, were the causes of the annual congestion. Having imparted this information, he very pertinently asked how I, a total stranger to the locality and without any capital—he brushed aside my hard-earned savings—proposed to accomplish what the Labour Company with all their resources had failed to do. The sheds at Mokameh Ghat, he added, were stacked to the roof with goods, there were four hundred wagons

in the yard waiting to be unloaded, and a thousand wagons on
the far side of the river waiting to be ferried across. 'My advice
to you', he concluded, 'is to catch the early steamer to Samaria
Ghat and go straight back to Gorakhpur. Tell the Railway you
will have nothing to do with the handling contract.'

I was up early next morning but I did not catch the steamer
to Samaria Ghat. Instead, I went on a tour of inspection of the
sheds and of the goods yard. Storrar had not overpainted the
picture: in fact the conditions were even worse than he had said
they were, for in addition to the four hundred metre-gauge
wagons there were the same number of broad-gauge wagons
waiting to be unloaded. At a rough calculation I put the goods
at Mokameh Ghat waiting to be dealt with at fifteen thousand
tons, and I had been sent to clear up the mess. Well, I was not
quite twenty-one years of age, and summer was starting, a season
when all of us are a little bit mad. By the time I met Ram Saran
I had made up my mind that I would take on the job, no matter
what the result might be.

Ram Saran was station-master at Mokameh Ghat, a post he
had held for two years. He was twenty years older than I was,
had an enormous jet black beard, and was the father of five
children. He had been advised by telegram of my arrival, but
had not been told that I was to take over the handling contract.
When I gave him this bit of news his face beamed all over and
he said, 'Good, Sir. Very good. We will manage.' My heart warmed
towards Ram Saran on hearing that 'we', and up to his death,
thirty-five years later, it never cooled.

When I told Storrar over breakfast that morning that I had
decided to take on the handling contract he remarked that fools
never took good advice, but added that he would do all he
could to help me, a promise he faithfully kept. In the months

that followed he kept his ferry running day and night to keep me supplied with wagons.

The journey from Gorakhpur had taken two days, so when I arrived at Mokameh Ghat I had five days in which to learn what my duties were, and to make arrangements for taking over the handling contract. The first two days I spent in getting acquainted with my staff which, in addition to Ram Saran, consisted of an assistant station-master, a grand old man by the name of Chatterji who was old enough to be my grandfather, sixty-five clerks, and a hundred shunters, pointsmen, and watchmen. My duties extended across the river to Samaria Ghat where I had a clerical and menial staff a hundred strong. The supervising of these two staffs, and the care of the goods in transit, was in itself a terrifying job and added to it was the responsibility of providing a labour force sufficient to keep the five hundred thousand tons of goods that passed through Mokameh Ghat annually flowing smoothly.

The men employed by the big Labour Company were on piece work, and as all work at Mokameh Ghat was practically at a standstill, there were several hundred very discontented men sitting about the sheds, many of whom offered me their services when they heard that I was going to do the handling for the metre-gauge railway. I was under no agreement not to employ the Labour Company's men, but thought it prudent not to do so. However, I saw no reason why I should not employ their relatives, so on the first of the three days I had in hand I selected twelve men and appointed them headmen. Eleven of these headmen undertook to provide ten men each, to start with, for the handling of goods, and the twelfth undertook to provide a mixed gang of sixty men and women for the handling of coal. The traffic to be dealt with consisted of a variety of commodities, and this meant employing different castes to deal with the different classes of goods. So of the twelve headmen, eight were Hindus, two Mohammedans, and two men of the depressed class; and as only one of the twelve was literate I employed one Hindu and one Mohammedan clerk to keep their accounts.

While one Labour Company was doing the work of both railways the interchange of goods had taken place from wagon to wagon. Now each railway was to unload its goods in the sheds, and reload from shed to wagon. For all classes of goods, excluding heavy machinery and coal, I was to be paid at the rate of Re I-7-0 (equivalent to Is. IId. at the rate of exchange then current) for every thousand maunds of goods unloaded from wagons to shed or loaded from shed to wagons. Heavy machinery and coal were one-way traffic and as these two commodities were to be trans-shipped from wagon to wagon and only one contractor could be employed for the purpose, the work was entrusted to me, and I was to receive Re I-4-0 (Is. 8d.) for unloading, and the same for loading, one thousand maunds. There are eighty pounds in a maund, and a thousand maunds therefore are equal to over thirty-five tons. These rates will appear incredible, but their accuracy can be verified by a reference to the records of the two railways.

A call-over on the last evening revealed that I had eleven headmen, each with a gang of ten men, and one headman with a mixed gang of sixty men and women. This, together with the two clerks, completed my force. At day-break next morning I telegraphed to Gorakhpur that I had assumed my duties as Trans-shipment Inspector, and had taken over the handling contract.

Ram Saran's opposite number on the broad-gauge railway was an Irishman by the name of Tom Kelly. Kelly had been at Mokameh Ghat for some years and though he was very pessimistic of my success, he very sportingly offered to help me in every way he could. With the sheds congested with goods, and with four hundred wagons of each railway waiting to be unloaded, it was necessary to do something drastic to make room in the sheds and get the traffic moving, so I arranged with Kelly that I would take the risk of unloading a thousand tons of wheat on the ground outside the sheds and with the wagons so released clear a space in the sheds for Kelly to unload a thousand tons of salt and sugar. Kelly then with his empty wagons would clear a space in sheds for me. This plan worked admirably. Fortunately for me it did not rain while my thousand tons of wheat were exposed to the weather, and in ten days we had not only cleared the accumulation in the sheds but also the accumulation of wagons. Kelly and I were then able to advise our respective headquarters to resume the booking of goods via Mokameh Ghat, which had been suspended for a fortnight.

I took over the contract at the beginning of the summer, the season when traffic on Indian railways is at its heaviest, and as soon as booking was opened a steady stream of downwards traffic from the Bengal and North Western Railway and an equally heavy stream from the broad-gauge railway started pouring into Mokameh Ghat. The rates on which I had been given the contract were the lowest paid to any contractor in India, and the only way in which I could hope to keep my labour was by cutting it down to the absolute minimum and making it work harder in order that it would earn as much, or possibly a little more, than other labour on similar work. All the labour at Mokameh Ghat was on piece work, and at the end of the first week my men and I were overjoyed to find that they had earned, on paper, fifty per cent more than the Labour Company's men had earned.

When entrusting me with the contract the Railway promised to pay me weekly, and I on my part promised to pay my labour weekly. The Railway, however, when making their promise, failed to realize that by switching over from one handling contractor to another they would be raising complications for their Audit Department that would take time to resolve. For the Railway this was a small matter, but for me it was very different. My total capital on arrival at Mokameh Ghat had been one hundred and fifty rupees, and there was no one in all the world I could call on to help me with a loan, so until the Railway paid me I could not pay my men.

I have entitled this story Loyalty and I do not think that anyone has ever received greater loyalty than I did, not only from my labour, but also from the railway staff, during those first three months that I was at Mokameh Ghat. Nor do I think that men have ever worked harder. The work started every morning, weekdays and Sundays alike, at 4 a.m., and continued without interruption up to 8 p.m. The clerks whose duty it was to check and tally the goods took their meals at different hours to avoid a stoppage of work and my men ate their food, which was brought to them by wives, mothers, or daughters, in the sheds. There were no trade unions or slaves and slave-drivers in those days and every individual was at liberty to work as many, or as few, hours as he or she wished to. And everyone worked cheerfully and happily; for no matter whether it was the procuring of more and better food and clothing for the family, the buying of a new ox to replace a worn-out one, or the paying-off of a debt, the incentive, without which no man can work his best, was there. My work and Ram Saran's did not end when the men knocked off work, for there was correspondence to attend to, and the next day's work to be planned and arranged for, and during those first three months neither of us spent more than four hours in bed each night. I was not twenty-one and as hard as nails, but Ram Saran was twenty years older and soft, and at the end of the three months he had lost a stone in weight but none of his cheerfulness.

Lack of money was now a constant worry to me, and as week succeeded week the worry became a hideous nightmare that never left me. First the headmen and then the labourers pledged their cheap and pitiful bits of jewellery and now all credit had gone; and to make matters worse, the men of the Labour Company, who were jealous that my men had earned more than they did, were beginning to taunt my men. On several occasions ugly incidents were narrowly avoided, for semi-starvation had not impaired the loyalty of my men and they were willing to give battle to anyone who as much as hinted that I had tricked them into working for me, and that they would never see a pice of the money they had earned.

The monsoon was late in coming that year and the red ball in the sky, fanned by a wind from an unseen furnace, was making life a burden. At the end of a long and a very trying day I received a telegram from Samaria Ghat informing me that an engine had been derailed on the slipway that fed the barges on which wagons were ferried across to Mokameh Ghat. A launch conveyed me across the river and twice within the next three hours the engine was replaced on the track, with the aid of hand jacks, only to be derailed again. It was not until the wind had died down and the powdery sand could be packed under the wooden sleepers that the engine was re-railed for the third time, and the slipway again brought into use. Tired and worn out, and with eyes swollen and sore from the wind and sand, I had just sat down to my first meal that day when my twelve headmen filed into the room, and seeing my servant placing a plate in front of me, with the innate courtesy of Indians, filed out again. I then, as I ate my dinner, heard the following conversation taking place in the veranda.

One of the headmen. What was on the plate you put in front of the sahib?

My servant. A *chapatti* and a little *dal*.

One of the headmen. Why only one *chapatti* and a little *dal*?

My servant. Because there is no money to buy more.

One of the headmen. What else does the sahib eat?

My servant. Nothing.

After a short silence I heard the oldest of the headmen, a Mohammedan with a great beard dyed with henna, say to his companions, 'Go home. I will stay and speak to the sahib.'

When my servant had removed the empty plate the old headman requested permission to enter the room, and standing before me spoke as follows: 'We came to tell you that our stomachs have long been empty and that after tomorrow it would be no longer possible for us to work. But we have seen tonight that your case is as bad as ours and we will carry on as long as we have strength to stand. I will, with your permission, go now, sahib, and, for the sake of Allah, I beg you will do something to help us.'

Every day for weeks I had been appealing to headquarters at Gorakhpur for funds and the only reply I could elicit was that steps were being taken to make early payment of my bills.

After the bearded headman left me that night I walked across to the Telegraph Office, where the telegraphist on duty was sending the report I submitted each night of the work done during the day, took a form off his table and told him to clear the line for an urgent message to Gorakhpur. It was then a few minutes after midnight and the message I sent read: 'Work at Mokameh Ghat ceases at midday today unless I am assured that

twelve thousand rupees has been dispatched by morning train.'
The telegraphist read the message over and looking up at me
said: 'If I have your permission I will tell my brother, who is on
duty at this hour, to deliver the message at once and not wait
until office hours in the morning.' Ten hours later, and with two
hours of my ultimatum still to run, I saw a telegraph messenger
hurrying towards me with a buff-coloured envelope in his hand.
Each group of men he passed stopped work to stare after him,
for everyone in Mokameh Ghat knew the purport of the
telegram I had sent at midnight. After I had read the telegram
the messenger, who was the son of my office peon, asked if the
news was good; and when I told him it was good, he dashed
off and his passage down the sheds was punctuated by shouts
of delight. The money could not arrive until the following
morning, but what did a few hours matter to those who had
waited for long months?

The pay clerk who presented himself at my office next day,
accompanied by some of my men carrying a cash chest slung
on a bamboo pole and guarded by two policemen, was a jovial
Hindu who was as broad as he was long and who exuded good
humour and sweat in equal proportions. I never saw him without
a pair of spectacles tied across his forehead with red tape. Having
settled himself on the floor of my office he drew on a cord tied
round his neck and from somewhere deep down in his person
pulled up a key. He opened the cash chest, and lifted out twelve
string-bags each containing one thousand freshly minted silver
rupees. He licked a stamp, and stuck it to the receipt I had
signed. Then, delving into a pocket that would comfortably have
housed two rabbits, he produced an envelope containing bank
notes to the value of four hundred and fifty rupees, my arrears
of pay for three months.

I do not think anyone has ever had as great pleasure in paying out money as I had when I placed a bag containing a thousand rupees into the hands of each of the twelve headmen, nor do I think men have ever received money with greater pleasure than they did. The advent of the fat pay clerk had relieved a tension that had become almost unbearable, and the occasion called for some form of celebration, so the remainder of the day was declared a holiday—the first my men and I had indulged in for ninety-five days. I do not know how the others spent their hours of relaxation. For myself, I am not ashamed to admit that I spent mine in sound and restful sleep.

For twenty-one years my men and I worked the handling contract at Mokameh Ghat, and during the whole of that long period, and even when I was absent in France and in Waziristan during the 1914–18 war, the traffic flowed smoothly through the main outlet of the Bengal and North Western Railway with never a hitch. When we took over the contract, between four and five hundred thousand tons of goods were passing through Mokameh Ghat, and when I handed over to Ram Saran the traffic had increased to a million tons.

Those who visit India for pleasure or profit never come in contact with the real Indian—the Indian whose loyalty and devotion alone made it possible for a handful of men to administer, for close on two hundred years, a vast subcontinent with its teeming millions. To impartial historians I will leave the task of recording whether or not that administration was beneficial to those to whom I have introduced you, the poor of my India.

BUDHU

Budhu was a man of the Depressed Class, and during all the years I knew him I never saw him smile: his life had been too hard and the iron had entered deep into his very soul. He was about thirty-five years of age, a tall gaunt man, with a wife and two young children, when he applied to me for work. At his request I put him on to trans-shipping coal from broad-gauge trucks to metre-gauge wagons at Mokameh Ghat, for in this task men and women could work together, and Budhu wanted his wife to work with him.

The broad-gauge trucks and metre-gauge wagons stood opposite each other with a four-foot-wide sloping platform between, and the coal had to be partly shovelled and partly carried in baskets from the trucks into the wagons. The work was cruelly hard, for there was no covering to the platform. In winter the men and women worked in bitter cold, often wet with rain for days on end, and in summer the brick platform and the iron floors of the trucks and wagons blistered their bare feet. A shovel in the hands of a novice, working for his bread and the bread of his children, is a cruel tool. The first day's work leaves the hands red and sore and the back with an ache that is a torment. On the second day blisters form on the hands, and the ache in the back becomes an even greater torment. On the third day the blisters break and become septic, and the back can with difficulty be straightened. Thereafter for a week or ten days only guts, and plenty of them, can keep the sufferer at work—as I know from experience.

Budhu and his wife went through all these phases, and often, when they had done sixteen hours' piece work and were dragging themselves to the quarters I had provided for them, I was tempted to tell them they had suffered enough and should look for other less strenuous work. But they were making good wages, better (Budhu said) than they had made before, so I let them carry on, and the day came when with hardened hands and backs that no longer ached they left their work with as brisk and as light a step as they had approached it.

I had some two hundred men and women trans-shipping coal at that time, for the coal traffic was as heavy as it always was in the summer. India was an exporting country in those days, and the wagons that took the grain, opium, indigo, hides, and bones to Calcutta returned from the collieries in Bengal loaded with coal, five hundred thousand tons of which passed through Mokameh Ghat.

One day Budhu and his wife were absent from work. Chamari, the headman of the coal gang, informed me that Budhu had received a postcard the previous day and had left that morning with his family, saying he would return to work as soon as it was possible for him to do so. Two months later the family returned and reoccupied their quarters, and Budhu and his wife worked as industriously as they had always done. At about the same time the following year Budhu, whose frame had now filled out, and his wife, who had lost her haggard look, again absented themselves from work. On this occasion they were absent three months, and looked tired and worn out on their return.

Except when consulted, or when information was voluntarily given, I never inquired into the private affairs of my workpeople, for Indians are sensitive on this point; so I did not know why Budhu periodically left his work which he invariably did after receiving a postcard. The post for the workpeople was delivered to the headmen and distributed by them to the men and women working under them, so I instructed Chamari to send Budhu to me the next time he received a card. Nine months later, when the coal traffic was unusually heavy and every man and woman in my employ was working to full capacity, Budhu, carrying a postcard in his hand, presented himself at my office. The postcard was in a script that I could not read so I asked Budhu to read it to me. This he could not do, for he had not been taught to read and write, but he said Chamari had read it to him and that it was an order from his master to come at once as the crops were ready to harvest. The following was Budhu's story as he told it to me that day in my office, and his story is the story of millions of poor people in India.

'My grandfather, who was a field labourer, borrowed two rupees from the *bania* of the village in which he lived. The *bania* retained one of the rupees as advance interest for one year, and made my grandfather put his thumb-mark to an entry in his *bhai khata*.[1] When my grandfather was able to do so from time to time, he paid the *bania* a few annas by way of interest. On the death of my grandfather my father took over the debt, which then amounted to fifty rupees. During my father's lifetime the debt increased to one hundred and fifteen rupees. In the mean

---

[1]Register of accounts.

time the old *bania* died and his son, who reigned in his place, sent for me when my father died and informed me that as the family debt now amounted to a considerable sum it would be necessary for me to give him a stamped and duly executed document. This I did, and as I had no money to pay for the stamped paper and for the registration of the document the *bania* advanced the required amount and added it to the debt, which together with interest now amounted to one hundred and thirty rupees. As a special favour the *bania* consented to reduce the interest to twenty-five per cent. This favour he granted me on the condition that my wife and I helped him each year to harvest his crops, until the debt was paid in full. This agreement, for my wife and I to work for the *bania* without wages, was written on another piece of paper to which I put my thumb-mark. For ten years my wife and I have helped to harvest the *bania*'s crops, and each year after the *bania* has made up the account and entered it on the back of the stamped paper he takes my thumb impression on the document. I do not know how much the debt has increased since I took it over. For years I was not able to pay anything towards it, but since I have been working for you I have paid, five, seven, and thirteen rupees—twenty-five rupees all together.'

Budhu had never dreamed of repudiating the debt. To repudiate a debt was unthinkable; not only would it blacken his own face, but, what was far worse, it would blacken the reputation of his father and grandfather. So he continued to pay what he could in cash and in labour, and lived on without hope of ever liquidating the debt; on his death, it would be passed on to his eldest son.

Having elicited from Budhu the information that there was

a *vakil*[2] in the village in which the *bania* lived, and taken his name and address, I told Budhu to return to work and said I would see what could be done with the *bania*. Thereafter followed a long correspondence with the Vakil, a stout-hearted Brahmin, who became a firm ally after the *bania* had insulted him by ordering him out of his house and telling him to mind his own business. From the Vakil I learnt that the *bhai khata* inherited by the *bania* from his father could not be produced in a court of law as evidence, for it bore the thumb-marks of men long since dead. The *bania* had tricked Budhu into executing a document which clearly stated that Budhu had *borrowed* one hundred and fifty rupees at a rate of twenty-five per cent interest. The Vakil advised me not to contest the case for the document Budhu had executed was valid, and Budhu had admitted its validity by paying three instalments as part interest, and putting his thumb-marks to these payments on the document. When I had sent the Vakil a money order in full satisfaction of the debt, plus interest at twenty-five per cent, the *bania* surrendered the legal documents; but he refused to surrender the private agreement binding Budhu and his wife to work without wages on harvesting his crops. It was only when I threatened, on the Vakil's advice, to prosecute for extortion, that he handed the agreement over to the Vakil.

Budhu was very uneasy while these transactions were dragging on. He never spoke to me on the subject but I could see from the way in which he looked at me whenever I passed him at work that he was speculating as to whether he had been wise in leaving me to deal with the all-powerful *bania*, and what his position would be if the *bania* suddenly appeared and demanded an explanation for his conduct. And then one day I received by

[2]An advocate, or lawyer.

registered post a heavily sealed letter containing a much thumb-marked, legal document, an agreement also thumb-marked, a stamped receipt for the Vakil's fees, and a letter informing me that Budhu was now a free man. The whole transaction had cost me two hundred and twenty-five rupees.

Budhu was leaving work that evening when I met him, took the documents out of the envelope, and told him to hold them while I set a match to them. 'No, Sahib, no', he said. 'You must not burn these papers, for I am now your slave and, God willing, I will one day pay off my debt to you.'

Not only did Budhu never smile but he was also a very silent man. When I told him that, as he would not let me burn the papers, he could keep them, he only put his hands together and touched my feet; but when he raised his head and turned to walk away, tears were ploughing furrows down his coal-grimed face.

Only one of millions freed of a debt that had oppressed three generations, but had the number been legion my pleasure could not have been greater, nor could any words have affected me more deeply than Budhu's mute gesture, and the tears that blinded him as he stumbled away to tell his wife that the *bania*'s debt had been paid and that they were free.

LALAJEE

The passenger streamer was late in arriving from Samaria Ghat. I was standing on the landing stage, watching the passengers disembark and hurry up the ramp to the broad-gauge train, which I had arranged to detain a few minutes for them. Last to leave the steamer was a thin man with eyes sunk deep in their sockets, wearing a patched suit which in the days of long ago had been white, and carrying a small bundle tied up in a coloured handkerchief. By clutching the handrail of the gangway for support, he managed to gain the landing stage, but he turned off at the ramp, walked with slow and feeble steps to the edge of the river, and was violently and repeatedly sick. Having stooped to wash his face, he opened his bundle, took from it a sheet, spread it on the bank, and lay down with the Ganges water lapping the soles of his feet. Evidently he had no intention of catching the train, for when the warning bell rang and the engine whistled, he made no movement. He was lying on his back, and when I told him he had missed his train he opened his sunken eyes to look up at me and said, 'I have no need of trains, Sahib, for I am dying'.

It was the mango season, the hottest time of the year, when cholera is always at its worst. When the man passed me at the foot of the gangway I suspected he was suffering from cholera, and my suspicions were confirmed when I saw him being violently sick. In reply to my questions the man said he was travelling alone, and had no friends at Mokameh Ghat, so I helped him to his feet and led him the two hundred yards that separated my bungalow from the Ganges. Then I made him comfortable in my *punkah* coolie's house, which was empty, and detached from the servants' quarters.

I had been at Mokameh Ghat ten years, employing a large labour force. Some of the people lived under my supervision in houses provided by me, and the balance lived in surrounding villages. I had seen enough of cholera among my own people and also the villagers to make me pray that if I ever contracted the hateful and foul disease some Good Samaritan would take pity on me and put a bullet through my head, or give me an overdose of opium.

Few will agree with me that of the tens of thousands of people reported as having died of cholera each year at least half die not of cholera but of fear. We who live in India, as distinct from those who visit the country for a longer or shorter period, are fatalists, believing that a man cannot die before his allotted time. This, however, does not mean that we are indifferent to epidemic diseases. Cholera is dreaded throughout the land, and when it comes in epidemic form as many die of stark fear as die of the actual disease.

There was no question that the man in my *punkah* coolie's house was suffering from a bad attack of cholera and if he was to survive, his faith and my crude treatment alone would pull him through; for the only medical aid within miles was a brute of a doctor, as callous as he was inefficient, and whose fat oily throat I am convinced I should have one day had the pleasure of cutting had not a young probationer clerk, who had been sent to me to train, found a less messy way of removing this medico who was hated by the whole staff. This young hopeful gained the confidence of the doctor and of his wife, both of whom were thoroughly immoral, and who confided to the clerk that they greatly missed the fleshpots of Egypt and the pleasures they had enjoyed before coming to Mokameh Ghat. This information set the clerk thinking, and a few nights later, and a little before the passenger steamer was due to leave for Samaria Ghat, a letter was delivered to the doctor, on reading which he told his wife that he had been summoned to Samaria Ghat to attend an urgent case and that he would be absent all night. He spruced himself up before leaving the house, was met outside by the clerk, and conducted in great secrecy to an empty room at the end of a block of buildings in which one of my pointsmen had died a few nights previously of coal-gas poisoning.

After the doctor had been waiting some time in the room, which had a single solid door and a small grated window, the door opened to admit a heavily veiled figure and was then pulled to and locked on the outside.

I was returning late that night through the goods sheds and overheard part of a very animated conversation between the probationer clerk and a companion he was relieving on night duty. Next morning on my way to work I saw a crowd of men in front of the late pointsman's quarters and was informed, by a most innocent-looking spectator, that there appeared to be someone inside, though the door was padlocked on the outside. I told my informant to get a hammer and break the lock off and

hurried away on my lawful occasions, for I had no desire to witness the discomfiture, richly as it was deserved, of the man and his wife when the door was broken open. Three entries appear in diary for that date: '(I) Doctor and his wife left on urgent private affairs. (2) Shiv Deb probationer confirmed as a Tally clerk on salary of twenty rupees per month. (3) Lock, points, alleged to have been run by the engine, replaced by the new one.' And that was the last Mokameh Ghat ever saw of the man who was a disgrace to the honourable profession he claimed to belong to.

I could not spare much time to nurse the thin man for I already had three cholera patients on my hands. From my servants I could expect no help, for they were of a different caste to the sufferer, and further, there was no justification for exposing them to the risk of infection. However, this did not matter, provided I could instil sufficient confidence into the man that my treatment was going to make him well. To this end I made it very clear to him that I had not brought him into my compound to die, and to give me the trouble of cremating him, but to make him well, and that it was only with his co-operation that this could be effected. That first night I feared that in spite of our joint efforts he would die, but towards morning he rallied and from then on his condition continued to improve and all that remained to be done was to build up his strength, which cholera drains out of the human body more quickly than any other disease. At the end of a week he was able to give me his story.

He was a *lala*, a merchant, and at one time possessed a flourishing grain business; then he made the mistake of taking as partner a man about whom he knew nothing. For a few years the business prospered and all went well, but one day when he returned from a long journey he found the shop empty, and his partner gone. The little money in his possession was only sufficient to meet his personal debts, and bereft of credit he had to seek employment. This he found with a merchant with whom he had traded, and for ten years he had worked on seven rupees a month, which was only sufficient to support himself and his son—his wife having died shortly after his partner robbed him. He was on his way from Muzaffarpur to Gaya, on his master's business, when he was taken ill in the train. As he got worse on board the ferry steamer, he had crawled ashore to die on the banks of the sacred Ganges.

Lalajee—I never knew him by any other name—stayed with me for about a month, and then one day he requested permission to continue his journey to Gaya. The request was made as we were walking through the sheds, for Lalajee was strong enough now to accompany me for a short distance each morning when I set out for work, and when I asked him what he would do if on arrival at Gaya he found his master had filled his place, he said he would try to find other employment. 'Why not try to get someone to help you to be a merchant once again?' I asked; and he replied: 'The thought of being a merchant once again, and able to educate my son, is with me night and day, Sahib, but there is no one in all the world who would trust me, a servant on seven rupees a month and without any security to offer, with the five hundred rupees I should need to give me a new start.'

The train for Gaya left at 8 p.m. and when that evening I returned to the bungalow a little before that hour, I found Lalajee with freshly washed clothes, and a bundle in his hand a little bigger than the one he had arrived with, waiting in the veranda to say goodbye to me. When I put a ticket for Gaya and five one-hundred rupee notes into his hand he, like the man with the coal-grimed face, was tongue tied. All he could do was to keep glancing from the notes in his hand to my face, until the bell that warned passengers the train would leave in five minutes rang; then, putting his head on my feet, he said: 'Within one year your slave will return you this money.'

And so Lalajee left me, taking with him the greater part of my savings. That I would see him again I never doubted, for the poor of India never forget a kindness; but the promise Lalajee had made was, I felt sure, beyond his powers of accomplishment. In this I was wrong, for returning late one evening I saw a man dressed in spotless white standing in my veranda. The light from the room behind him was in my eyes, and I did not recognize him until he spoke. It was Lalajee, come a few days before the expiry of the time limit he had set himself. That night as he sat on the floor near my chair he told me of his trading transactions, and the success that had attended them. Starting with a few bags of grain and being content with a profit of only four annas per bag he had gradually, and steadily, built up his business until he was able to deal in consignments up to the thirty tons in weight, on which he was making a profit of three rupees per ton. His son was in a good school, and as he could now afford to keep a wife he had married the daughter of a rich merchant of Patna; all this he had accomplished in a little under twelve months. As the time drew near for his train to leave he laid five one-hundred rupee notes on my knee. Then, he took a bag from his pocket, held it out to me and said, 'This is the interest, calculated at twenty-five per cent, that I owe you on the money you lent me'. I believe I deprived him of half the pleasure he had anticipated from his visit when I told him it was not our custom to accept interest from our friends.

Before leaving me Lalajee said, During the month I stayed with you I had talks with your servants, and with your workmen, and I learnt from them that there was a time when you were reduced to one *chapatti* and a little *dal*. If such a time should ever come again, which Parmeshwar forbid, your slave will place all that he has at your feet.'

Until I left Mokameh Ghat, eleven years later, I received each year a big basket of the choicest mangoes from Lalajee's garden, for he attained his ambition of becoming a rich merchant once again, and returned to the home he had left when his partner robbed him.

CHAMARI

Chamari, as his name implies, belonged to the lowest strata of India's sixty million Untouchables. Accompanied by his wife, an angular person whose face was stamped with years of suffering and whose two young children were clutching her torn skirts, he applied to me for work. Chamari was an undersized man with a poor physique, and as he was not strong enough to work in the sheds I put him and his wife on to trans-shipping coal. Next morning I provided the pair of them with shovels and baskets, and they started work with courage and industry far beyond their strength. Towards evening I had to put others on to finishing their task, for the delay in unloading one of a rake of fifty wagons meant hanging up the work of several hundred labourers.

For two days Chamari and his wife laboured valiantly but ineffectively. On the third morning when, their blistered hands tied up in dirty rags, they were waiting for work to be allotted to them I asked Chamari if he could read and write. When he said that he knew a little Hindi, I instructed him to return the shovels and baskets to the store and to come to my office for orders. A few days previously I had discharged the headman of the coal gang for his inability to keep sober— the only man I ever discharged—and as it was quite evident that neither Chamari nor his wife would be able to make a living at the job they were on, I decided to give Chamari a trial as a headman.

Chamari thought he had been summoned to the office to be sacked and was greatly relieved, and very proud, when I handed him a new account book and a pencil and told him to take down the numbers of the rake of broad-gauge wagons from which coal was being unloaded, together with the names of the men and women who were engaged on each wagon. Half an hour later he returned with the information I had asked for, neatly entered in the book. When I had verified the correctness of these entries I handed the book back to Chamari, told him I had appointed him headman of the coal gang, at that time numbering two hundred men and women, and explained his duties to him in detail. A humble man who one short hour earlier had laboured under all the disqualifications of his lowly birth walked out of my office with a book tucked under his arm, a pencil behind his ear and, for the first time in his life, his head in the air.

Chamari was one of the most conscientious and hard-working men I have ever employed. In the gang he commanded there were men and women of all castes including Brahmins, Chattris, and Thakurs, and never once did he offend by rendering less respect to these high-caste men and women than was theirs by birthright, and never once was his authority questioned. He was responsible for keeping the individual accounts of everyone working under him, and during the twenty years he worked for me the correctness of his accounts was never disputed.

On Sunday evenings Chamari and I would sit, he on a mat and I on a stool, with a great pile of copper pice between us, and ringed round by coal-grimed men and women eagerly waiting for their week's wages. I enjoyed those Sunday evenings as much as did the simple hard-working people sitting round me, for my pleasure in giving them the wages they had earned with the sweat of their brows was as great as theirs in receiving them. During the week they worked on a platform half a mile long, and as some of them lived in the quarters I had built for them, while others lived in the surrounding villages, they had little opportunity for social intercourse. Sunday evenings gave them this opportunity, and they took full advantage of it. Hardworking people are always cheerful, for they have no time to manufacture imaginary troubles, which are always worse than real ones. My people were admittedly poor, and they had their full share of troubles; none the less they were full of good cheer, and as I could understand and speak their language as well as they could, I was able to take part in their light-hearted banter and appreciate all their jokes.

The railway paid me by weight and I paid my people, both those who worked in the sheds and those who worked on the coal platform, at wagon rates. For work in the sheds I paid the headmen, who in turn paid the gangs employed by them, but the men and women working on coal were paid individually by me. Chamari would change the currency notes I gave him for pice in the Mokameh bazaar, and then, on Sunday evenings, as we sat with the pile of pice between us he would read out the names of the men and women who had been engaged on unloading every individual wagon during the week, while I made a quick mental calculation and paid the amount due to each worker. I paid forty pice (ten annas) for the unloading of each wagon, and when the pice would not divide up equally among the number that had been engaged on unloading any particular wagon I gave the extra pice to one of their number, who would later purchase salt to be divided among them. This system of payment worked to the satisfaction of everyone, and though the work was hard, and the hours long, the wage earned was three times as much as could be earned on the field work, and further, my work was permanent while field work was seasonal and temporary.

I started Chamari on a salary of fifteen rupees a month and gradually increased it to forty rupees, which was more than the majority of the clerks employed by the railway were getting, and in addition I allowed him to employ a gang of ten men to work in the sheds. In India a man's worth is assessed, to a great extent, by the money he is earning and the use he makes of it. Chamari was held in great respect by all sections of the community for the good wages he was earning, but he was held in even greater respect for the unobtrusive use he made of his money. Having known hunger he made it his business to see that no one whom he could succour suffered as he had suffered. All of his own lowly caste who passed his door were welcome to share his food, and those whose caste prohibited them from eating the food cooked by his wife were provided with material to enable them to prepare their own food. When at his wife's request I spoke to Chamari on the subject of keeping open house, his answer invariably was that he and his family had found the fifteen rupees per month, on which I had engaged him, sufficient for their personal requirements and that to allow his wife more than that sum now would only encourage her to be extravagant. When I asked what form her extravagance was likely to take he said she was always nagging him about his clothes and telling him he should be better dressed than the men who were working under him, whereas he thought money spent on clothes could be better spent on feeding the poor. Then to clinch the argument he said; 'Look at yourself, Maharaj,'—he had addressed me thus from the first day, and continued so to address me to the end— 'you have been wearing that suit for years, and if you can do that, why can't I?' As a matter of fact he was wrong about the suit, for I had two of the same material, one being cleaned of coal dust while the other was in use.

I had been at Mokameh Ghat sixteen years when Kaiser Wilhelm started his war. The railway opposed my joining up but gave their consent when I agreed to retain the contract. It was impossible to explain the implications of the war to my people at the conference to which I summoned them. However, each and every one of them was willing to carry on during my absence, and it was entirely due to their loyalty and devotion that traffic through Mokameh Ghat flowed smoothly and without a single hitch during the years I was serving, first in France, and later in Waziristan. Ram Saran acted as Trans-shipment Inspector during my absence, and when I returned after four years I resumed contact with my people with the pleasant feeling that I had only been away from them for a day. My safe return was attributed by them to the prayers they had offered up for me in temple and mosque, and at private shrines.

The summer after my return from the war cholera was bad throughout Bengal, and at one time two women and a man of the coal gang were stricken down by the disease. Chamari and I nursed the sufferers by turns, instilling confidence into them, and by sheer will power brought them through. Shortly thereafter I heard someone moving in my veranda one night—I had the bungalow to myself, for Storrar had left on promotion—and on my asking who it was, a voice out of the darkness said, 'I am

Chamari's wife. I have come to tell you that he has cholera'. Telling the woman to wait I hastily donned some clothes, lit a lantern, and set off with her armed with a stick, for Mokameh Ghat was infested with poisonous snakes.

Chamari had been at work all that day and in the afternoon had accompanied me to a nearby village in which a woman of his coal gang, by the name of Parbatti, was reported to be seriously ill. Parbatti, a widow with three children, was the first woman to volunteer to work for me when I arrived at Mokameh Ghat and for twenty years she had worked unflaggingly. Always cheerful and happy and willing to give a helping hand to any who needed it, she was the life and soul of the Sunday evening gatherings, for, being a widow, she could bandy words with all and sundry without offending India's very strict Mother Grundy. The boy who brought me the news that she was ill did not know what ailed her, but was convinced that she was dying, so I armed myself with a few simple remedies and calling for Chamari on the way hurried to the village. We found Parbatti lying on the floor of her hut with her head in her grey-haired mother's lap. It was the first case of tetanus I had ever seen, and I hope the last I shall ever see. Parbatti's teeth, which would have made the fortune of a film star, had been broken in an attempt to lever them apart, to give her water. She was conscious, but unable to speak, and the torments she was enduring are beyond any words of mine to describe. There was nothing I could do to give her relief beyond massaging the tense muscles of her throat to try to ease her breathing, and while I was doing this, her body was convulsed as though she had received an electric shock. Mercifully her heart stopped beating, and her sufferings ended. Chamari and I had no words to exchange as we walked away from the humble home in which preparations were already under way for the cremation ceremony, for though an ocean of prejudices had lain between the high-caste woman and us it had made no difference to our affection for her, and we both knew that we would miss the cheerful hardworking little woman more than either of us cared to admit. I had not seen Chamari again that evening, for work had taken me to Samaria Ghat; and now his wife had come to tell me he was suffering from cholera.

We in India loathe and dread cholera but we are not frightened of infection, possibly because we are fatalists, and I was not surprised therefore to find a number of men squatting on the floor round Chamari's string bed. The room was dark, but he recognized me in the light of the lantern I was carrying and said, 'Forgive the woman for having called you at this hour.'— it was 2 a.m.—'I ordered her not to disturb you until morning, and she disobeyed me.' Chamari had left me, apparently in good health, ten hours previously and I was shocked to see the change those few hours had made in his appearance. Always a thin, lightly built man, he appeared to have shrunk to half his size; his eyes had sunk deep into their sockets, and his voice was weak and little more than a whisper. It was oppressively hot in the room, so I covered his partly naked body with a sheet and made the men carry the bed out into the open courtyard. It was a public place for a man suffering from cholera to be in, but better a public place than a hot room in which there was not sufficient air for a man in his condition to breathe.

Chamari and I had fought many cases of cholera together and he knew, none better, the danger of panicking and the necessity for unbounded faith in the simple remedies at my command. Heroically he fought the foul disease, never losing hope and taking everything I offered him to combat the cholera and sustain his strength. Hot as it was, he was cold, and the only way I was able to maintain any heat in his body was by placing a brazier with

hot embers under his bed, and getting helpers to rub powdered
ginger into the palms of his hands and the soles of his feet. For
forty-eight hours the battle lasted, every minute being desperately
contested with death, and then the gallant little man fell into a
coma, his pulse fading out and his breathing becoming hardly
perceptible. From midnight to a little after 4 a.m. he lay in this
condition, and I knew that my friend would never rally. Hushed
people who had watched with me during those long hours were
either sitting on the ground or standing round when Chamari
suddenly sat up and in an urgent and perfectly natural voice
said, 'Maharaj, Maharaj! Where are you'? I was standing at the
head of the bed, and when I leant forward and put my hand in
his shoulder he caught it in both of his and said, 'Maharaj,
Parmeshwar is calling me, and I must go'. Then, putting his hands
together and bowing his head, he said, 'Parmeshwar, I come'.
He was dead when I laid him back on the bed.

Possibly a hundred people of all castes were present and heard
Chamari's last words, and among them was a stranger, with
sandalwood caste-marks on his forehead. When I laid
the wasted frame down on the bed the stranger asked
who the dead man was and, when told that he
was Chamari, said: 'I have found what I have
long been searching for. I am a priest of the
great Vishnu temple at Kashi. My master the
head priest, hearing of the good deeds of
this man, sent me to find him and take
him to the temple, that he might have
darshan of him. And now I will go back
to my master and tell him Chamari is
dead, and I will repeat to him the words I heard
Chamari say'. Then having laid the bundle he

was carrying on the ground, and slipped off his sandals, this
Brahmin priest approached the foot of the bed and made
obeisance to the dead Untouchable.

There will never again be a funeral like Chamari's at Mokameh
Ghat, for all sections of the community, high and low, rich and
poor, Hindu, Mohammedan, Untouchable, and Christian, turned
out to pay their last respects to one who had arrived friendless
and weighed down with disqualifications, and who left respected
by all and loved by many.

Chamari was a heathen, according to our Christian belief,
and the lowest of India's Untouchables, but if I am privileged
to go where he has gone, I shall be content.

LIFE AT MOKAMEH GHAT

My men and I did not spend all our time at Mokameh Ghat working and sleeping. Work at the start had been very strenuous for all of us, and continued to be so, but as time passed and hands hardened and back-muscles developed, we settled down in our collars, and as we were pulling in the same direction with a common object—better conditions for those dependent on us—work moved smoothly and allowed of short periods for recreation. The reputation we had earned for ourselves by clearing the heavy accumulation of goods at Mokameh Ghat, and thereafter keeping the traffic moving, was something that all of us had contributed towards, and all of us took a pride in having earned this reputation and were determined to retain it. When therefore an individual absented himself to attend to private affairs, his work was cheerfully performed by his companions.

One of my first undertakings, when I had a little time to myself and a few rupees in my pocket, was to start a school for the sons of my workmen, and for the sons of the lower-paid railway staff. The idea originated with Ram Saran, who was a keen educationist, possibly because of the few opportunities he himself had had for education. Between us we rented a hut, installed a master, and the school—known ever afterwards as Ram Saran's school—started with a membership of twenty boys. Caste prejudices were the first snag we ran up against, but our master soon circumnavigated it by removing the sides of the hut. For whereas high-and low-caste boys could not sit together in the same hut, there was no objection to their sitting in the same shed. From the very start the school was a great success, thanks entirely to Ram Saran's unflagging interest. When suitable buildings had been erected, an additional seven masters employed, and the students increased to two hundred, the Government relieved us of our financial responsibilities. They raised the school to the status of a Middle School and rewarded Ram Saran, to the delight of all his friends, by conferring on him the title of Rai Sahib.

Tom Kelly, Ram Saran's opposite number on the broad-guage railway, was a keen sportsman, and he and I started a recreation club. We cleared a plot of ground, marked out a football and a hockey ground, erected goal-posts, purchased a football and hockey sticks, and started to train each his own football and hockey team. The training for football was comparatively easy, but not so the training for hockey, for as our means did not run to the regulation hockey stick we purchased what at that time was known as Khalsa stick; this was made in Punjab from a black-thorn or small oak tree, the root being bent to a suitable angle to form the crook. The casualities at the start were considerable, for 98 per cent of the players were bare footed, the sticks were heavy and devoid of lapping, and the ball used was made of wood. When our teams had learnt the rudiments of the two games, which amounted to no more than knowing in which direction to propel the ball, we started inter-railway matches. The matches were enjoyed as much by the spectators as by us who took part in them. Kelly was stouter than he would have admitted to being and always played in goal for his side, or for our team when we combined to play out-station teams. I was thin and light and played centre forward and was greatly embarrassed when I was accidentally tripped up by foot or by hockey stick, for when this happened all the players, with the exception of Kelly, abandoned the game to set me on my feet and dust my clothes. On this occasion while I was receiving these attentions, one of the opposing team dribbled the ball down the field and was prevented from scoring a goal by the spectators, who impounded the ball and arrested the player!

Shortly after we started the recreation club the Bengal and North Western Railway built a club house and made a tennis court for the European staff which, including myself, numbered four. Kelly was made an honorary member of the club, and a very useful member he proved, for he was good at both billiards and tennis. Kelly and I were not able to indulge in tennis more than two or three times a month, but when the day's work was done we spent many pleasant evenings together playing billiards.

The goods sheds and sidings at Mokameh Ghat were over a mile and a half long, and to save Kelly unnecessary walking his railway provided him with a rail trolly and four men to push it. This trolly was a great joy to Kelly and myself, for during the winter months, when the barheaded and greylag geese were in, and the moon was at or near the full, we trollied down the main line for nine miles to where there were a number of small tanks. These tanks, some of which were only a few yards across while others were an acre or more in extent, were surrounded by lentil crops which gave us ample cover. We timed ourselves to arrive at the tanks as the sun was setting, and shortly after we had taken up our positions—Kelly at one of the tanks and I at another—

we would see the geese coming. The geese, literally tens of thousands of them, spent the day on the islands in the Ganges and in the evening left the islands to feed on the weeds in the tanks, or on the ripening wheat and grain crops beyond. After crossing the railway line, which was half-way between our positions and the Ganges, the geese would start losing height, and they passed over our heads within easy range. Shooting by moonlight needs a little practice, for birds flighting overhead appear to be farther off than they actually are and one is apt to fire too far ahead of them. When this happened, the birds, seeing the flash of the gun and hearing the report, sprang straight up in the air and before they flattened out again were out of range of the second barrel. Those winter evenings when the full moon was rising over the palm-trees that fringed the river, and the cold brittle air throbbed and reverberated with the honking of geese and the swish of their wings as they passed overhead in flights of from ten to a hundred, are among the happiest of my recollections of the years I spent at Mokameh Ghat.

My work was never dull, and time never hung heavy on my hands, for in addition to arranging for the crossing of the Ganges, and the handling at Mokameh Ghat of a million tons of goods, I was responsible for the running of the steamers that ferried several hundred thousand passengers annually between the two banks of the river. The crossing of the river which after heavy rains in the Himalayas was four to five miles wide, was always a pleasure to me, not only because it gave me time to rest my legs and have a quiet smoke but also because it gave me an opportunity of indulging in one of my hobbies—the study of human beings. The ferry was a link between two great systems of railways, one radiating north and the other radiating south, and among the seven hundred passengers who crossed at each trip were people from all parts of India, and from countries beyond her borders.

One morning I was leaning over the upper deck of the steamer watching the third-class passengers taking their seats on the lower deck. With me was a young man from England who had recently joined the railway and who had been sent to me to study the system of work at Mokameh Ghat. He had spent a fortnight with me and I was now accompanying him across the river to Samaria Ghat to see him off on his long railway journey to Gorakhpur. Sitting cross-legged, or tailorwise, on a bench next to me and also looking down on the lower deck was an Indian. Crosthwaite, my young companion, was very enthusiastic about everything in the country in which he had come to serve, and as we watched the chattering crowds accommodating themselves on the open deck he remarked that he would dearly love to know who these people were, and why they were travelling from one part of India to another. The crowd, packed like sardines, had now settled down, so I said I would try to satisfy his curiosity. Let us start, I said, at the right and work round the deck, taking only the outer fringe of people who have their backs to the rail. The three men nearest to us are Brahmins, and the big copper vessels, sealed with wet clay, that they are so carefully guarding, contain Ganges water. The water on the right bank of the Ganges is considered to be more holy than the water on the left bank and these three Brahmins, servants of a well-known Maharaja, have filled the vessels on the right bank and are taking the water eighty miles by river and rail for the personal use of the Maharaja who, even when he is travelling , never uses any but Ganges water for domestic purposes. The man next to the Brahmins is a Mohammedan, a *dhoonia* by profession. He travels from station to station teasing the cotton in old and lumpy mattresses with the harp-like implement lying on the deck beside him. With this

implement he teases old cotton until it resembles floss silk. Next
to him are two Tibetan lamas who are returning from a pilgrimage
to the sacred Buddhist shrine at Gaya, and who, even on this
winter morning, are feeling hot, as you can see from the beads
of sweat standing out on their foreheads. Next to the lamas are
a group of four men returning from a pilgrimage to Benares, to
their home on the foothills of Nepal. Each of the four men, as
you can see, had two blown-glass jars, protected with wickerwork,
slung to a short bamboo pole. These jars contain water which
they have drawn from the Ganges at Benares and which they
will sell drop by drop in their own and adjoining villagers for
religious ceremonies.

And so on round the deck until I came to the last man on
the left. This man, I told Crosthwaite, was an old friend of
mine, the father of one of my workmen, who was crossing the
river to plough his field on the left bank.

Crosthwaite listened with great interest to all I had told him
about the passengers on the lower deck, and he now asked me
who the man was who was sitting on the bench near us. 'Oh', I
said, 'he is a Mohammedan gentleman. A hide merchant on his
way from Gaya to Muzaffarpur.' As I ceased speaking the man on
the bench unfolded his legs, placed his feet on the deck and
started laughing. Then turning to me he said in perfect English,
'I have been greatly entertained listening to the description you
have given your friend of the men on the deck below us, and
also of your description of me'. My tan hid my blushes, for I
had assumed that he did not know English. 'I believe that with
one exception, myself, your descriptions were right in every case.
I am a Mohammedan as you say, and I am travelling from Gaya
to Muzaffarpur, though how you know this I cannot think for I
have not shown my railway ticket to anyone since I purchased it

at Gaya. But you were wrong in describing me as a hide merchant.
I do not deal in hides. I deal in tobacco.'

On occasions special trains were run for important personages,
and in connexion with these trains a special ferry steamer was
run, for the timings of which I was responsible. I met one
afternoon one of these special trains, which was conveying the
Prime Minister of Nepal, twenty ladies of his household, a
Secretary, and a large retinue of servants from Kathmandu, the
capital of Nepal, to Calcutta. As the train came to a standstill a
blond-headed giant in Nepalese national dress jumped down from
the train and went to the carriage in which the Prime Minister
was travelling. Here the man opened a big umbrella, put his back
to the door of the carriage, lifted his right arm and placed his
hand on his hip. Presently the door behind him opened and the
Prime Minister appeared, carrying a gold-headed cane in his
hand. With practised ease the Prime Minister took his seat on
the man's arm and when he had made himself comfortable the
man raised the umbrella over the Prime Minister's head and set
off. He carried his burden as effortlessly as another would have
carried a celluloid doll on his 300-yard walk, over loose sand,
to the steamer. When I remarked to the Secretary, with whom
I was acquainted, that I had never seen a greater feat of strength,
he informed me that the Prime Minister always used the blond
giant in the way I had just seen him being used, when other
means of transport were not available. I was told that the man
was a Nepalese, but my guess was that he was a national of
northern Europe who for reasons best known to himself, or to
his masters, had accepted service in an independent state on the
borders of India.

While the Prime Minister was being conveyed to the steamer,

four attendants produced a rectangular piece of black silk, some twelve feet long and eight feet wide, which they laid on the sand close to a carriage, which had all its windows closed. The rectangle was fitted with loops at the four corners, and when hooks at the ends of four eight-foot silver staves had been inserted into the loops and the staves stood on end, the rectangle revealed itself as a boxlike structure without a bottom. One end of this structure was now raised to the level of the door of the closed carriage, and out of the carriage and into the silk box stepped the twenty ladies of the Prime Minister's household. With the stave-bearers walking on the outside of the box and only the twinkling patent-leather-shod feet of the ladies showing, the procession set off for the steamer. On the lower deck of the steamer one end of the box was raised and the ladies, all of whom appeared to be between sixteen and eighteen years of age, ran lightly up the stairway on to the upper deck, where I was talking to the Prime Minister. On a previous occasion I had suggested leaving the upper deck when the ladies arrived and had been told there was no necessity for me to do so and that the silk box was only intended to prevent the common men from seeing the ladies of the household. It is not possible for me to describe in details the dress of the ladies, and all I can say is that in their gaily coloured, tight-fitting bodices and wide spreading trousers, in the making of each of which forty yards of fine silk had been used, they looked, as they flitted from side to side of the steamer in an effort to see all that was to be seen, like rare and gorgeous butterflies. At Mokameh Ghat the same procedure was adopted to convey the Prime Minister and his ladies from the steamer to their special train, and when the whole party, and their mountain of luggage, were on board, the train steamed off on its way to Calcutta. Ten days later the party returned and I saw them off at Samaria Ghat on their way to Kathmandu.

A few days later I was working on a report that had to go in that night when my friend the Secretary walked into my office. With his clothes dirty and creased, and looking as though they had been slept in for many nights, he presented a very different appearance from the spruce and well-dressed official I had last seen in company with the Prime Minister. He accepted the chair I offered him and said, without any preamble, that he was in great trouble. The following is the story he told me.

'On the last day of our visit to Calcutta the Prime Minister took the ladies of his household to the shop of Hamilton and Co., the leading jewellers in the city, and told them to select the jewels they fancied. The jewels were paid for in silver rupees for, as you know, we always take sufficient cash with us from Nepal to pay all our expenses and for everything we purchase. The selection of the jewels, the counting of the cash, the packing of the jewels into the suit-case I had taken to the shop for the purpose, and the sealing of the case by the jeweller, all took more time than we had anticipated. The result was that we had to dash back to our hotel, collect our luggage and retinue, and hurry to the station where our special train was waiting for us.

'We arrived back in Kathmandu in the late evening, and the following morning the Prime Minister sent for me and asked for the suit-case containing the jewels. Every room in the palace was searched and everyone who had been on the trip to Calcutta was questioned, yet no trace of the suit-case was found, nor would anyone admit having seen it at any time. I remembered having taken it out of the motor-car that conveyed me from the shop to the hotel, but thereafter I could not remember having seen it at any stage of the journey. I am personally responsible for the case and its contents and if it is not recovered I may lose more than my job, for according to the laws of our land I have committed a great crime.

'There is in Nepal a hermit who is credited with second sight, and on the advice of my friends I went to him. I found the hermit, an old man in tattered clothing, living in a cave on the side of a great mountain, and to him I told my troubles. He listened to me in silence, asked no questions, and told me to return next morning. The following morning I again visited him and he told me that as he lay asleep the previous night he had a vision. In the vision he had seen the suit-case, with its seals intact, in a corner of a room hidden under boxes and bags of many kinds. The room was not far from a big river, had only one door leading into it, and this door was facing the east. This is all the hermit could tell me, so', the Secretary concluded, with tears in his eyes and a catch in his throat, 'I obtained permission to leave Nepal for a week and I have come to see if you can help me, for it is possible that the Ganges is the river the hermit saw in his vision.'

In the Himalayas no one doubts the ability of individuals alleged to be gifted with second sight to help in recovering property lost or mislaid. That the Secretary believed what the hermit had told him there was no question, and his anxiety now was to regain possession of the suit-case, containing jewellery valued at Rs 150,000 (£10,000), before others found and rifled it.

There were many rooms at Mokameh Ghat in which a miscellaneous assortment of goods was stored, but none of them answered to the description given by the hermit. I did, however, know of one room that answered to the description, and this room was the parcel office at Mokameh Junction, two miles from Mokameh Ghat. Having borrowed Kelly's trolly, I sent the Secretary to the junction with Ram Saran. At the parcel office the clerk in charge denied all knowledge of the suit-case, but he raised no objection to the pile of luggage in the office being taken out on to the platform, and when these had been done, the suit-case was revealed with all its seals intact.

The question then arose as to how the case came to be in the office without the clerk's knowledge. The station master now came on the scene and his inquiries elicited the fact that the suit-case had been put in the office by a carriage sweeper, the lowest-paid man on the staff. This man had been ordered to sweep out the train in which the Prime Minister had travelled from Calcutta to Mokameh Ghat, and tucked away under the seat in one of the carriages he had found the suit-case. When his task was finished he carried the suit-case a distance of a quarter of a mile to the platform, and there being no one on the platform at the time to whom he could hand over the case he had put it in a corner of the parcel office. He expressed regret, and asked for forgiveness if he had done anything wrong.

Bachelors and their servants, as a rule, get into more or less set habits and my servants and I were no exception to the rule. Except when work was heavy I invariably returned to my house at 8 p.m. and when my house servant, waiting on the veranda, saw me coming he called to the waterman to lay my bath, for whether it was summer or winter I always had a hot bath. There were three rooms at the front of the house opening on to the veranda: a dining room, a sitting room, and a bedroom. Attached to the bedroom was a small bathroom, ten feet long and six feet wide. This bathroom had two doors and one small window.

One of the doors opened on to the veranda, and the other led to the bedroom. The window was opposite the bedroom door, and set high up in the outer wall of the house. The furniture of the bathroom consisted of an egg-shaped wooden bath, long enough to sit in, a wooden bath-mat with holes in it, and two earthen vessels containing cold water. After the waterman had laid the bath my servant would bolt the outer door of the bathroom and on his way through the bedroom pick up the shoes I had discarded and take them to the kitchen to clean. There he would remain until I called for dinner.

One night after my servant had gone to the kitchen I took a small hand-lamp off the dressing table, went into the bathroom and there placed it on a low wall, six inches high and nine inches wide, which ran half-way across the width of the room. Then I turned and bolted the door, which like most doors in India sagged on its hinges and would not remain shut unless bolted. I had spent most of that day on the coal platform so did not spare the soap, and with a lather on my head and face that did credit to the manufacturers I opened my eyes to replace the soap on the bath-mat and, to my horror, saw the head of a snake projecting up over the end of the bath and within a few inches of my toes. My movements while soaping my head and splashing the water about had evidently annoyed the snake, a big cobra, for its hood was expanded and its long forked tongue was flicking in and out of its wicked-looking mouth. The right thing for me to have done would have been to keep my hands moving, drawn my feet away from the snake, and moving very slowly stand up and step backwards to the

door behind me, keeping my
eyes on the snake all the time.
But what I very foolishly did
was to grab the sides of the
bath and stand up and step
backwards, all in one movement, on

to the low wall. On this cemented wall my foot slipped, and
while trying to regain my balance a stream of water ran off my
elbow on to the wick of the lamp and extinguished it, plunging
the room in the pitch darkness. So here I was shut in a small
dark room with one of the most deadly snakes in India. One
step to the left or one step to the rear would have taken me to
either of the two doors, but not knowing where the snake was I
was frightened to move for fear of putting my bare foot on it.
Moreover, both doors were bolted at the bottom, and even if
I avoided stepping on the snake I should have to feel about for
the bolts where the snake, in his efforts to get out of the room,
was most likely to be.

The servants' quarters were in a corner of the compound
fifty yards away on the dining-room side of the house, so shouting
to them would be of no avail, and my only hope of rescue was
that my servant would get tired of waiting for me to call for
dinner, or that a friend would come to see me, and I devoutly
hoped this would happen before the cobra bit me. The fact that
the cobra was as much trapped as I was in no way comforted me,
for only a few days previously one of my men had had a similar
experience. He had gone into his house in the early afternoon
in order to put away the wages I had just paid him. While he
was opening his box he heard a hiss behind him, and turning
round saw a cobra advancing towards him from the direction
of the open door. Backing against the wall behind him, for there
was only one door to the room, the unfortunate man had tried

to fend off the cobra with his hands, and while doing so was bitten twelve times on hands and on legs. Neighbours heard his cries and came to his rescue, but he died a few minutes later.

I learnt that night that small things can be more nerve-racking and terrifying than big happenings. Every drop of water that trickled down my legs was converted in my imagination into the long forked tongue of the cobra licking my bare skin, a prelude to the burying of his fangs in my flesh.

How long I remained in the room with the cobra I cannot say. My servant said later that it was only half an hour, and no sound has ever been more welcome to me than the sounds I heard as my servant laid the table for dinner. I called him to the bathroom door, told him of my predicament, and instructed him to fetch a lantern and ladder. After another long wait I heard a barbel of voices, followed by the scraping of the ladder against the outer wall of the house. When the lantern had been lifted to the window, ten feet above ground, it did not illuminate the room, so I told the man who was holding it to break a pane of glass and pass the lantern through the opening. The opening was too small for the lantern to be passed in upright. However, after it had been relit three times it was finally inserted into the room and, feeling that the cobra was behind me, I turned my head and saw it lying at the bottom of the bedroom door two feet away. Leaning forward very slowly, I picked up the heavy bath-mat, raised it high and let it fall as the cobra was sliding over the floor towards me. Fortunately I judged my aim accurately and the bath mat crashed down on the cobra's neck six inches from its head. As it bit at the wood and lashed about with its tail I took a hasty stride to the veranda door and in a moment was outside among a crowd of men, armed with sticks and carrying lanterns, for word had got round to the railway quarters that I was having a life-and-death struggle with a big snake in a locked room.

The pinned-down snake was soon dispatched and it was not until the last of the men had gone, leaving their congratulations, that I realized I had no clothes on and that my eyes were full of soap. How the snake came to be in the bathroom I never knew. It may have entered by one of the doors, or it may have fallen from the roof, which was made of thatch and full of rats and squirrels, and tunnelled with sparrows' nests. Anyway, the servants who had laid my bath and I had much to be thankful for, for we approached that night very near the gate of the Happy Hunting Grounds.

We at Mokameh Ghat observed no Hindu or Mohammedan holidays, for no matter what the day work had to go on. There was, however, one day in the year that all of us looked forward to with anticipation and great pleasure, and that day was Christmas. On this day custom ordained that I should remain in my house until ten o'clock, and punctually at this hour Ram Saran—dressed in his best clothes and wearing an enormous pink silk turban, specially kept for the occasion—would present himself to conduct me to my office. Our funds did not run to bunting, but we had a large stock of red and green signal flags, and with these flags and strings of marigold and jasmine flowers, Ram Saran and his band of willing helpers, working from early morning, had given the office and its surroundings a gay and festive appearance. Near the office door a table and a chair were set, and on the table stood a metal pot containing a bunch of my best roses tied round with twine as tight as twine could be tied. Ranged in front of the table were the railway staff, my headmen, and all my labourers. And all were dressed in clean clothes, for no matter how dirty we were during the rest of the year, on Christmas Day we had to be clean.

After I had taken my seat on the chair and Ram Saran had

put a garland of jasmine round my neck, the proceeding started with a long speech by Ram Saran, followed by a short one by me. Sweets were then distributed to the children, and after this messy proceeding was over to the satisfaction of all concerned, the real business of the day started—the distribution of a cash bonus to Ram Saran, to the staff, and to the labourers. The rates I received for my handling contract were woefully small, but even so, by the willing co-operation of all concerned, I did make a profit, and eighty per cent of this profit was distributed on Christmas Day. Small as this bonus was—in the good years it amounted to no more than a month's pay, or a month's earnings—it was greatly appreciated, and the goodwill and willing co-operation it ensured enabled me to handle a million tons of goods a year for twenty-one years without one single unpleasant incident, and without one single day's stoppage of work.

When I hear of the labour unrest, strikes, and communal disorders that are rife today, I am thankful that my men and I served India at a time when the interest of one was the interest of all, and when Hindu, Mohammedan, Depressed Class, and Christian could live, work, and play together in perfect harmony. As could be done today if agitators were eliminated, for the poor of India have no enmity against each other.

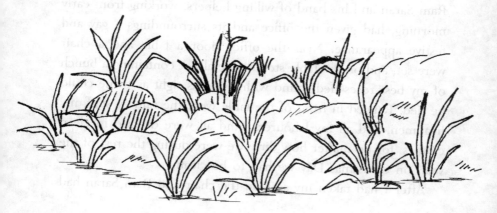

JUNGLE LORE

To Maggie

Contents

Contents

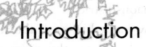

Introduction

IN THE SPRING OF 1985, I was sitting in a
courtyard in Kaladhungi, Jim Corbett's village
tucked against the first of the Himalayan foothills
to rise from plains: around me was strewn the
paraphernalia of the movie world. I was there
for the filming of a drama documentary I had
researched and written on the life of Jim Corbett,
the culmination of years of keen ambition and
a love and admiration for a man I never knew
but who had, through his writings, fundamentally
shaped my personal philosophy and attitude
towards the natural world.

It was a fearfully hot day, even though early
in the summer, and the film crew were hard at
work arranging another set, in a local person's
house, for the scene of Kunwar Singh's illness
and Jim's saving of him from his opium addiction.
Those not engaged in this work were squatting
in the short shadows of late morning. I was with

Frederick Treves, the actor playing Jim Corbett—and who looks remarkably like him, more so in costume and make-up—resting under the scant shade of some paw-paw trees, when one of the local staff on the film crew came up to us.

'Sir,' he announced to me, 'there is an old fellow come who wants to meet Carpet Sahib.' He pronounced Corbett as 'Carpet' as was the way in the Kumaon district.

I supposed the old fellow wanted to meet the actor—others had done so before him, drawn by the magnetism of the 'glamourous' movies—and so asked Freddie Treves if this would be in order. He, with the good grace of the generous man he is, agreed, although I know actors shun such public contact.

An incredibly old man appeared. He must have been in his eighties, wizen and bent almost double by age. He walked with a stick newly cut from a tree and weeping sticky sap. As soon as he saw Freddie, he bowed low and sought to press his forehead to the actor's feet.

I said to the crew member, foolishly assuming the old man to be perhaps a little senile, 'I think you'd better tell him this is only an actor.'

This information was translated and a gabble of Kumaoni dialect made in reply.

'I have told the old fellow,' the crewman reported, 'that this is an actor from England, but he refuses to believe this. It is, he says, a legend that Carpet Sahib will return one day and he believes this is the true Sahib come back.' Then, with obvious reverential astonishment, for the crewman was a city dweller from New Delhi, he added, 'This old fellow has walked one hundred kilometres to see Carpet Sahib. *In just two days...*'

Anyone who has seen the Kumaon foothills will know that twenty kilometres would be a feat for an average fit man yet this old sage had walked virtually non-stop for forty-eight hours on hearing over the jungle grapevine that Corbett was returned to his home. It was Carpet Sahib's magnetism, still vibrant over the forty years since his departure from India, which had drawn the old man and not the spurious trappings of movies and modernity. This is the reverence with which the Kumaoni people viewed Corbett, and still do. It is the veneration afforded to a *sadhu*, a saintly man who has earned his reputation by example: in Corbett's case, by the example he set in the jungles of northern India.

Corbett's famous stories of man-eating tigers and leopard hunting make such exciting reading one tends to overlook in them, in the heat of the chase retold with such simplicity of style and immediacy of effect, the minutiae of detail appertaining to the hunter's skill. And, sadly, his man-eater books tend to overshadow his other volumes, *My India* and *Jungle Lore*. In these are shown, to an even greater extent, not only the hunter but also the man Corbett was.

The former volume deals, as every Corbett reader knows, with the author's familiarity with and love of India, his home for all but the last eight years of his very long life. Here is revealed his immense knowledge of India in all her variety: although he never travelled to the south of the subcontinent, he knew the north and centre well. Yet it is in this book, *Jungle Lore*, that one sees the real soul of Corbett, the core of his love affair with the land of his birth—the jungles of the north and the people (in his mind, both human and animal folk) who inhabit it.

Jungle Lore is probably the least known of Corbett's books. It does not contain sustained anecdotes of hunting dangerous cats or in-depth stories of jungle or forest encounters. Instead, it deals quite simply—occasionally almost naïvely—with the close relationship between Corbett and the natural world and the immense value such an intimacy bears for all men. It is also the nearest he came to an autobiography.

Much of Corbett's childhood, as regards his experiences in the jungle, is here—his early forays with catapult and bow-and-arrow, his first gun and first adventures: but these are not presented as thrilling episodes (although they are) but as lessons attended in the jungle's classroom. For Corbett, term-time at the jungle school never ended and he never graduated, for it is impossible ever to do so: there is always more to learn, more to discover and more to observe because the jungle and the world of nature is in permanent flux.

The crux of *Jungle Lore*, however, is not restricted to learning and seeing. It is more to do with feeling, with sensibility and sensitivity—and it is here that Corbett stakes his claim to fame and posterity—and with presenting nature's case to a world fast ignoring the wonders of the animal (and plant) kingdoms. For, in *Jungle Lore*, written thirty-seven years ago, Jim Corbett is lamenting the divorce of modern man from his environment. He learns the lessons and, like all good teachers, he seeks to share his knowledge and the implications of it with others.

This book has not dated with the passing years. Its import is as vibrant today as ever it was, the morality even more seminal. Sadly, the morals Corbett espouses are still blatantly ignored. Much of Corbett's jungle has gone: the Siwalik Hills which he roamed are mostly denuded of trees, ravaged by erosion and mostly devoid of tigers and game. He would not recognize his Kumaon homeland now.

Yet pockets do remain. The reader can still wander a little way down the wooded firetrack to Powalgarh, still sit on the Boar River bridge, still see the wall Corbett and the villagers built around their fields to keep the wild pigs out of the crops—though the absence of these creatures has long since rendered that defence redundant.

Jungle Lore has a poignant and very pertinent message. It begs us to stop the disaster of raping the earth mother, entreats us to re-assert and re-affirm our contacts with the natural world, to get to know, understand and use to a mutual advantage the ways—the lore—of the wild.

MARTIN BOOTH

chapter one

FOURTEEN OF US—BOYS AND girls ranging
in age from eight to eighteen—were sitting on
the wing wall of the old wooden cantilever bridge
over the Boar river at Kaladhungi, listening to
Dansay telling ghost stories. The bonfire we had
made in the middle of the road, from brushwood collected in the nearby jungle, had burnt
down to a red glow and with darkness closing
down Dansay had selected just the right time
and setting for his stories, as was evident from
the urgent admonition of one of the nervous
girls to her companion: 'Oh *don't* keep looking
behind. You *do* make me feel so nervous.'

Dansay was an Irishman steeped to the
crown of his head in every form of
superstition, in which he had utter and
complete belief, and it was therefore
natural for him to tell his ghost stories
in a very convincing manner. The

stories he was telling that night related to shrouded figures and rattling bones, the mysterious opening and closing of doors, and the creaking of boards on stairways in old ancestral halls. As there was no possibility of my ever seeing a haunted ancestral hall, Dansay's ghost stories held no terrors for me. He had just finished telling his most blood-curdling story and the nervous girl had again admonished her companion not to look behind, when the old horned fish owl who spent all his days dozing on the dead branch of a tree roofed over with creepers—where he was safe from the attention of crows and other birds that love to bait owls—started on his nightly quest for fish and frogs in the Boar river by giving vent to his deep-throated call of *Ho Har Ho* from the topmost branch of the *haldu* tree that had been blasted by lightning and that was a landmark to those of us who, armed with catapult or butterfly net, ventured into the dense jungle in which it stood. The call of the owl, often mistaken by the ignorant for the call of a tiger, was answered by his mate who, except in the mating season, lived in a *pipal* tree on the bank of the canal, and was an excuse for Dansay to end his ghost stories and switch over to stories about banshees, which to him were even more real and more to be feared than ghosts. According to Dansay a banshee was an evil female spirit that resided in dense forests and was so malignant that the mere hearing of it brought calamity to the hearer and his family, and the seeing of it death to the unfortunate beholder. Dansay described the call of a banshee as a long drawn-out scream, which was heard most frequently on dark and stormy nights. These banshee stories had a fearful fascination for me, for they had their setting in the jungles in which I loved to roam in search of birds and their eggs and butterflies.

I do not know what form the banshees took that Dansay heard in Ireland, but I know what form two of them took that he heard in the jungles at Kaladhungi. About one of these banshees I will tell you later, the other is known to all the people who live along the foothills of the Himalayas, and in many other parts of India, as a *churail*. The *churail*, the most feared of all evil spirits, appears in the form of a woman. Having cast her eyes on a human being this woman, whose feet are turned the wrong way, mesmerizes her victims, as a snake does a bird, and walking backwards lures them to their doom. When danger of seeing the woman threatens, the only defence against her wiles is to shield the eyes with the hands, any piece of cloth that is handy, or, if indoors, to pull a blanket over the head.

Whatever the human race may have been in the days of the cave man, we of the present day are essentially children of the daylight. In daylight we are in our element and the most timid among us can, if the necessity arises, summon the courage needed to face any situation, and we can even laugh and make light of the things that a few hours previously made our skin creep. When daylight fades and night engulfs us the sense of sight we depended on no longer sustains us and we are at the mercy of our imagination. Imagination at the best of times can play strange tricks, and when to imagination is added a firm belief in the supernatural it is not surprising that people surrounded by dense forests, whose only means of transport is their own feet, and whose field of vision at night is limited to the illumination provided by a pine torch, or a hand lantern when paraffin is available, should dread the hours of darkness.

Living among the people and for months on end speaking only their language, it was natural for Dansay to have superimposed their superstitions on his own. Our hillmen do not lack courage, and Dansay was as brave as man could be; but because of their belief in the supernatural, I am convinced that neither the hillmen nor Dansay ever dreamed of investigating what the former called a *churail* and the latter believed was a banshee.

During all the years I have lived in Kumaon, and the many hundreds of nights I have spent in the jungles, I have heard the *churail* only three times—always at night—and I have seen it only once.

It was the month of March. A bumper mustard crop had just been harvested, and the village in the midst of which our cottage is situated was alive with happy sounds. Men and women were singing and children were calling to each other. The moon was a night or two from the full, and visibility was nearly as good as in daylight. Maggie and I were on the point of calling for dinner—the time was close on 8 p.m.—when clear and piercing on the night air came the call of the *churail*, and instantly every sound in the village was hushed. In the right-hand corner of the compound, and some fifty yards from our cottage, stands an old *haldu* tree. Generations of vultures, eagles, hawks, kites, crows, and glossy ibis, have worn the bark off and killed the upper branches of the old tree. Opening our front door, which had been closed against the cold wind blowing down from the north, Maggie and I stepped out on to the veranda, and as we did so, the *churail* called again. The call came from the *haldu* tree and there, sitting on the topmost branch in brilliant moonlight was the maker of the call, the *churail*.

It is possible to describe some sounds by a combination of

letters or of words, as for instance the 'cooee' of a human being, or the 'tap, tap, tapping' of a woodpecker, but no words of mine can describe the call of the *churail*. If I said it resembled the cry of a soul in torment, or of a human being in agony, it would convey no meaning to you, for neither you nor I have heard either of these sounds. Nor can I liken the call to any other sounds heard in the jungles, for it is something apart, something that does not appear to have any connexion with our world and that has the effect of curdling the hearer's blood and arresting his heart-beats. On the previous occasions on which I had heard the call I knew it emanated from a bird and I suspected the bird to be an owl, possibly a migrant, for I know every bird in Kumaon and its call, and this was no bird of our jungles. Stepping back into the room I returned with a pair of field-glasses which had been used during the Kaiser's war for spotting for artillery and which were therefore as good as glasses could be. With these I examined the bird very carefully. I will describe what I saw in the hope that someone, more knowledgeable than myself, will be able to identify it.

(a) In size the bird was a little smaller than a golden eagle.

(b) It stood upright on its rather long legs.

(c) Its tail was short, but not as short as an owl's tail.

(d) Its head was not round and big like the head of an owl, nor did it have a short neck.

(e) On its head there was no crest or 'horns'.

(f) When it called—which it did at regular intervals of about half a minute—it put its head up facing the heavens, and opened its beak wide.

(g) In colour it was an overall black, or possibly a dark brown which looked black by moonlight.

I had a 28-bore shot gun, and a light rifle in the gun rack. The gun was useless, for the bird was out of range of it, and I was frightened to use the rifle. Accuracy of aim cannot be depended on in moonlight, and if I missed the bird everyone within hearing distance would be more convinced than ever that the call was being made by an evil spirit which even a rifle bullet was of no avail. After calling about twenty times the bird spread its wings, and gliding off the tree, vanished into the night.

The village sounds were not resumed, and next day no references was made to the *churail*. 'When in the jungles,' warned my poacher friend Kunwar Singh when I was a small boy, 'never speak of a tiger by its name, for if you do, the tiger is sure to appear.' For the same reason the people of our foothills never talk of the *churail*.

The younger members of the two large families who spent the winter months in Kaladhungi numbered fourteen, excluding my younger brother who was too small to take part in the nightly bonfire or to bathe in the river, and who therefore did not count. Of these fourteen, seven were girls, ranging in age from nine to eighteen, and seven were boys, ranging in age from eight to eighteen, of whom I was the youngest. This handicap, of being the youngest of the males, saddled me with tasks that I disliked intensely, for we were living in the Victorian age and when, for instance, the girls went bathing in the canal that formed one boundary of our estate, which they did every day except Sunday— why girls should not bathe on Sunday I do not know—it was deemed necessary for them to be accompanied by a male whose age would offer no offence to Mother Grundy. The selected victim being myself, it was my duty to carry the towels and nightdresses of the girls— for there were no swim- suits in those days—and to keep guard while the girls were bathing and warn them of the approach of males, for there was a footpath on the opposite bank of the canal which was occasionally used by men on their way to collect firewood in the jungles, or to work on the canal when it needed repair or cleaning. The canal was a masonry one, ten feet wide and three feet deep, and where there was an inlet for irrigating our garden the King of Kumaon, General Sir Henry Ramsay, had had the bed of the canal scooped out for a few yards to a depth of six feet, and every day before I set out with the girls I was cautioned not to allow any of them to get drowned in this deep part. The entering of running water while wearing a thin cotton nightdress is a difficult feat, if the proprieties are to be maintained, for if the unwary step into three feet of water and sit down—as all girls appear to want to do the moment they get into the water—the nightdress rises up and flows over the head, to the consternation of all beholders. When this happened, as it very frequently did, I was under strict orders to look the other way.

While I was guarding the girls, and looking the other way when the necessity arose, the other boys armed with catapults and fishing-rods were making their way up the canal bank to the deep pool at the head of the canal, competing as they went as to who could shoot down the highest flower off the *samal* trees they passed, or put the first pellet into the ficus tree on the canal bank, a hit only being allowed when the milk-like sap— the best medium for the making of bird-lime—trickled down the bole of the tree. And there were birds to be fired at, hair-crested drongos, golden orioles, and rosy pastors that drink the nectar of the *samal* flowers; common, slaty, and rose-headed paroquets that nipped off the *samal* flowers and, after nibbling a small portion, dropped the flowers to the ground for deer and pigs to eat; crested pied kingfishers who when disturbed went skimming up the canal, and always the horned owl—the mate of the one who lived on the far side of the Boar bridge—whose perch was on a branch of the *pipal* tree overhanging the canal, and who had never been known to let anyone get within catapult range but who nevertheless was always fired at. Arrived at the big pool there would be fierce competition to see who could land the most fish on improvised tackle of thread borrowed from their respective mother's or sister's work baskets, bent pins for those who could not afford the regulation hook, and rods made from the side-shoots of bamboos. The fishing ended when the supply of paste, used as bait, was exhausted or had been dropped by a careless hand into the water, and with a catch of a few small *mahseer*—for our rivers were full of fish—clothes were hastily discarded and all lined up on the big rock overhanging the pool and, at a signal, dived off to see who could reach the far bank first. And while the others were indulging in these fascinating sports I, a mile lower down the canal, was being told to look the other way or being reprimanded for not having given warning of the approach of the old villager who had passed carrying a load of wood on his head. One advantage I derived from my enforced labour, it let me into all the secret plans the girls made for the playing of practical jokes on the boy members of the two families in general, and on Dansay and Neil Fleming in particular.

Dansay and Neil were both mad Irishmen, and here their similarity ended, for while Dansay was short, hairy, and as strong as a grizzly bear, Neil was tall and willowy and as fair as a lily. The difference even went deeper, for whereas Dansay would think nothing of shouldering his muzzle-loading rifle and stalking and shooting tigers on foot, Neil had a horror of the jungles and had never been known to fire a gun. One thing they had in common, hatred of each other, for both were madly in love with all the girls. Dansay—who had been disinherited by his father, a General, for refusing to go into the Army—had been at a Public School with my elder brothers and was at that time resting between the job he had lost in the Forest Service and the one he hoped some day to get in the Political Service. Neil on the other hand was a working man, assistant to my brother Tom in the Postal Service; and the fact that neither was in a position to dream of matrimony in no way damped their affection for the girls or lessened their jealousy of each other.

From conversations overheard on the canal bank I learned that friend Neil on his last visit to Kaladhungi had been too full of himself and was beginning to imagine things, whereas Dansay on the other hand was too subdued and very slow in coming forward. To rectify this unsatisfactory state of affairs it was thought necessary to pull Neil down a whole row of pegs, and elevate Dansay a little: 'Not too much, my dear, or he will then begin to imagine things.' What 'imagining things' meant I did not know, and I thought it best not to ask. To accomplish these desired ends, with one stroke if possible, it would be necessary to include both the too ardent Neil, and the too slow Dansay in the same practical joke. Many plans were discussed and the one eventually agreed on needed the co-operation of brother Tom. Work during the winter months was not heavy in Naini Tal and Tom was in the habit of allowing Neil to absent himself every alternate week from Saturday evening to Monday morning. This brief holiday Neil spent with one or other of the two families in Kaladhungi, in both of which he was welcome for his genial nature and his grand voice. Accordingly a letter was sent to Tom asking him to detain Neil on one pretext or another on the coming Saturday evening, and to send him off on his fifteen-mile walk to Kaladhungi so as to arrive at the end of his journey as night was falling. Further, Tom was to hint to Neil that the girls would probably get alarmed at his late arrival and would walk up the road to meet him. The plan that had been agreed on for this, the greatest of all practical jokes, was that Dansay, sewn up in one of his bear skins, was to be conducted by the girls two miles up the Naini Tal road to where there was a sharp bend on the road. At this point Dansay was to take up position behind a rock and, when Neil arrived, roar at him in a bear-like manner. Neil, on seeing the bear, was expected to dash down the road into the arms of the waiting girls who, on hearing his story, would pass uncomplimentary remarks on his bravery, and scream with laughter in which Dansay would join when he arrived on the scene a minute later. Dansay raised objections, which he withdrew when he was told that the strip of red flannel he had found in his ham sandwich, and which had caused him a lot of embarrassment at a picnic two weeks previously, had been inserted at Neil's suggestion.

Traffic on the Kaladhungi-Naini Tal road ceased at sundown and on the appointed evening Dansay, sewn into one of his bear skins, was led by the girls, at times on all fours and at times on his flat feet, to the pre-arranged spot where——the evening being warm and the skin having been sewn over his clothes——he arrived in a bath of sweat. In the meantime up in Naini Tal Neil was chafing at being given one job after another until the time had passed when he usually started on his walk to Kaladhungi. Eventually he was told that he could go, and before he left, Tom produced his shot gun and putting two cartridges into it placed it in Neil's hands and warned him that it was only to be used in emergency. The road from Naini Tal to Kaladhungi is downhill most of the way and for the first eight miles passes through patches of cultivation; thereafter, and right down to Kaladhungi, it runs through more or less dense forest. Dansay and the girls had been in their respective positions for some time, and the light was beginning to fade, when down the road came Neil singing 'Killarney' at the top of his voice, to keep his courage up. The singing came nearer and nearer—the girls said later that they had never heard Neil in better voice—and then round the bend where Dansay was waiting for him came Neil. Acting on instructions, Dansay stood up on his hind legs and roared at Neil in a bear-like manner, and Neil *threw up his gun and fired off both barrels*. A cloud of smoke obscured Neil's vision and as he started to run away he heard the 'bear' go rolling down the hill out of sight. At that moment the girls came running up the road, and at the sight of them, Neil brandished his gun and said he had just shot a huge bear that had made a furious attack upon him. Asked by the horrified girls what had become of the bear Neil pointed down the hill and invited the girls to accompany him to have a look at his bag, adding that it would be quite safe to do so for he had shot the bear dead. Declining the invitation the girls told Neil to go down alone and nothing loth Neil—who was greatly touched by the tears of the girls which he thought were being shed at his narrow escape from the bear—went down the hill. What Dansay said to Neil and what Neil said to Dansay is not on record; but when, after a long interval, they scrambled up to the road—where the girls were anxiously waiting—Dansay was carrying the gun, and Neil was carrying the bear's skin. Dansay, who in his roll down the steep hillside had been saved from injury by the bear's skin, asserted that Neil had shot him in the chest and knocked him off his feet. And when Neil explained how he came into possession of the gun, which had so nearly caused a fatal accident, the blame for the miscarriage of the whole enterprise was heaped on brother Tom's absent head.

Monday was a government holiday and when Tom arrived on Sunday night to spend the holiday at home, he was confronted by a bevy of angry girls who demanded to know what he meant by entrusting a man like Neil with a loaded gun and thereby endangering the life of Dansay. Tom listened while the storm broke over his head, and when the narrator got to the part where Dansay had been shot in the chest and knocked off his feet and the girls had wept in each others arms at his untimely death, Tom scandalized all present by bursting into peals of laughter, in which all but Dansay joined when he explained that suspecting—from the letter he had received—that mischief was on foot he had extracted the bullets from the cartridges, and loaded them with flour. So the net result of the great practical joke was not what had been expected, for Neil got more full of himself, while Dansay got more subdued.

chapter two

OWING TO MY ASSOCIATION WITH the girls Dansay suspected me, quite wrongly, of having had a hand in the bear incident out of which he had not come with as much credit to himself as had been expected, for the only contribution I had made was to suggest that strong twine be used to sew him into the bear's skin instead of thread. To no other reason can I ascribe his invitation to me one morning—while I was showing my companions how to swing from one branch of a tree to another—to accompany him on a shoot. Uplifted to the seventh heaven at having been selected for this great honour I set out with Dansay who—after we had started—said he would show me how to shoot a tiger on foot. At the Dhunigar canebrakes—the home of tigers as I found in subsequent years—we saw many pug marks but no tigers, and on the way home Dansay, who was a friend of the family, decided to give me my first lesson in firing a gun. At the time he came to this decision we were standing at one end of an open glade, at the other end of which a number of white-capped laughing thrushes were turning up the dead leaves in search of white ants. While we had been after the tigers Dansay had carried his muzzle-loading rifle in his hands and his shotgun—also a muzzle-loader—slung over his shoulder. He now unslung the shotgun and placing it in my hands pointed to the thrushes and instructed me to put my left foot a little in advance of the right, raise the gun to my shoulder, hold it steady, and gently press the trigger, all of which I did. Even after this long lapse of years I am not sure in my mind whether the gun had been specially loaded for my benefit or whether Dansay who, as I have told you, was as strong as a grizzly bear, was in the habit of over-charging his gun. Anyway, when I recovered sufficiently to pick myself up and take an interest in my surroundings I saw Dansay running his hands along the barrels of the gun to see if they had got dented on the stones on to which I flung the gun as I went heels over head on pressing the trigger. The thrushes had all gone but on the ground on which they had been feeding we found a white-browed flycatcher, a bird about the size of a robin. On examining the little bird we found no signs of injury and Dansay concluded it had died of shock, a conclusion with which I was in entire agreement, for I too had nearly died of shock.

Shortly after my experience with Dansay's muzzle-loader my eldest brother Tom who, on the death of my father when I was four years of age, had taken over the responsibilities of the family, announced one evening that he was going to take me out bear shooting. The announcement was received with consternation by my mother who, though she had the courage of Joan of Arc and Nurse Cavell combined, was as gentle and as timid as a dove.

I listened interestedly while Tom—on whom I lavished all of a
small boy's hero worship—assured my mother that there was
no danger, that he would take great care of me, and that I
would come to no harm. When my mother eventually gave her
consent to my going bear shooting I determined I would keep
out of harm's way by sticking to brother Tom's heels like glue.

We proceeded that evening—Tom carrying both his own
rifle and a gun for me—along a game track that ran across the
face of a great mountain. Half-way across the mountain we came
to a deep, dark, and evil-looking ravine. Tom stopped at the edge
of the ravine and whispered to me that it was a grand place for
bears, who either went up or down the ravine or came along the
game track. He then pointed to a rock on the side of the track
for me to sit on, put the gun and two ball cartridges into my
hands, and warned me to be very careful to kill and not wound
any bears I fired at. Then, pointing to a solitary oak tree on
the shoulder of the mountain eight hundred yards away, he said
he was going there and that if during the course of the evening
I saw a bear anywhere in his vicinity and in a position in which
I thought he could not see it, I was to go and tell him, and
with these parting words *Tom left me.*

A wind was blowing, rustling the dry grass and dead leaves,
and my imagination filled the jungle round me with hungry
bears. (During that winter nine bears were shot on that mountain.)
That I would presently be eaten I had no doubt whatever, and
I was quite sure the meal would prove a very painful one for
me. Time dragged on leaden feet, each moment adding to my
terror, and when the glow from the setting sun was bathing the
mountain side in red, I saw a bear slowly making its way along
the skyline a few hundred yards above Tom's tree. Whether Tom
had seen the bear or not mattered no jot to me. The opportunity
I had been praying for to get away from that terrifying spot

had come, and I was going while the going was still good. So, shouldering the gun, which after my experience with Dansay's muzzle-loader I had been too frightened to load, I set off to tell Tom about the bear and to reattach myself to him.

The Himalayan black bear, in our part of the world, live throughout the winter on acorns. Bears are heavy and acorns grow at the extremities of oak branches, and in order to get at the acorns bears bend the branches inwards towards the centre of the tree. Some of these branches are only cracked and remain green for years, others are torn right off and fall to the ground when released, while others again are left dangling by a strand of bark. I had crossed the ravine and entered a dense patch of undergrowth when I heard a rushing sound. Petrified, I stood quite still while the sound grew louder and louder, and then with a crash a big object fell right in front of me. It was only a branch which a bear had left dangling on the tree under which I was passing, and which the wind had dislodged, but had it been the biggest bear in Asia it could not have frightened me more. The courage I had summoned to take me to brother Tom had all gone, so back to my rock I crept. If a human being in normal health can die of fear, I would have died that night and many times since.

The red glow had faded off the mountain and the light gone out of the sky, when a figure loomed out of the darkness and a cheery voice hailed me. 'You have not been feeling frightened,

have you?' Tom asked as he took my gun, and when I said I
was not feeling frightened *now*, Tom left it at that, for he was a
wise and a very understanding brother.

Tom was a great believer in making an early start when he
went shooting, and the morning he took me with him to shoot
peafowl he roused me at 4 a.m., made me wash and dress as
silently as possible in order not to disturb the rest of the family
and, half an hour later, with a hot cup of tea and home-made
biscuits to sustain us, we set out in the dark on our seven-mile
walk to Garuppu.

In my lifetime I have seen great changes in the forests of
the Tarai and Bhabar. Some of these changes have resulted from
exploitation, others have been brought about in a natural manner.
In some areas where there were dense virgin forests there is now
scrub jungle, and where there were wide open stretches of grass
and plum bushes there is now forest. To the south east of
Garuppu where there is now tree jungle, there was (at the time
I am writing about), waist-high grass and plum bushes. It was
this area that Tom was making for on that December morning,
for the plums were ripe and were an irresistible attraction, not
only to deer and pigs but also to peafowl.

It was still dark when we arrived at Garuppu so we sat near
the well while light gradually appeared in the east, listening to
the jungle awakening. On all sides red jungle-cocks were
crowing, arousing from their slumbers a multitude of smaller
birds each of which, as it shook the
dew from its feathers and the sleep
out of its eyes, joined the cocks in
heralding the new-born day.
Presently the peafowl, who
were roosting on the giant
samal trees, scattered over

the wide grass area, added their piercing call to the growing volume of jungle sounds, and when the rising sun touched the topmost branches of a *samal* tree within our view, the twenty or more peafowl that were clustered on the widespreading branches flew down among the plum bushes. Getting to his feet Tom knocked the ashes out of his pipe, and said it was time for us to enter the jungle. The dew in this low-lying area rises to a height of about thirty feet, and when going through tree jungle in the early morning the moisture dripping from the leaves resembles both in sound and in volume a shower of rain. The grass, waist-high for Tom and chin-high for me, into which we stepped from the road was saturated with dew and we had only gone a few yards into it when my clothes were clinging to me, and adding to the discomfort of wet clothes the morning was bitterly cold.

Going in the direction of the *samal* tree we put up ten or a dozen peafowl all of which, with one exception, flew low for some distance and resettled in the grass. The exception, a peacock in full plumage, rose at a steep angle and alighted on a branch of the *samal* tree. Tom now filled me with delight by putting his 12-bore breach-loading hammer gun into my hands, and telling me to go forward and shoot the peacock. I had a distance of a hundred and fifty yards to go and when I had covered forty yards I stopped, and as I was trying to cock the gun I heard a low whistle and on looking round saw Tom beckoning to me. On my rejoining him he said I was out of range where I had stopped, and when I told him I had not stopped to fire the gun, but to cock it, he said I must never cock a gun until I was ready to fire for it was dangerous anywhere to carry a cocked gun and most of all in grass where one was liable to trip up or stumble into unseen holes. 'Now,' he said, 'go forward and have another try.' On this second occasion—taking advantage of a big plum bush—I crept up to within easy range. The *samal* tree was leafless but was covered with big red flowers, and sitting on a branch on my side of the tree, with the slanting rays of the sun shining on it, was the most beautiful peacock I had ever seen. The time had now come to cock the gun but what with excitement and my frozen fingers I found it impossible to draw back the hammers, and while I was wondering what to do next the peacock flew away. 'Never mind,' Tom said when he came up to me. 'You will have better luck next time.' But no more birds obliged me by flying into trees that morning, and after Tom had shot a red jungle-cock and three peafowl we left the grass and plum jungle and regaining the road made for home and a late breakfast.

chapter three

WITH THE THREE LESSONS I have detailed, my jungle training—as far as my elders were concerned—was over. I had been shown how to handle and to fire a gun, and I had been taken into jungles in which there were tigers and bears with the object, I believe, of showing me that no danger was to be apprehended from unwounded animals. Lessons well learnt when young are never afterwards forgotten, and I had learnt my lessons well. Whether or not from now onwards I took advantage of these lessons to interest myself in any form of field sport was entirely my own concern, and I am glad it was so. I am glad the decision was left with me and that I was not told I must do this or must do that not because of any desire on my part, but because my elders considered it was the right thing for a boy of my age to do.

Boys are not lacking in intelligence, and where

facilities for field sports exist—as they do in most parts of India—they should not be deprived of the pleasure of selecting the form of sport that most appeals to them and for which they are physically fitted, or of eschewing field sports altogether if they have no interest in them and are averse to taking life. Compulsion—no matter how well veiled—even though it follows the lines of an individual's inclinations, takes, in my opinion, all the joy out of any form of sport.

Tom helped my mother and my sisters to nurse me through a life-and-death struggle with pneumonia, and when an incentive was needed to make me take an interest in the life that had so nearly slipped through my fingers, he gave me my first catapult. Sitting on my bed Tom produced the catapult from his pocket, and putting it into my hands, took a cup of beef juice off the bed-side table and told me I must drink it in order to get strong enough to use the catapult. Thereafter I took without protest all that was offered me, and as I regained strength Tom assisted the other members of the family to keep my interest alive by telling me about the jungles and instructing me in the use of my catapult.

From Tom I learned that the year—for sportsmen—was divided into two seasons, a close season and an open season. During the close season my catapult would have to be put away, for at this time birds were nesting and it was cruel to kill them while they were sitting on their eggs or caring for their young. During the open season I could use my catapult freely to kill birds, provided I made use of every bird I killed. Green pigeons and blue rockpigeons, which abounded in our hills, could be shot to eat, but all other birds would have to be skinned and set up and for this purpose, when the time came, Tom provided me with a skinning knife and a pot of arsenical soap. Tom did not include taxidermy among his many accomplishments, however, but his demonstration with a cock *kalege* pheasant as subject gave me a general idea of how to remove a bird's skin, and practice later made me perfect. A cousin of ours, Stephen Dease, was at that time compiling a book of the birds of Kumaon and most of the four hundred and eighty coloured illustrations in his book were made from birds in my collection, or from specimens I specially collected for him.

Tom had two dogs: Poppy, a red pi dog which he found starving in the streets of Kabul during the second Afghan war and which he brought back to India with him; and Magog, a liver and white spaniel with a great plume of a tail. Poppy had no use for small boys, but Magog—who was strong enough to carry me for short distances—was more liberal minded and in addition to constituting himself my protector, lavished all his affection on me. It was Magog who taught me it was unwise to pass close to dense cover in which animals who were sleeping might resent being disturbed, and it was he who showed me that a dog can learn to walk as noiselessly through a jungle as a cat. With Magog to give me confidence I penetrated deep into the jungles where previously I had been afraid to go, and during the catapult days we met with one exciting experience which nearly cost Magog his life.

We were out that morning trying to get a scarlet sun-bird for my collection when Dansay, out for a walk with his Scottie called Thistle, joined us. The two dogs were not good friends, but they refrained from fighting and after we had proceeded a short distance together Thistle put up a porcupine and Magog, disregarding my urgent call to him, joined in the chase. Dansay was armed with his muzzle-loading shotgun but was afraid to use it for fear of hitting the dogs which were running one on either side of the porcupine and biting at it. Running was not Dansay's strong point and, further, he was hampered with his gun so it was not long before the porcupine, the two dogs, and I, had left him far behind. Porcupines are very unpleasant animals to deal with, for though they cannot project or 'shoot' their quills they are tough and very agile on their feet, and their method of defence, or attack, is to erect their quills and run backwards.

Before joining in the chase I had stuffed my catapult into my pocket and armed myself with a stout stick, but I was able to do little to help the dogs, for every time I got near the porcupine it ran at me and I was several times saved by the dogs from being impaled on its quills. When the chase had covered half a mile and we were approaching a deep ravine in which there were porcupine burrows, Magog got the porcupine by the nose and Thistle got hold of its throat. Dansay arrived when the fight was practically over, and, for good measure, he put a charge of shot into the porcupine. Both dogs were streaming with blood, and after we had pulled from them all the quills we could we hurried home—Dansay carrying the porcupine slung over his shoulder—to try to pull out with pincers the quills that had broken off short and resisted all our attempts to pull them out with our fingers, for porcupine quills are barbed and difficult to extract.

Magog passed a very restless day and night sneezing frequently and, each time he did so, leaving a big clot of blood on the straw on which he was lying. The following day was fortunately a Sunday and when Tom arrived from Naini Tal to spend the day at home, he found that a quill had broken off short inside

Magog's nose. After many fruitless attempts Tom eventually got hold of the broken end with the princers and extracted a six-inch length of quill, of the thickness of the quills that are used for the making of penholders. Blood spurted out after the quill had been removed, and as we had no means of stopping the flow Magog's life was despaired of. However, with careful nursing and feeding he recovered, as did also Thistle who had not come as badly out of the fight with the porcupine as Magog had done.

After I had been given the muzzle-loading gun, about which I shall tell you later, Magog and I met with two exciting experiences, one at Kaladhungi and the other at Naini Tal. Naya Gaon village, which I have mentioned elsewhere, was at that time fully cultivated and between the cultivation and the Dhunigar stream there was a strip of jungle, intercepted with open glades. Through this strip of jungle which was from a quarter to half a mile wide runs a game track parallel to, and midway between, the cultivation and the stream. The jungles on both sides of the stream were teeming with game in the way of red jungle-fowl, peafowl, deer, and pig, that took heavy toll of the crops and that crossed the game track on their way to or from the fields. It was on this game track that Magog and I met with our first experience.

Naya Gaon is three miles from our home at Kaladhungi and at crack of dawn one morning Magog and I set out to try to bag a peafowl. Keeping to the middle of the wide road, for the light was not good and the jungle through which the road ran was the haunt of leopards and tigers, we arrived at the point where the game track met the road just as the sun was rising. Here I proceeded to load the gun, a long business, for first the powder had to be measured and poured down the barrel and a thick felt wad firmly rammed down on it. The shot then had to be measured and poured down on to the felt wad and a thin cardboard wad rammed down on the shot. When the ramrod bounced off the charge in the barrel, the gun was considered to be well and truly loaded. The big cumbersome hammer was then put at half-cock and a percussion cap firmly fixed on the nipple. When these several items had been performed to my satisfaction I stowed away the loading materials in my haversack, and Magog and I set off on the game track. A number of jungle-fowl and several peafowl crossed the track in front of us but none of them stood to give me a shot, and we had proceeded for about half a mile when we came to an open glade and as we stepped out on it seven peafowl, in single file, crossed its further end. Waiting for a few moments we crept forward to where the peafowl had crossed, and I then sent in Magog to put them up.

Peafowl when put up by a dog in thick jungle invariably settle on the branches of trees, and as I was at the stage when even a sitting bird was difficult to shoot, it took Magog's and my combined efforts to bring a peafowl to bag. Magog loved peafowl above all other game, and after treeing the birds he invariably dashed round barking at them, and while he engaged their attention I crept up to do my part.

The seven peafowl after crossing the glade had evidently taken to their legs, for Magog had gone at least a hundred yards into the dense scrub and tree jungle before I heard a flutter of wings and the squark of the peafowl, followed immediately afterwards by a frightened yelp from Magog and the angry roar of a tiger. The peafowl had quite evidently led Magog on to a sleeping tiger, and birds, dog, and tiger, were each expressing their surprise, fear, and resentment, in their own particular way. Magog after his first yelp of fear was barking furiously and running, and the tiger was emitting roar upon roar and chasing him, and both were coming towards me. In the general confusion a peacock—giving its alarm call—came sailing through the trees and alighted on a branch just above my head, but for the time being I had lost all interest in birds and my one and only desire was to go somewhere, far away, where there were no tigers. Magog had four legs to carry him over the ground whereas I only had two, so without any feeling of shame—for deserting a faithful companion—I picked up my feet and ran as I had never run before. Magog soon overtook me and the roaring behind us ceased.

I can picture the tiger now, though I could not do so at the time, sitting down on his haunches on reaching the open glade and laughing, a tiger's laugh, at the sight of a big dog and a small boy running for what they thought was dear life, while all that he was doing was to shoo away a dog that had disturbed his slumbers.

I met with one more experience that winter before we left Kaladhungi for our summer home in Naini Tal and on that occasion I was alone, for Magog had taken french leave to visit a lady friend in the village and was absent when I started. I had been avoiding dense jungle for some time and keeping to more open stretches, and on this particular morning I was looking for jungle-fowl near the Garuppu road below Naya Gaon. Many birds were scratching about on the road but none of them let me get close enough for a shot, so I left the road and entered the jungle which here consisted of trees, a few scattered bushes, and short grass. Before leaving the road I removed my shoes and stockings, and I had only proceeded a short distance when I caught sight of a red jungle-cock scratching up the dead leaves under a tree.

When a jungle-fowl, or a farmyard chicken, scratches up in the one case dead leaves and in the other litter, it holds its head high when looking round for danger and if there is no danger near it lowers its head to feed on the exposed insects or corn. The cock that was feeding under the tree was out of range so I started on my bare feet to stalk it. Gaining a yard or two each time the cock lowered his head and freezing each time he raised it, I had nearly got within shooting range when I came on a shallow depression. One step into the depression—which was masked on both sides with knee-high grass—and two steps on the far side and I would be in range, and would in addition have a small tree against which to rest the heavy gun and take careful aim. So waiting until the cock again lowered his head I stepped into the depression, *and put my bare foot on the coils of a big python*. A few days previously I had run as no boy had ever run, and I now jumped as no boy had ever jumped, and as I landed on the far side of the depression I whipped round and fired into the writhing mass and ran until I regained the safety of the road.

In all the years I have spent in the jungles of Northern India I have never heard of a python killing a human being; even so, I know I had a very lucky escape that morning, for if the python had caught me by the leg, as it would undoubtedly have done if it had not been asleep, there would have been no necessity for it to kill me, for I should have died of fright, as a full-grown *cheetal* hind died near my tent one night when a python caught it by the tail. How big the python was that I stepped on, and whether I killed it or not, I do not know for I never went back to look. In that same area I have seen python eighteen feet in length, and I have seen one that had swallowed a *cheetal* and another that had swallowed a *kakar*.

Magog and I met with our second experience shortly after we returned to Naini Tal from Kaladhungi. The forests round Naini Tal at that time teemed with *kalege* pheasants and game of all kinds, and as there were few sportsmen and no restrictions with regard to shooting areas it was possible for Magog and me to go out in the evening after school hours and bag a brace of pheasants or hill-partridge for the larder.

One evening Magog and I walked down the Kaladhungi road and though Magog put up several pheasants, none of them remained seated on a tree long enough to give me a shot. At Sarya Tal, the little lake nestling at the foot of the valley, we left the road and entered the jungle with the object of working back to the gorge at the upper end of the valley. Near the lake I shot a pheasant, and going through dense brushwood and over great piles of rocks we had got back to within two hundred yards of the road when, on emerging from some thick cover on to an open grassy glade, we saw several pheasants jumping up from a bed of wild balsam to eat the berries off a low bush. The birds were only visible while they were in the air, and as I had not reached the stage when I could hit a moving target I sat down on the ground, with Magog lying alongside, to wait for one of the birds to come out on to the glade.

We had been in position for some time and the birds were still jumping up to reach the berries when on the road—which ran diagonally across the face of the hill—we heard a number of men talking and laughing. From the rattling of their tin cans I knew they were milkmen who had been up to Naini Tal to sell milk and were now on their way home to their villages below Sarya Tal. I first heard the men when they turned a corner in the road four hundred yards away, and they had reached a point above and a little to our left front when they all shouted together as though they were driving some animal off the road. Next minute, in the jungle immediately above us, we heard some big animal coming in our direction. The undergrowth was too dense for me to see what the animal was until it dashed into the bed of balsam and put up the pheasants, which went skimming over our heads: then out on to the open glade bounded a big leopard. The leopard saw us while he was still in the air, and as he touched the ground he lay flat and froze in that position. The glade sloped upwards at an angle of thirty degrees, and as the leopard was above and some ten yards from us every inch of him from his chin to the tip of his tail was visible. As the leopard appeared I released my left hand from the gun and placed it on Magog's neck and I could now feel tremors running through him, as I could feel them running through myself.

This was the first leopard that Magog and I had ever seen, and as the wind was blowing up the hill I believe our reactions to it were much the same—intense excitement, but no feeling of fear. This absence of fear I can now, after a lifetime's experience, attribute to the fact that the leopard had no evil intentions towards us. Driven off the road by the men, he was quite possibly making for the mass of rocks over which Magog and I had recently come, and on clearing the bushes and finding a boy and a dog directly in his line of retreat he had frozen, to take stock of the situation. A glance at us was sufficient to satisfy him that we had no hostile intensions towards him, for a leopard can size up a situation more quickly than any other animal in our jungles. And now, satisfied from our whole attitude that he had nothing to fear from us, and satisfied also that there were no other human beings in the direction that he wanted to go, he leapt from his crouching position and in a few graceful bounds disappeared into the jungle behind us. The wind blowing from this direction carried the scent of the leopard to Magog and in a second he was on his feet growling fiercely and with all the hair on his neck and back on end. Only now he realized that the beautiful animal he had watched without any feeling of fear and that could have killed him, big as he was, without any difficulty, had been a leopard, his most deadly and most feared enemy in all the jungles.

chapter four

BETWEEN THE CATAPULT AND THE muzzle-loader periods there was a bow-and-arrow interlude which I look back on with very great pleasure, for though I never succeeded in impaling bird or beast with an arrow I opened my credit account—with my small savings—with the bank of Nature during that period, and the Jungle Lore I absorbed during the interlude, and later, has been a never-ending source of pleasure to me.

I have used the word 'absorbed', in preference to 'learnt', for jungle lore is not a science that can be learnt from textbooks; it can, however, be absorbed, a little at a time, and the absorption process can go on indefinitely, for the book of nature has no beginning, as it has no end. Open the book where you will, and at any period of your life, and if you have the desire to acquire knowledge you will find it of intense interest, and no matter how long or how intently you study the pages your interest will not flag, for in nature there is no finality.

Today it is spring, and the tree before you is bedecked with gay bloom. Attracted by this bloom a multitude of birds of many colours are flitting from branch to branch, some drinking the nectar from the flowers, others eating the petals, and others again feeding on the bees that are busily collecting honey. Tomorrow the bloom will have given place to fruit and a different multitude of birds will be in possession of the tree. And each member of the different multitudes has its allotted place in the scheme of nature. One to beautify nature's garden, another to fill it with melody, and yet another to regenerate the garden.

Season after season, year after year, the scene changes. A new generation of birds in varying numbers and species adorn the tree. The tree loses a limb—torn off in a storm—gets stackheaded and dies, and another tree takes its place; and so the cycle goes on.

On the path at your feet is the track of a snake that passed that way an hour before sunrise. The snake was going from the right-hand side of the path to the left, was three inches in girth, and you can be reasonably certain that it was of a poisonous variety. Tomorrow the track on the same path, or on another, may show that the snake that crossed it five minutes earlier was travelling from left to right, that it was five inches in girth, and that it was non-poisonous.

And so the knowledge you absorb today will be added to the knowledge you will absorb tomorrow, and on your capacity for absorption, not on any fixed standard, will depend the amount of knowledge you ultimately accumulate. And at the end of the accumulating period—be that period one year or fifty—you will find that you are only at the beginning, and that the whole field of nature lies before you waiting to be explored and to be absorbed. But be assured that if you are not interested, or if you have no desire to acquire knowledge, you will learn nothing from nature.

I walked with a companion for twelve miles through a beautiful forest from one camp to another. It was the month of April and nature was at her best. Trees, shrubs, and creepers were in full bloom. Gaily coloured butterflies flitted from flower to flower, and the air, filled with the scent of the flowers, throbbed with the song of birds. At the end of the day my companion was asked if he had enjoyed the walk, and he answered, 'No. The road was very rough.'

I was travelling, shortly after World War I, from Bombay to Mombasa in the British India liner *Karagola*. There were five of us on the upper deck. I was going to Tanganyika to build a house, the other four were going to Kenya—three to shoot and one to look at a farm he had purchased. The sea was rough and I am a bad sailor, so I spent most of my time dozing in a corner of the smoke room. The others sat at a table nearby playing bridge, smoking, and talking, mostly about sport. One day, on being awakened by a cramp in my leg, I heard the youngest member of the party say, 'Oh, I know all about tigers. I spent a fortnight with a Forest Officer in the Central Provinces last year.'

Admittedly two extreme cases, but they will serve to emphasize my contention that if you are not interested you will see nothing but the road you walk on, and if you have no desire to acquire knowledge and assume you can learn in a fortnight what cannot be learnt in a lifetime, you will remain ignorant to the end.

chapter five

DURING MY CHILDHOOD DAYS, AND the ten years I spent at school, and again while I was working in Bengal, and later between the two world wars, I spent all my holidays and leave in the jungles in and around Kaladhungi. If during those years I did not absorb as much jungle lore as I might have done, the fault is mine, for I had ample opportunities of doing so. Opportunities which will never be enjoyed by another, for pressure of population has brought under cultivation large areas on which in my time game wandered at will; while standardization of forests, with all the evils it brings in its train of wild life, has resulted in the total destruction of the trees that bore the flowers and the fruit that birds and animals live on. One result of this destruction, which in my opinion was quite unnecessary, has been to drive millions of monkeys out of the forests on to cultivated land,

presenting Government with a problem which they are finding it difficult to deal with owing to the religious prejudices of the population, who look upon monkeys as sacred animals. A day will come when this problem will have to be faced, and the lot of those who have to face it will not be an enviable one, for in the United Provinces alone the monkey population—in my opinion—is less than ten million, and ten million monkeys living on crops and garden fruit present a very major problem.

Had I realized in those far-off days that a time would come when I would write this book, I would have tried to learn more than I did, for the time I spent in the jungles held unalloyed happiness for me, and that happiness I would now gladly share. My happiness, I believe, resulted from the fact that all wild life is happy in its natural surroundings. In nature there is no sorrow, and no repining. A bird from a flock, or an animal from a herd, is taken by hawk or by carnivorous beast and those that are left rejoice that their time had not come today, and have no thought of tomorrow. When I was ignorant I tried to rescue birds and young animals caught by hawks or by eagles, and deer caught by carnivorous beasts, but soon found that in trying to rescue one I caused the death of two. For the talons of hawk and eagle, and the teeth and claws of carnivorous beasts, hold poison in the form of decayed flesh or blood, and unless expert treatment is immediately applied—which is not possible in a jungle—only one in a hundred of rescued birds or animals survive, and the killer, being deprived of its prey, immediately finds another victim to satisfy its hunger or the hunger of its young.

It is the function of certain birds and animals to maintain the balance in nature, and in order to carry out this function and at the same time provide themselves with the only food they can assimilate it is necessary for them to kill. This killing is—whenever possible—expeditiously and very expertly performed. From the killer's point of view expeditious killing is necessary to avoid attracting enemies, and I see no reason why it should not also be a provision of nature designed to minimize suffering.

Each species has its own method of killing and the method employed in individual cases depends to a great extent on the relative size of the killer and its victim. For instance, a peregrine falcon that does most of its killing on the ground will, on occasion, take a small bird on the wing and kill and eat it in the air. Again, a tiger that on occasion finds it necessary to hamstring an animal before overpowering and killing it will on another occasion strike down a victim with a single blow.

The jungle folk, *in their natural surroundings,* do not kill wantonly. Killing for sport is, however, occasionally indulged in, and some animals, notably pine-marten, civet cats, and mongoose, will, *in abnormal circumstances,* kill in excess of their needs. Sport has a wide meaning and can be interpreted in many ways. In the two instances I am going to narrate it should be interpreted liberally.

When Percy Wyndham was Commissioner of Kumaon he was asked by Sir Harcourt Butler, Governor of the then United Provinces, to provide a python for the recently-opened Lucknow Zoo. Wyndham was on his winter tour when he received the request and on arrival at Kaladhungi he asked me if I knew of a python that would be a credit to our jungles and a suitable gift for a commissioner to present to a Governor. It so happened that I did know of such a python, and next day Wyndham and two of his *shikaris* and I set out on an elephant to look at the python I had in mind. I had known this python for several years and I had no difficulty in guiding the elephant to it.

We found the python lying full stretch on the bed of a shallow stream with an inch or two of gin-clear water flowing over it, and it looked for all the world like a museum specimen in a glass case. When Wyndham saw it he said it was just the kind of python he had hoped to secure, and he ordered the mahout to undo a length of rope from the trappings of the elephant. When this had been done, Wyndham made a noose at one end of the rope and handing it to the *shikaris* told them to dismount from the elephant and noose the snake. With an exclamation of horror the two men said it would be *quite* impossible for them to do this. 'Don't be frightened,' Wyndham said, adding that if the snake showed any sign of attacking them he would shoot it—he was armed with a heavy rifle. This, however, did not appeal to the men, so turning to me Wyndham asked me if I would like to help them. Very emphatically I assured him there was nothing in all the world that I would like less, so handing his rifle to me he joined the two men on the ground.

I greatly regret that instead of the rifle I did not have a movie camera in my hands to make a record of the following few minutes, for I have never witnessed a more amusing scene. Wyndham's plan was to noose the python's tail and haul it to dry land, and then tie it up so that it could be loaded on to the elephant. When he explained this plan to the two *shikaris* they handed the noose to Wyndhom and said that if he would pass the noose under the snake's tail they would haul on the rope. Wyndham, however, was firm in his opinion that the noosing could be done more expertly by the *shikaris*. Eventually, after a lot of advancing and retreating and dumb play to avoid alarming the python, all three men entered the water, each attempting to hold the rope as far away from the noose as possible, and very gingerly they approached the python upstream. When they got to within an arm's length of it, and while each was urging the other to take the noose and pass it under the tail, the python raised its head a foot or two out of the water, and started to turn and glide towards them. With a yell of '*Bhago Sahib*' ('Run sir') the *shikaris* splashed out of the water, followed by Wyndham, and all three dashed into the thick brushwood on the side of the stream while the python glided under the roots of a big *jamun* tree and disappeared from view, and the mahout and I nearly fell off the elephant laughing.

A month later I received a letter from Wyndham informing me he was arriving in Kaladhungi the following day, and that he would like to have another try to capture the python. Geoff Hopkins and a friend of his who had recently arrived from England were with me when I received the letter, and the three of us set off to see if the python was still in the place where I had last seen it. Near the tree under the roots of which the python lived was a *sambhar*'s stamping ground. On this ground, the earth of which had been churned to fine dust by the hooves of generations of *sambhar*, we found the python lying dead, killed a few minutes before our arrival by a pair of otters.

The method employed by otters in killing python, and also crocodiles, for sport—for I have never known of their using either of these reptiles for food—is to approach, one on either side of their intended victim. When the python or crocodile turns its head to defend itself against the attack of, say, the otter on the right, the otter on the left jumps in—otter are very agile— and takes a bite at the victim's neck as close to its head as possible. Then when the victim turns and tries to defend itself against its assailant on the left the one on the right jumps in and takes a bite. In this way, biting alternately and a little at a time, the neck of the victim is bitten away right down to the bone before it is dispatched, for both python and crocodiles are very tenacious of life.

In the case I am narrating the python measured 17 feet 6 inches in length and 26 inches in girth, and the pair of otters must have run a considerable risk while killing it. Otter, however, are big-hearted animals and quite possibly—like human beings—they value their sport in proportion to the risk involved.

The second instance concerns a big bull elephant and a pair of tigers, and unless my theory of 'sport' is accepted I can give no reason for the encounter between the lord and the king and queen of the Indian jungle. The encounter received wide publicity in the Indian press and many letters on the subject were written by renowned sportsmen to the editors of *The Pioneer* and *The Statesman*. The theories advanced for the encounter were: old vendetta, revenge for the killing of a cub, and killing for food. None of the writers of the articles and letters witnessed the encounter, and as a similar case from which deductions might have been made had never been known, the theories remained just theories and proved nothing.

I first heard of the encounter between the elephant and the tigers, which resulted in the death of the elephant, when the Superintendent, Tarai, and Bhabar asked me if it would take 200 gallons of paraffin oil to cremate the body of an elephant. Inquiries at the Superintendent's office in Naini Tal elicited the information that an elephant had been killed by the tigers at Tanakpur on rocky ground where it could not be buried, hence the claim for the cost of cremating it. This information was intensely interesting to me hut unfortunately the trail was ten days old, and, further, the evidence had been burnt and heavy rain had obliterated all tracks.

The Naib-Tahsildar of Tanakpur, who had heard but not witnessed the encounter, was a friend of mine and I am indebted to him for the particulars that enable me to narrate the incident.

Tanakpur, terminus of a branch line of the Oudh-Tirhut Railway and a trading centre of considerable importance, is situated on the right bank of the Sarda river where it emerges from the foothills. Thirty years ago the river flowed along the foot of the high bank on which Tanakpur is built, but like all big rivers where they leave the foothills the Sarda keeps making new channels for itself, and at the time these events took place the river was two miles from Tanakpur. Between the main bank, which is about a hundred feet high, and the river there were several small channels and on the islands formed by these channels there was moderate to heavy tree, scrub, and grass jungle.

One day two *malhas* (boatmen) living in Tanakpur went to the Sarda river to net fish. They stayed out longer than they had intended and the sun was setting when they started on their two-mile walk home. On emerging from a dense patch of grass on to the last channel that lay between them and the high bank, they saw two tigers standing on the far side of the channel, which here was about forty yards wide, with a trickle of water

in it, and as the tigers were between them and their objective the men crouched down where they were, intending to wait until the tigers moved away. These men had seen tigers on many occasions and were not unduly alarmed. This point is important for when anyone suffers from nerves in a jungle, imagination is liable to play strange tricks. At this stage of the proceedings there was still a little light from the recently set sun, and the full moon having just risen behind the two men the tigers standing on the open ground were in clear view. Presently there was a movement in the grass through which they had just come and out on to their side of the channel, stepped an elephant with big tusks. This tusker was well known in the Tanakpur forests and it had made itself unpopular with the Forest Department owing to its habit of pulling down the pillars supporting the roof of the Chene forest bungalow. It was not, however, a rogue in the sense of molesting human beings.

When the elephant stepped out on to the channel and saw the tigers on the far side it raised its trunk and trumpeted and started to move towards them. The tigers now turned to face the elephant and as it approached them one demonstrated in front of it while the other circled round behind and sprang on its back. Swinging its head round, the elephant tried to get at the tiger on its back with its trunk, and the one in front then sprang on to its head. The elephant was now screaming with rage, while the tigers were giving vent to full-throated roars. When tigers roar with anger it is a very terrifying sound, and since the screaming of the maddened elephant was added to this terrifying sound, it is little wonder that the *malhas* lost their nerve and, abandoning their nets and catch of fish, sprinted for Tanakpur at their best speed.

In Tanakpur preparations were being made for the evening meal when the sounds of the fight were first heard. Shortly thereafter, when the *malhas* arrived with the news that an elephant and two tigers were fighting, a few bold spirits went to the edge of the high bank to try to see the fight. When it was realized, however, that the contestants were coming towards them, a stampede took place and in a few minutes every door in Tanakpur was fast closed. Opinions on the duration of the fight differed. Some maintained that it lasted all night, while others maintained that it ended at midnight. Mr Matheson, a retired gentleman whose bungalow was on the high bank immediately above where the fight took place, said it lasted for many hours, and that he had never heard more appalling or terrifying sounds. Guns shots were heard during the night, but it is not clear whether they were fired by the police or by Mr Matheson; anyway, they did not have the desired effect of stopping the fight and driving the animals away.

In the morning the residents of Tanakpur again assembled on the high ground, and at the foot of the hundred-foot boulder-strewn bank they saw the elephant lying dead. From the injuries described by the Naib-Tahsildar, it was evident that it had died of loss of blood. No portion of the elephant had been eaten, and no dead or injured tigers were found at the time or subsequently in the vicinity of Tanakpur.

I do not think that the tigers, at the onset, had any intention of killing the elephant. The theory of an old vendetta, anger at the killing of a cub, and killing for food are not convincing. The fact remains, however, that a big bull elephant, carrying tusks weighing ninety pounds, was killed near Tanakpur by two tigers and I am of the opinion that what started as a lark—by a pair of mating tigers when an elephant tried to shoo them out of his way—developed into a real fight. I am also of the opinion that when the second tiger sprang on the elephant's head it clawed out the elephant's eyes and that thereafter the blinded animal dashed about aimlessly until it came to the high bank. Here on the round loose boulders, which afforded no foothold, it was practically anchored and at the mercy of the tigers who—possibly because of injuries received in the fight—showed no mercy.

All carnivorous animals kill their victims with their teeth, and those that stalk their prey depend on their claws not only to catch and hold but also, on occasion, to disable a victim before dispatching it with their teeth. The act of killing, except in the case of animals that run down their prey, is so seldom witnessed in the jungles, and, when witnessed, the initial movements of the killer are so rapid and consequently so difficult to follow that after witnessing, possibly, twenty kills by tigers and leopards I can give no precise description of the movements of the killer at the actual moment of contact with its victim. In only one of the cases I have witnessed—a *cheetal* hind feeding down-wind— was a head-on attack made. This is understandable, for the horns of the animals usually killed by tigers and leopards are capable of inflicting very serious wounds. The attacks in the other cases witnessed were made by the killers coming up from behind, or at an angle, and with a single spring or short rush getting hold of their victims with their claws, and then with a lightning-fast movement seizing them by the throat and bringing them to the ground.

In bringing an animal to the ground great care has to be exercised, for a full-grown *sambhar* or *cheetal* could with a single kick disembowel a tiger or a leopard. To avoid injury, and also to prevent the victim from struggling to its feet, the head, in the act of pulling it to the ground, is twisted round, as shown in the sketch. When an animal is thus brought down and held it can kick indefinitely without doing its assailant any injury, and it cannot rise or roll over without dislocating its neck. It occasionally happens that when a heavy animal is brought to the ground the fall dislocates the neck, and it also occasionally happens that the neck is dislocated by the canine teeth of the assailant. When the neck is not dislocated either by its fall or by the attacker's teeth, the victim is killed by strangulation.

I have never seen an animal hamstrung by a leopard, but have seen many cases of hamstringing by tigers. In all those cases

the hamstringing was done by the claws and not by the teeth of tigers. A friend once brought me news of the killing of one of his cows on the Semdhar ridge six miles from Naini Tal. He owned a big herd of cattle and had seen many kills by tigers and leopards and from the absence of injuries on this particular cow's neck and from the way the flesh had been torn in shreds he suspected that it had been killed and partly eaten by some unknown animal. The day was still young when he brought me the news, and two hours later we arrived at the kill. The cow, a full-grown animal, had been killed on a fifty-foot-wide fire track and no attempt had been made to drag it away. When the condition of the kill had been described to me I had come to the conclusion that the cow had been killed by a Himalayan black bear. Bears are not habitual meat-eaters but they do occasionally kill, and not being equipped for killing, as tigers and leopards are, their method of killing is very clumsy. The cow had not been killed by a bear, however, but by a tiger, and killed in a very unusual way. It had first been hamstrung, and then killed by being disembowelled. Having killed the cow the tiger had eaten a portion of the hindquarters by tearing away the flesh with its claws. Tracking on the hard ground was not possible, so I spent the rest of the day searching the surrounding forests to try to get a shot at the tiger on foot. Near sundown I returned to the kill and sat up over it all night on the branch of a tree. The tiger did not return to his kill, nor did he return to the kills of nine other animals—six cows and three young buffaloes—that he killed in identically the same way.

This method of killing was intensely cruel from a human being's point of view, but not from the point of view of the tiger. He had to kill to provide himself with food, and his method of killing was dependent on his physical condition. The fact that the tiger could not use his canine teeth to kill, or to drag away his kills, and that he had to use his claws instead of his teeth to tear the flesh from his kills, was proof that he was suffering from some physical defect. This defect, I am convinced, had resulted from a carelessly fired high velocity bullet having shot away a portion of his lower jaw. I came to this conviction on seeing the tiger's first kill and my conviction—that he was wounded and that he was still suffering from his wound—was strengthened by the lengthening period between the kills, and the fact that he was able to eat less from each succeeding kill.

His wound had evidently been received over a kill and this would account for his never returning for a second meal. The killing stopped after the tenth kill and as no tiger was shot or found dead in that area I am inclined to think that the tiger crawled away into a cave, of which there were many on a nearby hill, and there succumbed to his wound.

Admittedly this was an unusual case, but it was not the only case I know of hamstringing, for two of the biggest buffaloes I have ever seen killed by tigers had been hamstrung by the claws of tigers before being pulled down and killed by the tiger's teeth.

chapter six

WHEN THE RUBBER OF THE catapult Tom gave me perished, I made myself a pellet bow. The difference between a bow that shoots a pellet and one that shoots an arrow is that the former is shorter and stiffer, and that it has two strings between which a small square of webbing is fixed to hold the pellet. Practice is needed to shoot with a pellet bow, for if the wrist of the hand holding the bow is not turned at the exact moment that the pellet is released, very serious injury can result to the thumb of the bow hand. A pellet bow can shoot with twice the velocity that a catapult can, but it is not as accurate as a catapult. The Naini Tal Treasury, which was guarded by Gurkhas of the Regular Army, was just across the road from our summer home. The Gurkhas were keen pellet bowmen and I was often invited into the Treasury grounds to compete with them. In the grounds was a short wooden post on which was hung a great circular gong for striking the hours. On this post a match-box used to be placed and from a range of twenty yards the man selected to compete with me, and I, each fired one shot in turn. The *Havildar* of the guard, a short stocky man as strong as a bull, was the best shot of them all, but—much to the delight of the onlookers— he never succeeded in beating me.

Necessity compelled me to use a pellet bow, and though I acquired sufficient accuracy with it to continue my collection of birds, I never took to it as I had taken to a catapult, and after reading Fennimore Cooper's thrilling books I supplemented my pellet bow with a bow to project arrows. If Cooper's Red Indians could shoot game with an arrow, I saw no reason why I should not be able to do the same. The people in our part of India do not use bows and arrows so I had no pattern to work on; however, after several attempts I made a bow to my liking and with this bow and two arrows—tipped with sharp nails— I set out to emulate a Red Indian. I had no illusions about the killing powers of my arrows, or their defensive value, so I walked warily, for in addition to the jungle fowl and peafowl that I hoped to shoot, there were in our jungles many animals of which I was mightily afraid. To enable me to approach the game I wanted to shoot, and to assist me in seeking protection in trees when danger threatened, I discarded my shoes, for there were no thin rubber-soled shoes in those days and the choice lay between bare feet and hard leather shoes which were neither suitable for stalking in nor for climbing trees.

Two watercourses, dry except after heavy rain, ran down from the foothills and met at the lower end of our estate. Both had sandy beds and in the jungle between them, which was a quarter of a mile wide at the bottom end, a mile wide at the top end, and two miles long, was game of all kinds. The canal in which the girls bathed formed a boundary between our estate and the jungle, and I had only to cross it by a fallen tree to get in touch with the game, which included the birds I hoped to shoot. In later years, when I had a cine-camera, I spent many days on a tree on our side of the canal, trying to film tigers that came down to the canal to drink. And it was in this jungle that I shot my last tiger, on my release from the army after Hitler's war. The tiger killed—at different times—a horse, a calf, and two bullocks, and as it resisted all my attempts to drive it away I shot it. Sister Maggie doubted my ability to hold a rifle steady, for many forms of malaria contracted in many jungles had, she thought, impaired the steadiness of my hands. However, to make quite sure of my shot I called the tiger up for judgement, found it guilty, and shot it through the eye as it was looking at me at the range of a few feet. It was murder, of course, but justifiable murder; for though I was willing to let the tiger live in the dense patch of lantana it had selected for its home—two hundred yards from the village—and pay compensation for all the animals it killed, it was difficult to replace these animals owing to the country-wide shortage of farm animals bought about by the war, and—as I have said—the tiger resisted all my attempts to drive it away.

Magog and I had explored the strip of jungle between the two watercourses very thoroughly and I knew all the places to be avoided; even so, I did not consider it was safe to cross the canal by the fallen tree and go hunting jungle-fowl and peafowl until I had satisfied myself that there were no tigers in it. And this I did by examining the watercourse on the left-hand side of the jungle. The tigers that frequented the strip invariably came from the west at about sunset and, unless they had made a kill, returned before sunrise to the heavy jungle from which they had come. By examining the sandy stretches along the bed of this watercourse it was possible to ascertain whether a tiger had crossed into the jungle that I looked on as my private preserve, and, if so, whether it had remained or left. On the occasions on which I found only a one-way track I left the jungle severely alone and went elsewhere to look for birds.

This watercourse was of never-ending interest to me for, in addition to tigers, all the animals and all the crawling creatures that lived in the jungles that stretched for many miles on either side, crossed it, and in doing so left a photographic record of their passage. It was here, first armed with a catapult, then with a bow, later with a muzzle-loader, and later still with a modern rifle, that I added—a little at a time—to my store of jungle lore. Starting out as the sun was rising, and moving noiselessly on my bare feet, I saw at one time or another all the animals and all the crawling creatures that crossed the watercourse, until a day came when I was able to identify each by the track it made. But here was only a small beginning for I had yet to learn the habits of the animals, their language, and the part they played in the scheme of nature. And while I was accumulating knowledge of these interesting subjects I was also absorbing the language of the birds and understanding their functions in nature's garden.

The first thing I did then was to divide the birds and animals and the crawling creatures into groups. Starting with the birds, I divided them into six groups:

(a) Birds that beautified nature's garden. In this group I put minivets, orioles, and sunbirds.

(b) Birds that filled the garden with melody: thrushes, robins, and *shamas*.

(c) Birds that regenerated the garden: barbets, hornbills, and *bulbuls*.

(d) Birds that warned of danger: drongos, red jungle-fowl, and babblers.

(e) Birds that maintained the balance in nature: eagles, hawks, and owls.

(f) Birds that performed the duty of scavengers: vultures, kites, and crows.

The animals I divided into five groups:

(g) Animals that beautified nature's garden. In this group I put deer, antelope, and monkeys.

(h) Animals that helped to regenerate the garden by opening up and aerating the soil: bears, pigs and porcupines.

(i) Animals that warned of danger: deer, monkeys, and squirrels.

(j) Animals that maintained the balance in nature: tigers, leopards, and wild dogs.

(k) Animals that acted as scavengers: hyaenas, jackals, and pigs.

The crawling creatures I divided into two groups:

(l) Poisonous snakes. In this group I put cobras, kraits, and vipers.

(m) Non-poisonous snakes: Pythons, grass-snakes, and *dhamin* (rat snakes).

Having divided the principal birds and animals into groups according to the functions they performed, the other members of the jungle folk that performed similar duties were added—as my knowledge increased—to the groups to which they belonged. The next step was to make myself familiar with the language of the jungle folk, and to learn to imitate the calls of those birds and animals whose calls are within the range of human lips and of a human throat. All birds and all animals have their own language and though—with few exceptions—one species cannot speak the language of another species, all the jungle folk understand each other's language. The best three of the exceptions are, the racket-tailed drongo, the rufous-backed shrike, and the gold-fronted green *bulbul*. To bird lovers the racket-tailed drongo is a never-ending source of pleasure and interest for, in addition to being the most courageous bird in our jungles, he can imitate to perfection the calls of most birds and of one animal, the *cheetal*, and he has a great sense of humour. Attaching himself to a flock of ground-feeding birds—jungle-fowl, babblers, or thrushes—he takes up a commanding position on a dead branch and, while regaling the jungle with his own songs and the songs of the other birds, keeps a sharp look-out for enemies in the way of hawks, cats, snakes, and small boys armed with catapults, and his warning of the approach of danger is never disregarded. His services are not disinterested, for in return for protection he expects the flock he is guarding to provide him with food. His sharp eyes miss nothing, and the moment he sees that one of the birds industriously scratching up or turning over the dead leaves below him has unearthed a fat centipede or a juicy scorpion he darts at it screaming like a hawk, or screaming as a bird of the species he is trying to dispossess does when caught by a hawk. Nine times out of ten he succeeds in wresting the prize from the finder, and returning to his perch kills and eats the titbit at his leisure, and having done so continues his interrupted song.

Racket-tailed drongos are also found in association with *cheetal*, feeding on the grasshoppers and other winged insects disturbed by the deer; and having heard the *cheetal* give their alarm call on seeing a leopard or a tiger, he learns the call and repeats it with great exactitude. I was present on one occasion when a leopard killed a yearling *cheetal*. Moving the leopard away for a few hundred yards I returned to the kill and breaking down a small bush tied the kill to the stump, and as there were no suitable trees nearby I sat on the ground with my back to a bush and my cine-camera resting on my drawn-up knees. Presently a racket-tailed drongo arrived in company with a flock of white-throated laughing thrush. On catching sight of the kill the drongo came close for a better look at it and, in doing so, saw me. The kill was a natural sight to him but my presence appeared to puzzle him; however, after satisfying himself that I did not look dangerous he flew back to the white-throats who were chattering noisily on the ground. The birds were on my left and I was expecting the leopard to appear from my right front when suddenly the drongo gave the alarm call of a *cheetal*, on hearing which the white-throats—some fifty in number— rose in a body and went screaming into the branches above them, whence they started giving their alarm call. By watching the drongo I was able to follow every move of the unseen leopard who, annoyed by the baiting of the birds, worked round until he was immediately behind me. The bush in front of which I was sitting had few leaves on it, and on catching sight of me the leopard gave a low growl and retreated into the jungle, followed by the drongo. The drongo was now thoroughly enjoying himself and his rendering of the alarm call of *cheetal* filled me with admiration and with envy, for though I could have competed with him on a single call I could not have rung the changes on the different ages of the deer he was imitating as quickly or as smoothly as he was doing.

When taking up my position on the ground, I knew the leopard would see me the moment he returned to his kill, and I expected to get my picture while he was trying to take the kill away. After shaking off the drongo the leopard returned a second time and though, by growling fiercely, he showed his resentment at my presence and at the sound my camera made, I succeeded in exposing fifty feet of film—at a range of twenty yards— while he was struggling to break the creeper with which I had tied the kill to the stump.

I do not know if racket-tailed drongos can learn to talk, but I do know that they can learn to whistle tunes. Some years ago the Anglo-Indian station-master of Mankapur Junction on the Bengal and North-Western Railway, now the Oudh-Tirhut Railway, supplemented his income by teaching drongos and *shamas* to whistle tunes. Trains halted at the junction for breakfast and lunch and it was a common sight to see passengers running over to the station-master's bungalow to hear his birds, and returning with a cage containing a bird that whistled the tune they fancied most. For these birds, plus an ornate cage, the station-master charged a flat rate of thirty rupees.

chapter seven

HAVING STATED THAT THE BOOK of Nature
has no beginning and no end, I would be the
last to claim that I have learned all that is to be
learnt of any of the subjects dealt with in *Jungle
Lore*, or that the book contains any expert
knowledge. But having spent so much of my
life with nature, and having made a hobby of
jungle lore, I have observed a little knowledge,
and that knowledge I am now imparting without
reservations. I do not flatter myself that all who
read these pages will agree with my deductions
and statements, but that need be no cause for
quarrel, for no two or more people look at any
object with the same eyes. Take, for example,
three people looking at a rose. One will see only
the colour of the flower, another will see only
the shape, while the third will see both the colour
and the shape. All three will have seen what they
were looking for, and all three will have been

right. When the present Prime Minister of the United Provinces of India and I differed on a subject under discussion, he said, 'We can agree to differ on this point, and still remain friends.' So if any reader differs with me on any point I raise, let us take the Prime Minister's advice and remain friends.

In the beginning I found it difficult to distinguish between the tracks of different animals that left more or less similar impressions on the bed of the watercourse. For instance, the tracks of a young *sambhar* and of a young blue-bull are very similar to the tracks of a big pig. But by watching each of these animals crossing the watercourse and then examining its tracks I soon found that I could, at a glance, distinguish between the tracks of a pig and the tracks of all the other cloven-hoofed animals in the jungle. A pig, like all deer, has rudimentary hoofs at the back of the main hoofs. In a pig these rudimentary hoofs are longer than they are in a deer, and except when a pig is crossing hard ground these rudimentary hoofs leave a distinct impression, whereas in the case of deer the rudimentary hoofs only leave an impression when the main hoofs have sunk in soft ground. Again, until one has gained some experience it is difficult to tell the difference between the pug marks of a tiger cub, and the pug marks of a leopard, when both are of the same superficial area. The difference between the two pug marks can be determined by looking at the imprint of the toes, for the toes of a tiger cub are larger and out of all proportion to the toes of a leopard when both pug marks cover the same superficial area.

The tracks of hyaenas and those of wild dogs are often

confused with the tracks of leopards. Here—when there is any doubt—two fundamental rules can be applied to determine the species of the animal that has made the track:

(a) All animals that run down their prey have big toes as compared with their pads, and all animals that stalk their prey have small toes as compared with their pads.

(b) The imprint of the toe-nails shows in the tracks of all animals that run down their prey, and—except when startled, or when in the act of springing—the imprint of the claws does not show in the tracks of animals that stalk their prey.

If you look at the tracks of a house dog and cat, you will see what I mean by big toes and small pads in the track of the former, and small toes and big pads in the track of the latter.

When living in an area in which snakes are plentiful, it is advisable on occasion to know—from its tracks—in which direction the snake has gone and to determine, more or less accurately, if the snake was poisonous or nonpoisonous. The girth of a snake can also be assessed from its track. I will deal with these three points in the order in which I have mentioned them:

(a) *Direction*: For the purpose of my illustration I should like you to imagine a field of closely-planted lucern, six inches high. If you were to run a roller across the field from right to left you would notice that the lucern plants were laid flat in the direction in which the roller had been run, so even if you had not been present when the roller was being run across the field you would have no difficulty in knowing that it had been run from right to left. If you are not blessed with good eyesight, take a magnifying glass and look carefully at any patch of sand or dust, and you will note that particles of the sand or dust stand up higher than other particles. Call these particles that stand upright the 'pile'. When a snake passes over sand or dust it lays the pile flat in the direction in which it has gone, in the same way as the roller did with the lucern, Every surface like sand, dust, ashes, and so on, on which a snake leaves a track, has a pile on it, and remembering this, you can always tell in which direction a snake has gone by looking at the flattened pile.

(b) *Poisonous or non-poisonous*: You will note that I have said you can determine *more or less* accurately from the track of a snake whether it is poisonous or non-poisonous. There is no hard and fast rule—as in the case of direction—by which the species of a snake can be determined from its track. For though I have only seen the tracks of a few of the three hundred or more varieties of snakes in India, I know of two exceptions from the general rule I apply to determine the species from the track. The two exceptions are the hamadryad or king cobra in the case of poisonous snakes, and the python in the case of non-poisonous snakes.

Poisonous snakes, with the exception I have mentioned, lie in wait for their victims or approach them unseen. They therefore have no need for speed and move over the ground comparatively slowly, and when a snake moves slowly it can only do so by excessive wriggling. Take for example a Russell's Viper, or a krait, India's most deadly snake. If you watch one of these snakes moving over the ground, say over sand or dust, you will note that it travels in a series of short curves, and if you examine the track left by the snake, you will observe that it shows as a series of short curves. When, therefore, you see the track of a snake that shows excessive wriggling,

you can be reasonably sure it is the track of a poisonous snake. Hamadryads live almost exclusively on other snakes and as many of their intended victims can move with speed, the hamadryad has acquired a turn of speed which is said to equal that of a horse. On this point I am ignorant for I have never chased or been chased on horseback by this king of snakes, which attains a length of seventeen feet. However, having killed a few hamadryads up to fourteen feet in length, I know they can travel fast, and this turn of speed I believe they have acquired to enable them to catch other fast-moving snakes. Non-poisonous snakes, with the exception I have mentioned, are slim-built, active, and speedy; and some, like the *dhamin* or rat snake and the black rock snake, can cover the ground at incredible speed. Speed in non-poisonous snakes may be essential partly to secure their prey and partly to outstrip their enemies, of whom they have many. When a snake covers the ground at great speed it leaves a more or less straight track, and where there are slight inequalities in the ground the belly of the snake only touches the hills, and not the valleys. When, therefore, you see a track that is comparatively straight you can be reasonably sure it is the track of a non-poisonous snake. The only poisonous snake whose track you might confuse with that of a non-poisonous one is a hamadryad, but the chances of your doing so are small, for the hamadryad is rare and is found only in a few localities.

(c) *Girth*: To estimate the girth of a snake from the track it makes, measure the width of the track at several points, and multiply the mean width by four. This will give the girth of the snake, though only approximately, for the width of the track will depend on the surface on which it is made. For instance, if the track is made on a light film of dust, it will be narrower than it would be if made on deep dust.

In India twenty thousand people die each year of snake-bite. Of these twenty thousand, I believe only half die of snake poison; the other half die of shock or fright, or a combination of the two, from the bite of non-poisonous snakes. Though Indians have lived with snakes for thousands of years it is surprising how little they know about them, and with very few exceptions Indians look upon all snakes as poisonous. The shock of a bite from a big snake is considerable, and when in addition to the shock the victim jumps to the conclusion that he has been bitten by a poisonous snake and that he is doomed, it is not surprising that such a large number of people succumb—as I believe they do—to the bite of non-poisonous snakes.

In most villages in India there are men who are credited with being able to cure people bitten by snakes. As only some ten per cent of the snakes in India are poisonous, these men build up a great reputation for themselves. They give their services free and do good work among the poor, for though they cannot with their nostrums and charms cure anyone who has received a lethal dose of snake poison, they do save the lives of many people bitten by non-poisonous snakes, by infusing them with courage and confidence.

Most hospitals in India are equipped to deal with snake-bite victims, but as the poor have no means of transport other than their own legs or the shoulders of companions, in many cases they arrive at hospital when they have passed the stage at which expert medical treatment would be of benefit to them. In all hospitals charts are exhibited of poisonous snakes. Except where rewards are paid for the destruction of poisonous snakes these charts are of little value, for most people are bitten while moving about barefoot at night, and therefore do not see the snakes that have bitten them. And again, there is a widespread belief that if the person bitten kills the snake, the snake in turn will kill him, so few snakes are produced in hospitals by snake-bite victims to enable doctors to determine whether the patient was bitten by a poisonous or a non-poisonous species.

My method—when I am in doubt—of determining whether a snake is poisonous or non-poisonous, is to kill it and look at its mouth. If it has two rows of teeth I class it as non-poisonous; while if it has two fangs on the upper jaw—hinged in the viper family and fixed in the cobra family—I class it as poisonous. A bite from the former class exhibits a number of teeth-marks; a bite from the latter class exhibits two fang-marks, though in some cases only one fang-mark, as happens occasionally when the striker is not at right angles to the object struck, or when the object struck, say a finger or a toe, is too small for both fangs to make contact.

chapter eight

LEARNING THE CALLS OF THE jungle folk was not difficult, nor was it difficult to imitate some of the birds and a few of the animals, for I had a good ear, and being young my lips and vocal chords were pliant. Learning the calls and being able to identify every bird and animal by its call was not sufficient, however, for, with the exception of those birds whose function it is to fill nature's garden with melody, birds and animals do not call without a reason, and the call differs according to the reason for which it is made.

I was sitting one day on a tree watching a herd of *cheetal* in an open glade. There were fifteen stags and hinds in the herd, and five young ones all about the same age. One of the young ones that had been sleeping in the sun got to its feet, stretched itself, and kicking up its heels raced across the glade towards a fallen tree; this was a signal to the other young ones that a game of 'follow the leader' was on. Nose to tail the five cleared the tree, circled around, raced through the glade and again cleared the tree. After the second jump the leader carried on into the jungle beyond, followed by its companions. A hind that had been lying down now got to her feet, looked in the direction in which the young ones had gone, and gave a sharp bark. The bark brought the truants racing back to the glade, but it had not the slightest effect on the grown animals, who continued to lie down or to crop the short grass. A footpath used by woodcutters passed within a short distance of the glade and presently along this path came a man carrying an axe over his shoulder. From my raised position I saw the man while he was still a long way off, for the jungle in the direction in which  he was coming was comparatively open. When the man was a hundred yards from the glade one of the hinds saw him; gave a sharp bark and the whole herd without a moment's hesitation dashed away into thick cover.

The bark of the anxious mother recalling her young one and the bark of the hind warning the herd of the presence of a human being had, to my untrained ears, sounded exactly alike and it was not until I had gained experience that I detected that the difference in the call of animals, and also of birds, when calling for different reasons was not to be found in the call itself, but in the intonation of the call. A dog barks, and all who hear it know it is barking to welcome its master; or barking with excitement at being taken for a run; or barking with frustration at a treed cat; or barking with anger at a stranger; or just barking because it is chained up. In all these cases it is the intonation of the bark that enables the hearer to determine why the dog is barking.

When I had absorbed sufficient knowledge to enable me to identify all the jungle folk by their calls, ascribe a reason for the call, and imitate many of them sufficiently well to get some birds and a few animals to come to me or to follow me, the jungles took on an added interest, for not only was I able to take an interest in the surroundings within sight but also in the surroundings to the limit of my hearing. But first it was necessary to be able to locate, or pinpoint sound. Animals who live day and night with fear can pinpoint sound with exactitude, and fear can teach human beings to do the same. Sounds that are repeated—as, for instance, a *langor* barking at a leopard, or a *cheetal* barking at a suspicious movement, or a peafowl calling at a tiger—are not difficult to locate, nor do they indicate immediate danger calling for instant action. It is the sound that is only heard once, like the snapping of a twig, a low growl, or the single warning call of bird or of animal, that is difficult to locate, is of immediate danger, and calls for instant action. Having acquired the ability—through fear—of being able to pinpoint sound, that is, to assess the exact direction and distance of all sounds heard, I was able to follow the movement of unseen leopards and tigers, whether when in the jungle by daylight, or in bed at night, for the situation of our home enabled me to hear all the jungle sounds.

In return for the birds I collected for him, Stephen Dease gave me the gun I have already referred to. This gun was a double-barrelled muzzle-loader which in its young days must have been quite a good weapon, but whose efficiency had been reduced by half by an over-charge of powder which had split the right barrel. The explosion had also evidently broken the stock, and when Stephen passed the old warrior over to me the barrels and stock were held precariously together with lappings of brass wire. However, as Kunwar Singh—my poacher friend—pointed out to me, the left barrel was sound and capable of rendering good service; a prediction that proved correct for I kept the larder for a considerable family supplied for two winters with jungle-fowl and pea-fowl, and on one memorable occasion I crept up close enough to a *cheetal* to shoot it with No. 4 shot.

I am not ashamed to admit that all the birds I shot with the muzzle-loader were shot sitting. Ammunition was not easy to come by and to eke out my scanty supply every shot had to be effective. If during a morning or an evening I fired two or three shots, I brought back two or three birds, and no other method of shooting the birds could possibly have given me more pleasure.

I was returning one evening from the foothills at the upper end of the jungle between the two watercourses I have mentioned. The weather for several weeks had been very dry, making stalking difficult, and the sun was near setting when I turned my face for home, with a jungle-fowl and a *kalege* pheasant in the string bag in which I carried my powder and shot. A blue-black cloud was showing over a shoulder of the foothills to the west as I emerged from a deep ravine in which I had shot the *kalege* pheasant. This ominous-looking cloud, following a spell of dry weather and a sultry day when not a leaf or a blade of grass had stirred, presaged a hailstorm. Hailstorms along the foothills are feared by man and beast, for in a few minutes a belt of cultivation, maybe only a quarter of a mile wide or maybe ten miles, can be laid waste and children and cattle killed if caught in the open. I have never seen a wild animal killed by hailstones, but I have seen the jungle strewn with dead birds, including vultures and peafowl.

I had three miles to go, but by taking a direct line for home and cutting the corners in the winding game-tracks I could reduce the distance by half a mile. I was now facing the oncoming blue-black cloud, across the face of which forked lightning was continuous. The birds and animals were silent and the only sound to be heard as I entered a thick belt of heavy timber was the distant rumble of thunder. Under the dense canopy of leaves the light was fading and as I loped along, taking care to see where I placed my feet for I was running barefoot, I heard the wind that always precedes a hailstorm. When I was half-way through the timber the wind struck the forest, sending the carpet of tinder-dry dead leaves swirling along the ground with the noise of a suddenly released torrent of water, and at the same moment I heard a scream—Dansay's 'banshee', without a doubt. Starting on a minor note the scream developed into a terrifying shriek, and then died away on a long-drawn-out sobbing note. Some sounds have the effect of petrifying one, others galvanize one into instant action: the scream—which I placed as being above and a little behind me—had the latter effect on me. A few weeks previously—in company with Magog—I had run from a tiger as I thought I should never run again, but I did not know then that terror of the unknown could lend wings to one's feet. To my credit be it noted that I did not throw away my gun and the heavy string bag, and regardless of thorns and of stubbed toes I ran until I reached home. Thunder was booming overhead and the first of the hailstones were hissing down as I ran up the steps of the veranda, and in the general confusion of fastening doors and windows and making all secure against the storm, my breathless and excited condition escaped attention.

Dansay had said that hearing the banshee brought calamity to the hearer and his family, and fearing that I would be blamed for any calamity that befell the family, I said not a word about my experience. Danger of any kind has an attraction for everyone, including small boys, and though for many days I avoided the area in which I had heard the banshee, a day came when I found myself back at the edge of the heavy timber. As on the evening of the storm a wind was blowing, and after I had been standing with my back to a tree for some minutes, I again heard the scream. Restraining with difficulty my impulse to run away, I stood trembling behind the tree and after the scream had been repeated a few times, I decided to creep up and have a look at the banshee. No calamity had resulted from my hearing her and I thought that if by chance she saw me now, and saw that I was a very small boy, he would not kill me; so—with my heart beating in my throat—I crept forward as slowly and as noiselessly as a shadow, until I saw Dansay's banshee.

In some violent storm of long ago a giant of the forest had been partly uprooted and had been prevented from crashing to the ground by falling across another and slightly smaller giant. The weight of the bigger tree had given the smaller tree a permanent bend, and when a gust of wind lifted the bigger one and then released it, it swayed back on to the supporting tree. At the point of impact the wood of both trees had died and worn as smooth as glass, and it was the friction between these two smooth surfaces that was emitting the terrifying scream. Not until I had laid the gun on the ground and climbed the leaning tree and sat on it while the scream was being repeated below me, was I satisfied that I had found the terror that was always at the back of my mind when I was alone in the jungles. From that day I date the desire I acquired of following up and getting to the bottom of every unusual thing I saw or heard in the jungles, and for this I am grateful to Dansay for, by frightening me with his banshee, he started me on the compiling of many exciting and interesting jungle detective stories.

Detective stories of fiction usually start with the evidence of some violent crime or attempted crime, and the enthralled reader—oblivious for the time being that he is reading fiction— is carried along through exciting scene after scene until finally the criminal is detected and made to suffer for his crime. My jungle detective stories do not start in the same way, nor do they always end with punishment for the criminal. I will select at random two of these stories from memory's library.

(1)

I was camping at a Forest Department bungalow ten miles from Kaladhungi and had gone out early one morning to try to shoot a jungle-fowl or a peafowl for the pot. To the left of the road I was on was a densely-wooded low hill with game of all kinds on it, and to the right was cultivated land with a narrow strip of bush-covered ground between the cultivation and the road. When the village folk started moving about their fields in the morning, birds that were feeding on the crops rose and flew over the road, offering excellent shots. My luck was out that morning, for the birds that crossed the road were out of range of my small bore gun, and I got to the end of the cultivation without firing a shot.

While keeping an eye open for birds, I had also kept an eye on the road, and a hundred yards from where the chances of my shooting a bird ended I noted that a big male leopard had come down the hill from my left on to the road. For a few yards the leopard had kept to the left of the road, then crossed to the right and lain down near a bush. From this point the leopard had gone forward for twenty yards, and again lain down by a bush. The behaviour of the leopard indicated that he had been interested in something, and quite evidently that something had not been on the road, for if it had he would have gone forward through the bushes and not along the road. Going back to where he had first lain I knelt down to see the view he had obtained from this spot. Where the cultivation and the narrow strip of bushes ended there was an open stretch of ground, the grass on which had been cropped close by village cattle. This stretch of ground was visible from the leopard's first viewpoint, and I found it was also visible from his second viewpoint, so what he had been interested in was evidently on the open ground.

Keeping under cover of the screen of bushes, the leopard had gone forward for another fifty yards to where the bushes ended and where a shallow depression starting at the edge of the road ran across the open ground. Where the bushes ended the leopard had lain down for some time, changing his position several times, and eventually he had entered the depression and proceeded along it, stopping and lying down frequently. Thirty yards farther on the sand and dust that had been washed off the road into the depression ended and gave place to short grass. Here, from the particles of sand and dust adhering to the grass where the leopard had put his pads, it was reasonable to assume that he passed that way after the dew had started falling the previous evening, which would be at approximately 7 p.m. The grass in the depression extended for only a few yards and the light sand and dust beyond showed no pug marks, so it was evident the leopard had left the depression at this spot. Tracking on the open ground was not possible, but from where the leopard had left the depression I saw he had gone in the direction of a few coarse tufts of grass, a foot or two high. Going up to the tufts, I saw at a distance of about ten feet the deep imprints of a *sambhar*'s hoofs. From here on for thirty yards, and at regular intervals, all four hoofs of the *sambhar* had bitten deep into the ground as would naturally happen if the *sambhar* was trying, by shock tactics, to dislodge something from his back. At the end of the thirty yards the *sambhar* had turned to the left and dashed straight towards an isolated tree on the far side of the depression. On the bark of this tree, and at a height of about four feet, I found *sambhar* hairs and a small splash of blood.

I was now convinced that the leopard from his look-out on the hill had seen the *sambhar* feeding on the open ground, and after reconnoitring the position had set off to stalk it and, having sprung on its back from the cover of the tufts of grass, that he was now riding it until it took him to some sheltered spot where he could kill it and have the kill to himself. To have killed the *sambhar* where he caught it would have been easy but he could not have dragged a full-grown *sambhar* to cover—the hoof marks had shown me that the *sambhar* was full grown—and when daylight came he would have lost his kill, so he had wisely decided to ride it. Having failed to wipe the leopard off its back on the first tree the *sambhar* made three more attempts to get rid of his unwelcome rider before making for the main jungle two hundred yards away, where he evidently hoped that bushes would accomplish what the trees had failed to do. Twenty yards inside the bushes, and well screened from the prying eyes of human beings and vultures, the leopard had buried his teeth in the old *sambhar* hind's throat, and while holding on with his teeth and the claws of his fore-paws, had swung his body clear of the hind bringing her to the ground and, after killing her, had eaten his meal. The leopard was lying near his kill when I arrived and on seeing me moved off, but he had nothing to fear from me for I was out bird shooting and was armed with a 28-bore gun and No. 8 shot.

I know of many instances of leopards riding animals they intend to kill—*sambhar*, *cheetal*, and in one instance a horse—but I only know of one instance of a tiger having done so.

On that occasion I was camped near Mangolia Khatta, a cattle station twelve miles from Kaladhungi, and while I was having a late breakfast one morning I heard the distant boom of buffalo bells. Earlier in the morning, while returning to camp after taking a cinema picture of a leopard, I had passed through a herd of some hundred and fifty buffaloes that were grazing on a wide expanse of *tarai* grass through which ran a sandy *nullah*, with a trickle of water in it. In this *nullah* I had seen the fresh pug marks of a tiger and a tigress. From the violent booming of the bells it was evident that the herd of buffaloes was stampeding back to the cattle station, and mingled with the sound of the bells was the bellowing of a single buffalo. The men at the cattle station, some ten in number, had now taken alarm and started to shout and to beat tin cans, whereon the buffalo stopped bellowing but the herd continued to stampede until it reached the station.

Shortly after all the noise had died down I heard two shots, and on going to the station to investigate I saw a young European with a gun in his hand and a ring of Indians standing round a buffalo that was stretched on the ground. The European told me that he was employed by the Indian Wood Products at Izatnagar and that he had been talking to the cattle men when they heard the distant booming of the buffalo bells. As the sound drew nearer they heard the bellowing of a buffalo and the angry roar of a tiger (I was farther away and so had not heard the tiger), and fearing that the tiger was coming to the station they had started shouting and beating tin cans. On the arrival of the herd one of the buffaloes was seen to be smothered in blood and on the cattle men saying that nothing could be done for it, he had asked for and obtained permission to shoot it and had put two bullets into its head to end its suffering.

The buffalo the young man had shot was young and in perfect condition, and the cattle men were probably right when they informed me it was one of the best in the herd. I had never seen an animal in the condition it presented, so I examined it very thoroughly.

On the buffalo's neck and throat there was not a single mark of tooth or claw, but on its back were fifty or more deep cuts made by a tiger's claws. Some of these claw marks had been made while the tiger was facing towards the buffalo's head, others had been made while it had been facing towards the buffalo's tail. While riding the maddened animal the tiger had torn off and eaten some five pounds of flesh from its withers, and some ten to fifteen pounds from its hind quarters.

Going back to my camp I armed myself with a heavy rifle and went down the trail the buffaloes had made, and found that the stampede had started on the far side of the *nullah* in which I had seen the tiger's pug marks. But the grass here was unfortunately shoulder high, so I was not able to reconstruct the scene or to find any clue as to how the tiger came to be on the back of a buffalo it had no intention of killing, as was evident from the absence of marks on the buffalo's neck and throat. This failure to reconstruct the scene I greatly regret, for apart from its being the only occasion on which I have been at fault, I believe no other instance of a tiger riding an animal and having a meal while doing so has ever been known.

The pug marks in the *nullah* showed that both tigers were full grown, so it was not a case of a young and inexperienced tiger trying his hand; and, further, no young tiger would have dared to approach a herd of buffaloes at ten o'clock in the morning, or, for the matter of that, at any hour.

(2)

Evelyn Gill, son of my old friend Harry Gill, is one of the keenest butterfly collectors I know, and in a conversation I had with him while he was in Naini Tal on short leave I mentioned having seen on the Powalgarh road a butterfly with brilliant red spots on its upper wings. Evelyn said he had not seen a butterfly of this kind and he begged me to get him a specimen.

Some months later I was camped at Sandni Gaga, three miles from Powalgarh, trying to get a cinema picture of *cheetal* stags fighting, for at that time it was not unusual to see several battles between rival stags taking place at the same time on the Sandni Gaga plain. One morning after an early breakfast I set out with my butterfly net to try to get the specimen I had promised Evelyn. A hundred yards from my tent there was a forest road connecting Kaladhungi with Powalgarh, and in a hollow a mile along this road where there was a *sambhar* wallow I hoped to get the butterfly.

This forest road was little used by human beings and as there was an abundance of game in the forest through which it ran, an early morning walk along it was of great interest, for on the road, which was of hard clay with a light film of dust on it, was a record of all the animals that had used or crossed it during the night. When looking at tracks on a road or game path, with a trained eye, it is not necessary to stop at each track to determine the species, size, movement, and so on of the animal or animals that have made the track, for these details are subconsciously noted. For instance, the porcupine that had come out on to the road, a little beyond where I joined the road after leaving my camp, had evidently taken fright at something in the jungle on the right of the road and had scurried back. The reason for his fright was apparent a few yards farther on, where a bear had crossed the road from right to left. On entering the jungle on the left the bear had disturbed a sounder of pig and a small herd of *cheetal*, for they had dashed across the road into the jungle on the right. A little farther on, a *sambhar* stag had come out from the right and after browsing on a bush

had walked along the road for fifty yards, rubbed his antlers against a young sapling, and then gone back into the jungle. Near this spot a four-horned antelope, with a fawn at foot, had come on the road. The fawn, whose hoof-prints were no bigger than the finger nails of a child, had skipped about the road until the mother had taken fright, and after dashing down the road for a few yards mother and fawn had gone into the jungle. Here there was a bend in the road, and at the bend were the footprints of a hyaena who had come as far as this, and then turned and gone back the way it had come.

Reading the signs on the road and listening to the birds—Sandni Gaga in addition to being the most beautiful spot for a hundred miles round is noted for its bird life—I had covered half a mile when I came to a stretch of the road that had been cut out of the face of the hill. Here the surface was too hard to show normal tracks and I had gone a short distance along the road when my attention was arrested by an unusual mark. This was a little furrow three inches long and two inches deep where it started, and it was at right angles to the road. The furrow could have been made by a staff with an iron point, but no human being had been along the road for twenty-four hours and the furrow had been made within the past twelve hours. And again, if a human being had made it it would have been parallel with and not at right angles to the road, which at this point was fourteen feet wide with a more or less perpendicular bank some ten feet high on the right and a steep slope on the left. The earth thrown out of the furrow showed that the object that had made it had travelled from right to left.

Having satisfied myself that the furrow had not been made by a human being, I came to the conclusion that the only other thing that could have made it was the pointed tip of a horn, either of a *cheetal* or of a young *sambhar*. Had either of these deer jumped down the steep bank and made a bad landing, hard though the ground was the hoofs of the animal would have broken the surface and left a track, but there were no deer tracks anywhere near the furrow. The final conclusion that I arrived at, therefore—with the furrow as my only clue—was that it had been made by the horn of a *dead* deer, and made when a tiger had jumped down the bank with the deer in its mouth. That there were no drag marks on the road was not unusual, for whenever it is possible to do so both tigers and leopards when crossing a road with a kill lift the kill clear of the ground, and this I believe they do to avoid leaving a scent trail for bears, hyaenas, and jackals to follow.

To test the accuracy of my deductions I crossed the road and looked down the hill on the left of the road. No drag marks were to be seen, but on a bush twenty feet down the hill and at a height of about four feet I saw something glistening on a leaf in the morning sun; on going down to investigate I found this was a big drop of blood, not yet quite dry. From

here on, tracking was easy, and fifty yards farther down under
the shelter of a small tree and surrounded by thick bushes I
found the kill, a *cheetal* stag with horns that many a sportsman
would have prized as a good trophy. The tiger was taking no
chances of his kill—from which he had eaten both hind
quarters—being found by bird or beast, for he had scratched
together the dry leaves and twigs for a considerable distance
round, and had heaped them on the kill. When a tiger does
this it is an indication that he is not lying up nearby to keep an
eye on the kill.

I had been told by Fred Anderson and Huish Edye of a big
tiger in this area which Mrs (now Lady) Anderson had christened
the Bachelor of Powalgarh. I had long wished to see this famous
tiger that all the sportsmen in the province were trying to bag,
and which I knew lived in a deep ravine that started near the
sambhar wallow I was making for. As there were no pug marks
near the kill by which I could identify the tiger that had killed
the *cheetal*, it occurred to me that it was just possible that the
kill was the property of the Bachelor and, if so, that there was
now a reasonable chance of my having a look at this tiger to
see if he was as big as he was reputed to be.

Starting from near the kill a narrow glade ran down to a
small stream a hundred yards away. Beyond the stream was a
dense patch of wild lime. If the Bachelor had not gone back to
his ravine he would in all probability be lying up in this patch
of cover, so I decided to try to get the tiger to return to his kill.
Having come to this decision I went up towards the road and
buried my white butterfly net under dead leaves. The glade at
the upper end was about ten feet wide and the tree under
which the kill was lying was about the same distance from the
right-hand side of the glade. On the left-hand side, and nearly
opposite the kill was the dead stump of a tree roofed over with

creepers. First seeing that there were no holes in the dead stump to harbour snakes, I cleared away the dry leaves from the foot of the stump—to avoid sitting on scorpions—and then made myself comfortable with my back to the stump. From my seat I could see the kill, which was about thirty feet away, and I could also see down the glade to the stream, on the far side of which a troupe of red monkeys were feeding on the berries of a *pipal* tree.

When my preparations were completed, I gave the call of a leopard. Leopards will—when it is safe for them to do so—eat a tiger's kill, and of this tigers are very resentful. If the tiger was within hearing distance, and if my imitation was sufficiently good to deceive him, I expected him to come up the glade, and after I had had a good look at him I intended letting him know I was there and then make my getaway. The monkeys responded to my call by giving their alarm call, and three of them took up positions on a branch that jutted out from the *pipal* tree at right

angles at a height of about forty feet above ground. The alarm call of the monkeys which, as they could not see me, only lasted for a minute or so was all to the good, for if the tiger was in the vicinity he would now be assured

that a leopard was interfering with his kill. I kept my eye on the three monkeys, and presently I saw one of them turn round, peer into the jungle behind him, bob his head up and down several times, and then he gave an alarm call. A minute later the other two started calling and were followed by several others farther up the tree. The tiger was coming, and I greatly regretted not having my camera with me for he would make a grand picture, walking up the glade with the sun glinting on the water of the stream and the *pipal* tree with the excited monkeys on it in the background.

As usually happens on these occasions, however, the tiger did not do what I expected. After a long pause, during which I had the uneasy feeling that the tiger was approaching his kill from behind me, I caught a fleeting glimpse of him as he sprang across the stream and disappeared into the thick jungle on the right-hand side of the glade. After reconnoitring the position from the bushes beyond the stream the tiger had evidently concluded that if he came up the glade the leopard would see him, so he had started out to stalk the kill where he evidently expected to find the leopard. As far as I was concerned there was no objection to his doing this, though it would mean his coming closer to me than I had intended letting him.

The ground was carpeted with dry leaves, and the tiger accomplished his stalk without my hearing a sound. I next saw him as he was standing looking down at his kill but, to my great unease, I found I was not looking at the Bachelor, but at a big tigress. At the best of times a tigress's temper cannot be relied on, and this was not one of those 'best of times', for I was sitting too close to her kill for my comfort, and , further it was quite possible that she had cubs in the lime thicket, in which case she would resent my presence near her kill. However, if she went back the way she had come all would be well, but the tigress did not do this. After satisfying herself that the leopard had not touched her kill, she walked out on to the glade, halving the distance between us. For a long minute she stood undecided, while I held my breath and closed my eyes until I was looking through a slit, and then she quietly walked down the glade, lay down at the stream, had a drink, and then sprang across the stream and disappeared into the thick cover.

In both the incidents I have related in these stories I did not know, at the start, that a crime had been committed, and it is this uncertainty of not knowing what a small clue will lead up to that makes the compiling of jungle detective stories so interesting and so exciting.

Few can compile a detective story of fiction, but all can compile jungle detective stories provided they have eyes to see more than the road they walk on, and provided also that they do not start with the assumption that they know all, before in fact they know anything.

chapter nine

WHEN I WAS TEN YEARS of age I was considered old enough to join the school cadet company of the Naini Tal Volunteer Rifles. Volunteering was very popular and was taken very seriously in India in those days, and all able-bodied boys and men took pride and pleasure in joining the force. There were four cadet companies and one adult company in our battalion with a combined strength of 500 which, for a population of 6,000, meant that every one in twelve was a volunteer.

The Principal of our school of seventy boys was also captain of the school cadet company, which mustered fifty strong. The holder of these dual posts was an ex-army man and it was his burning, and very praiseworthy, ambition to have the best cadet company in the battalion and to satisfy this ambition we small boys suffered, and suffered greatly. Twice a week we drilled on the school playground, and once a week we drilled with the other four companies on the flats, an open stretch of ground at the upper end of the Naini Tal lake.

Our captain never missed, nor did he ever overlook a fault, and all mistakes made on the drill grounds were atoned for after evening school. Taking up a position four feet from his target and wielding a four-foot-long cane, the captain was a marksman of repute who had earned for himself the title of 'Dead Eye Dick'. I do not know if he made private bets with himself, but we small boys laid wagers of marbles, tops, pen-knives, and even on occasions the biscuit that formed our breakfast, that nine times out of ten our captain could lay his cane along the most painful weal left on the hand by the previous day's or previous week's caning, and the boy—usually a newcomer—who betted against the odds always lost. The cadets of the other three companies hotly disputed our reputation of being the best drilled company, but they did not dispute our claim of our being the best turned-out company. This claim was justified, for before being marched down to drill with the other companies we were subjected to an inspection that detected the minutest particle of dirt under a finger-nail, or speck of dust on the uniform.

Our uniforms—passed down when grown out of—were of dark blue serge of a quality guaranteed to stand hard wear and to chafe every tender part of the skin they came in contact with, and, further, to show every speck of dust. Hot and uncomfortable as the uniform was it was surpassed in discomfort by the helmet that was worn with it. Made of some heavy compressed material, this instrument of torture was armed with a four-inch-long fluted metal spike, the threaded butt end of which projected down inside the helmet for an inch or more. To keep the threaded end from boring into the brain the inner band had to be lined with paper, and when the helmet had been fixed to the head like a vice it was held in that position by a heavy metal chin strap mounted on hard leather. After three hours in the hot sun few of us left the drill ground without a splitting headache which made repetition of lessons prepared the previous night difficult, with the result that the four-foot cane was used more freely on drill days than on any other.

On one of our drill days on the flats the battalion was inspected by a visiting officer of senior rank. After an hour of musketry drill and marching and counter-marching, the battalion was marched up to the Suka Tal (dry lake) rifle range. Here the cadet companies were made to sit down on the hillside while the adult company demonstrated to the visiting officer their prowess with the 450 Martini rifle. The battalion prided itself on having some of the best rifle shots in India in its ranks, and this pride was reflected in every member of the force. The target, standing on a masonry platform, was made of heavy sheet-iron and the experts could tell from the ring of the bullet on the iron sheet whether it had struck the centre of the target or the edge of it.

Each cadet company had its hero in the adult company, and adverse comments against the marksmanship of a selected hero would that morning have resulted in many sanguinary fights, had fighting in uniform not been frowned on. After the scores of the best shots had been announced, the cadets were ordered to fall in and march down from the five-hundred- to the two-hundred-yard range. Here four senior cadets were selected from each company and we juniors were ordered to pile arms and sit down behind the firing point.

Inter-school competition in all forms of sport, and most of all on the rifle range, was very keen and every shot fired that morning by the four competing teams was eagerly watched and fiercely commented on by friend and foe alike. The scores ran close, for the best shots in each company had been selected by the respective company commanders, and there was great jubilation in our ranks when it was announced that our team had come out second in the competition and that we had been beaten by only one point by the school that had three times our membership.

While we—the rank and file—were commenting on the achievements of the recent competitors, the Sergeant-Major was seen to detach himself from the group of officers and instructors standing at the firing point, and come towards us bellowing in a voice that it was claimed could be heard a mile away, 'Corbett, Cadet Corbett!' Heavens! What had I done now that merited punishment? True I had said that the last shot that had put the rival company one point ahead of us had been a fluke, and someone had offered to fight me, but there had been no fight for I did not even know who the challenger was, and here now was that awful Sergeant-Major again bellowing, 'Corbett, Cadet Corbett!' 'Go on.' 'He's calling you.' 'Hurry up or you'll catch it,' was being said on all sides of me; and at last, in a very weak voice, I answered 'Yes sir.' 'Why didn't you answer? Where is your carbine? Fetch it at once,' were rapped out at me all in one breath. Dazed by these commands I stood undecided until a push from behind by a friendly hand and an urgent 'Go on you fool' set me off at a run for my carbine.

On our arrival at the two-hundred-yard range those of us who were not competing had been made to pile arms, and my carbine had been used to lock one of the piles. In my effort now to release my carbine the whole pile of arms clattered to the ground and while I was trying to set the pile up again the Sergeant-Major yelled, 'Leave those carbines you have mucked up alone, and bring yours here.' 'Shoulder arms, right turn, quick march', were the next orders I received. Feeling far worse

than any lamb could possibly ever have felt I was led off to the
firing point, the Sergeant-Major whispering over his shoulder
as we started, 'Don't you dare disgrace me.'

At the firing point the visiting officer asked if I was the
youngest cadet in the battalion, and on being told that I was,
he said he would like to see me fire a few rounds. The way in
which this was said—and the kindly smile that went with it—
gave me the feeling that of all the officers and instructors who
were standing round, the visiting officer was the only one who
realized how alone, and how nervous, a small boy suddenly
called upon to perform before a large and imposing gathering
can feel.

The 450 Martini carbine the cadets were armed with had
the most vicious kick of any small-arms weapon ever made,
and the musketry course I had recently been put through had
left my shoulder—which was not padded with overmuch flesh—
very tender and very painful, and the knowledge that it would
now be subjected to further kicks added to my nervousness.
However, I would have to go through with it now, and suffer for
being the youngest cadet. So on the command of the Sergeant-
Major I lay down, picked up one of the five rounds that had
been laid down for me, loaded the carbine and raising it very
gently to my shoulder took what aim I could and pressed the
trigger. No welcome ring came to my anxious ears from the
iron target, only a dull thud, and then a quiet voice said, 'All
right, Sergeant-Major, I will take over now,' and the visiting officer,
in his spotless uniform, came and lay down beside me on the
oily drugget. 'Let me have a look at your carbine,' he said, and
when I passed it over to him a steady hand carefully adjusted
the back-sight to two hundred yards, a detail I had omitted to
attend to. The carbine was then handed back to me with the
injunction to take my time, and each of the following four shots

brought a ring from the target. Patting me on the shoulder the visiting officer got to his feet and asked what score I had made and on being told that I had made ten, out of a possible twenty, with the first shot a miss he said, 'Splendid. Very good shooting indeed,' and as he turned to speak to the officers and instructors I went back to my companions, walking on air. But my elation was short lived, for I was greeted with, 'Rotten shot.' 'Disgraced the Company.' 'Could have done better with my eyes closed.' 'Crumbs, did you see that first shot, went and hit the hundred-yard firing point.' Boys are like that. They just speak their minds without any thought or intention of being cruel or unkind.

The visiting officer who befriended me that day on the Suka Tal rifle range when I was feeling lonely and nervous, later became the nation's hero and ended his career as Field-Marshal Earl Roberts. When I have been tempted, as many times I have been, to hurry over a shot or over a decision, the memory of that quiet voice telling me to take my time has restrained me and I have never ceased being grateful to the great soldier who gave me that advice.

The Sergeant-Major who for many years ruled the Naini Tal Volunteers with a rod of iron, was short and fat with a neck like a bull's and a heart of gold. After our last drill on the flats that term he asked me if I would like to have a rifle. Surprise and delight rendered me speechless; however, no reply appeared to be expected, and he went on to say, 'Come and see me before you leave for the holidays and I will give you a service rifle and all the ammunition you want, provided you promise to keep the rifle clean, and to return me the empties.'

So that winter I went down to Kaladhungi armed with a rifle, and without any anxiety about ammunition. The rifle the good Sergeant-Major had selected for me was dead accurate, and though a 450 rifle firing a heavy bullet may not have been the best type of weapon for a boy to train on, it served my purpose. The bow and arrow had enabled me to penetrate farther into the jungles than the catapult, and the muzzle-loader had enabled me to penetrate farther than the bow and arrow; and now, armed with a rifle, the jungles were open to me to wander in wherever I chose to go.

Fear stimulates the senses of animals, keeps them 'on their toes', and adds zest to the joy of life; fear can do the same for human beings. Fear had taught me to move noiselessly, to climb trees, to pin-point sound; and now, in order to penetrate into the deepest recesses of the jungle and enjoy the best in nature, it was essential to learn how to use my eyes, and how to use my rifle.

A human being has a field of vision of 180 degrees, and when in a jungle in which all forms of life are to be met with, including poisonous snakes and animals that have been wounded by others, it is necessary to train the eyes to cover the entire field of vision. Movements straight in front are easy to detect and easy to deal with, but movements at the edge of the field of vision are vague and indistinct and it is these vague and indistinct movements that can be most dangerous, and are most to be feared. Nothing in the jungle is deliberately aggressive, but circumstances may arise to make some creature so, and it is against the possibility of these chance happenings that the eye must be trained. On one occasion the darting in and out of the forked tongue of a cobra in a hollow tree, and on another occasion the moving of the tip of the tail of a wounded leopard lying behind a bush, warned me just in time that the cobra was on the point of striking and the leopard on the point of springing. On both these occasions I had been looking straight in front, and the movements had taken place at the extreme edge of my field of vision.

The muzzle-loader had taught me to economize ammunition and now, when I had a rifle, I considered it wasteful to practise on a fixed target, so I practised on jungle-fowl and on peafowl, and I can recall only one instance of having spoilt a bird for the table. I never grudged the time spent, or the trouble taken, in stalking a bird and getting a shot, and when I attained sufficient accuracy with the rifle to place the heavy 450 bullet exactly where I wanted to, I gained confidence to hunt in those areas of the jungle into which I previously been too frightened to go.

One of these areas, known to the family as the Farm Yard, was a dense patch of tree and scrub jungle several miles in extent, and reputed to be 'crawling' with jungle-fowl and tigers. Crawling was not an overstatement as far as the jungle-fowl were concerned, for nowhere have I seen these birds in greater numbers than in those days in the Farm Yard. The Kota-Kaladhungi road runs for a part of its length through the Farm Yard and it was on this road that the old dak runner, some years later, told me he had seen the pug marks of the 'Bachelor of Powalgarh'.

I had skirted round the Farm Yard in the bow-and-arrow and muzzle-loader days, but it was not until I was armed with the 450 that I was able to muster sufficient courage to explore this dense tree and scrub jungle. Through the jungle ran a deep and narrow ravine, and up this ravine I was going one evening intent on shooting a bird for the pot, or a pig for our villagers, when I heard jungle-fowl scratching among the dead leaves in the jungle to my right. Climbing on to a rock in the ravine I sat down, and on cautiously raising my head above the bank saw some twenty to thirty jungle-fowl feeding towards me, led by an old cock in full plumage. Selecting the cock for my target, I was waiting with finger on trigger for his head to come in line with a tree——I never fired at a bird until I had a solid background for the bullet to go into——when I heard a heavy animal on the left of the ravine and on turning my head I saw a big leopard bounding down the hill straight towards me. The Kota road here ran across the hill, two hundred yards above me, and quite evidently the leopard had taken fright at something on the road and was now making for shelter as fast as he could go. The jungle-fowl had also seen the leopard and as they rose with a great flutter of wings, I slewed round on the rock to face the leopard. Failing in the general confusion to see my movement the leopard came straight on, pulling up when he arrived at the very edge of the ravine.

The ravine here was about fifteen feet wide with steep banks twelve feet high on the left, and eight feet high on the right. Near the right bank, and two feet lower than it, was the rock on which I was sitting; the leopard was, therefore, a little above, and the width of the ravine from me. When he pulled up at

the edge of the ravine he turned his head to look back the way he had come, thus giving me an opportunity of raising the rifle to my shoulder without the movement being seen by him. Taking careful aim at his chest I pressed the trigger just as he was turning his head to look in my direction. A cloud of smoke from the black-powder cartridge obscured my view and I only caught a fleeting glimpse of the leopard as he passed over my head and landed on the bank behind me, leaving splashes of blood on the rock on which I was sitting, and on my clothes.

With perfect confidence in the rifle, and in my ability to put a bullet exactly where I wanted to, I had counted on killing the leopard outright and was greatly disconcerted now to find that I had only wounded him. That the leopard was badly

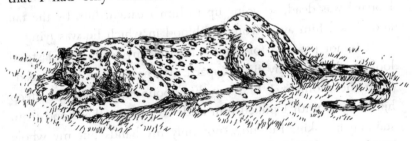

wounded I could see from the blood, but I lacked the experience to know—from the position of the wound, and the blood— whether the wound was likely to prove fatal or not. Fearing that if I did not follow him immediately he might get away into some inaccessible cave or thicket where it would be impossible for me to find him, I reloaded the rifle and stepping from my rock on to the bank, set off to follow the blood trail.

For a hundred yards the ground was flat, with a few scattered trees and bushes, and beyond this it fell steeply away for fifty yards before again flattening out. On this steep hillside there were many bushes and big rocks, behind any one of which the leopard might have been sheltering. Moving with the utmost caution, and scanning every foot of ground, I had gone half-way down the hillside when from behind a rock, some twenty yards away, I saw the leopard's tail and one hind leg projecting. Not knowing whether the leopard was alive or dead I stood stock still until presently the leg was withdrawn, leaving only the tail visible. The leopard was alive and to get a shot at him I would have to move either to the right or to the left. Having already hit the leopard in the body, and not killed him, I now decided to try his head, so inch by inch I crept to the left until his head came into view. He was lying with his back to the rock, looking away from me. I had not made a sound but the leopard appeared to sense that I was near, and as he was turning his head to look at me I put a bullet into his ear. The range was short, and I had taken my time, and I knew now that the leopard was dead, so going up to him I caught him by the tail and pulled him away from the blood in which he was lying.

It is not possible for me to describe my feelings as I stood looking down at my first leopard. My hands had been steady from the moment I first saw him bounding down the steep hillside and until I pulled him aside to prevent the blood from staining his skin. But now, not only my hands but my whole body was trembling: trembling with fear at the thought of what would have happened if, instead of landing on the bank behind me, the leopard had landed on my head. Trembling with joy at the beautiful animal I had shot, and trembling most of all with anticipation of the pleasure I would have in carrying the news of my great success to those at home who I knew would be as pleased and as proud of my achievement as I was. I could have screamed, shouted, danced, and sung, all at one and the same time. But I did none of these things, I only stood and trembled, for my feelings were too intense to be given expression in the jungle, and could only be relieved by being shared with others.

I had no idea how heavy a leopard was, but I was determined to carry my leopard home; so, laying the rifle down, I ran back

to the ravine where there was a bauhinia creeper, and stripping
off sufficient of the inner bark to make a strong rope, I returned
and tied the fore and the hind legs of the leopard together. Then
squatting down I got the legs across my shoulders but found I
could not stand up, so I dragged the leopard on to the rock
and again tried and found I could not lift it. Realizing that the
leopard would have to be left, I hastily broke some branches
and, covering it up, set off on my three-mile run for home. There
was great excitement and great rejoicing in the home when I
arrived with the news that I had shot a leopard, and within a
few minutes Maggie and I, accompanied by two hefty servants,
were on our way to the Farm Yard to bring home my first leopard.

It is fortunate that Providence does not exact retribution
for the mistakes of beginners or my first encounter with a leopard
would probably have been my last, for I made the mistake of
shooting at that first leopard when it was above and within
springing distance of me, without knowing where to hit it to
kill it outright. My total bag of animals up to that date was one
cheetal—shot with the muzzle-loader—and three pigs and one
kakar, shot with the 450 rifle. The pigs and the *kakar* I killed
stone dead, and I thought I could also kill the leopard stone
dead by shooting it in the chest, and there I made my mistake.
For I learnt subsequently that though a leopard can be killed
stone dead, it is seldom possible to do this by shooting it in
the chest.

When a leopard receives a body wound that does not kill it
outright or disable it, it springs wildly, and though leopards
never attack deliberately immediately on being shot at, there is
always a risk of their making accidental contact with the
sportsman, especially when they are above and within springing
distance, and this risk is increased when the wounded animal
is not aware of the position of its assailant. That the leopard in
his wild spring landed on the bank behind me and not on my

head was my good fortune, for not knowing where I was he might have made accidental contact with me, which would have been just as unpleasant as a deliberate attack.

As an example of how uncertain a chest shot is, I will relate another experience I had with a leopard I shot in the chest. Maggie and I were camped one winter at Mangolia Khatta, a cattle station to which the animals of our village were sent when grazing in the Kaladhungi jungles became scarce. One morning while we were having breakfast the barking of a herd of *cheetal* apprised me of the fact that one of their number had been killed by a leopard. I had gone to Mangolia Khatta to try to shoot a leopard that was taking toll of our cows, and as there appeared to be a chance of getting a shot at the leopard now, I left Maggie to finish her breakfast and, picking up a 275 rifle, set off to investigate.

The deer were calling four hundred yards due west of us, but to get to them I had to make a detour to avoid an impenetrable canebrake and swampy ground. Approaching the calling animals from the south, with the wind in my face, I saw some fifty stags and hinds standing on an open patch of burnt ground and looking in the direction of the canebrake. On the swampy ground between the canebrake and the open ground there was a belt of grass some two hundred yards wide, and from the open ground, and at a distance of sixty yards from me, a leopard was attempting to drag a *cheetal* stag towards this belt of grass. It was not possible to approach any nearer to the leopard without being seen by the herd of *cheetal*, who would have warned the leopard of my presence, so I sat down and raising my rifle waited for the leopard to give me a shot.

The stag was big and heavy and the leopard was having great difficulty in dragging it over the rough ground, and presently it released its hold and stood up facing me. A leopard's white

chest, flecked with black, is a perfect target for an accurate rifle
at sixty yards, and when I pressed the trigger I knew I had put
the bullet where I wanted to. On receiving my shot the leopard
sprang high into the air, and landing on all fours, dashed into
the belt of grass. Going to the spot where the leopard had been
standing I saw a blood trail leading to the grass, which here was

about waist-high. Breaking some
branches off a nearby tree, I
covered up the stag to prevent
vultures getting at it, for the stag
was in velvet and in prime
condition and I knew our men
would be glad to have it. Returning
to camp I finished my breakfast
and then, accompanied by four
of our tenants, went back to

recover the stag and to follow up the wounded leopard. As we
approached the spot from where I had fired, one of the men
touched me on the shoulder and pointed to our right front,
where the burnt ground ended and the belt of grass began.
After a little while I saw what he was pointing at. It was a leopard,
two hundred and fifty yards away, standing near the edge of
the belt of grass.

Our tenants, when in camp with us, stoutly refuse to accept
any payment for their services, but when out in the jungles we
compete among ourselves to see who will be the first to spot a
shootable animal, and when I lose they accept with great glee
the rupee I pay as forfeit. When I had paid my forfeit to the
two men who claimed to have seen the leopard at the same
time, I told them to sit down for the leopard had now turned
and was coming in our direction. Quite evidently this was the
mate of the one I had wounded and, attracted to the spot as I

had been, was coming to see what its mate had killed. A hundred yards from us a tongue of grass extended for a few yards on to the open ground, and on reaching this spot—from where the leopard could see the kill—it stopped for several minutes, offering me a shot at its chest, but as I already had one leopard with a chest wound on my hands I held my fire.

The leopard was very suspicious of the branches I had heaped on the kill; however, after a careful look all round, it cautiously approached the kill and as it stood broadside on to me I put a bullet into it an inch or two behind the left shoulder. It fell at my shot and did not move again and on going up to it I found it was dead. Telling the men to tie it to the bamboo pole they had brought and carry it to camp and return for the stag, I set out on the very unpleasant task of following up a wounded leopard in waist-high grass.

The unwritten law that a wounded animal must be recovered at all costs is accepted by all sportsmen and—where carnivora are concerned—each individual has his own method of accomplishing this end. Those who have the command of elephants find the task an easy one, but those like myself who shoot on foot have to learn by experience the best method of putting wounded carnivora out of their suffering, and avoiding injury while doing so. Burning a jungle to recover a wounded animal is, in my opinion, both cruel and wasteful, for if the animal is able to move the chances are that it will get away to die, maybe days or weeks later, and if it is too badly wounded to move there is a certainty of its being roasted alive.

It is not possible to follow the blood trail of carnivora in high grass with any degree of safety, and the method I adopted on the occasions on which I retrieved wounded carnivora in grass was to ignore the blood trail and to proceed inch by inch in the direction in which the animal had gone, hoping for the best while prepared for the worst. On hearing the slightest sound a wounded animal will either charge or betray its position by some movement. If a charge does not materialize and the looked-for movement is observed, a stone or a billet of wood, or even a hat, can be usefully used and the animal dealt with when it charges at the thrown object. This method can only be adopted when there is no wind to rustle the grass, and when the sportsman has had some experience of shooting in grass, for though wounded carnivora are very vocal when disturbed they keep close to the ground and seldom show themselves until the last moment.

There was no wind of any account that day at Mangolia Khatta, and after leaving my men I followed the blood trail over the burnt ground to where it entered the grass. Satisfying myself that my rifle was loaded and that it was working smoothly, I stepped very cautiously into the grass, and as I did so I heard a whistle behind me and on looking round saw my men beckoning to me. On my rejoining them they pointed to three

bullet holes they had found in the dead leopard while tying it to the bamboo pole. One was the bullet hole behind the left shoulder that had killed the leopard; of the other two, one was in the centre of the chest, while the other—an exit hole—was two inches from the root of the tail.

The leopard, I very greatly regret to say, had a reason for returning to its kill, and when I found what this reason was I was consumed with remorse. Leopard cubs can fend for themselves at a very young age by catching small birds, rats, mice, and frogs, and I can only hope that the cubs of the gallant mother, who after being wounded, risked her life to procure food for her young, were old enough to fend for themselves, for all my efforts to find them failed.

My statement that before entering the grass to follow up the wounded leopard, I satisfied myself that my rifle was loaded and working smoothly, will appear unusual to sportsmen in view of the fact that I had a minute previously walked up to a leopard I had just shot, and presumably I had not done so with an empty rifle without knowing whether the leopard was alive or dead. What necessity then was there for me to *satisfy* myself that my rifle was loaded? I will tell why I did so, not only on this occasion but on every occasion on which my life has depended on my rifle being loaded. Fortunately I learnt my lesson when I was comparatively young, and to this I attribute the fact that I have lived to tell the tale.

Shortly after starting work at Mokameh Ghat, of which I have told in *My India*, I invited two friends to shoot with me at Kaladhungi. Both men, Silver and Mann, had recently arrived in India and had never fired a shot in the jungles. The morning after their arrival I took them out, and two miles along the Haldwani road I heard a leopard killing a *cheetal* in the jungle to the right of the road. Knowing it would not be possible for my friends to stalk the leopard, I decided to put one of them up on a tree over the kill, and told them to draw lots. Silver was armed with a ·500 D.B. rifle which he had borrowed, while Mann was armed with a 400 S.B. black-powder rifle, also borrowed. I was armed with a ·275 magazine rifle. As Silver was a little older, and better armed than Mann, Mann very sportingly declined to draw, and the three of us set off to find the kill. The *cheetal*, a fine stag, was still twitching when we found it, and selecting a tree for Silver to sit on I left Mann to help him up, while I moved the leopard away to prevent it seeing Silver climbing the tree. The leopard was very hungry and disinclined to move; however, by zigzagging in front of him I drove him away and then returned to the kill. Silver had never before climbed a tree and was looking very unhappy, and I am not sure that I cheered him by remarking that the leopard was a big male, and cautioning him to be very careful over his shot. Then telling him that he would only have to wait a matter of five minutes, I took Mann away.

A hundred yards from the kill there was a fire track that met the Haldwani road at right angles. Going through the jungles to this track, Mann and I had only proceeded a short distance along it when Silver fired two shots in quick succession, and as we turned round to retrace our steps we saw the leopard dashing across the track. Silver did not know whether he had hit the leopard or not, but on going to the spot where Mann and I had seen it crossing the track we found a blood trail. Telling my companions to sit on the track and wait for me, I set off alone to deal with the leopard. There was nothing heroic in this, quite the contrary in fact, for when following wounded carnivora it is necessary to concentrate attention on the matter in hand and it is difficult to do this when accompanied by companions with fingers on the triggers of cocked rifles. When I had gone

a short distance Silver came after me and offered to accompany
me, and when I declined his offer he begged me to take his rifle,
saying he would never forgive himself if the leopard attacked
me and I was unable to defend myself with my light rifle. So,
to please him, we exchanged rifles. As Silver walked back to
the fire track I set off for the second time, but before doing so
I uncocked his rifle and opened the breach sufficiently to see
that there were two cartridges in the chambers.

The ground for a hundred yards was comparatively open,
and then the blood trail led into heavy cover. As I approached
this cover I heard the leopard moving in front of me, and for a
second I thought it was on the point of charging. The sound
was not repeated, however, so very cautiously I entered the
cover and twenty yards farther on found where the leopard had
been lying, and from where he had got up when I heard him.
It was now a case of moving step by step and I was thankful,
when a hundred and fifty yards farther on, the trail led out on
to more open ground. There I was able to move faster and I
had covered another hundred yards when, on approaching a
big *haldu* tree, I caught sight of the tip of the leopard's tail
projecting from the right-hand side of the tree. Finding he was
being followed the leopard had quite evidently taken up what
he considered would be the best position for his charge, and
that he would charge I had no doubt whatever.

Deciding it would be to my advantage to meet a head-on
charge, I moved to the left of the tree. As the leopard's head
came into view I saw he was lying flat down, facing me, with his
chin resting on his outstretched paws. His eyes were open, and
the tips of his ears and his whiskers were trembling. The leopard
should have sprung at me the moment I appeared round the
tree, and that he had not done so made me hold my fire, for it
had not been my intention to blow his head off at a range of a

few feet, but to put a bullet into his body and so avoid ruining Silver's trophy. As I continued to stare at him his eyes closed and I realized that he was dead, that in fact he had died as I was watching him. To make sure I was right I coughed and as there was no response, I picked up a stone and hit him on the head.

Silver and Mann came up at my call and before handing Silver's rifle back to him I opened the breach and extracted the two brass cartridges, and, to my horror, found that both were empty. Many sportsmen have suffered through pulling the triggers of empty rifles, and had I not been slowed down while following the blood trail through heavy cover, I would have added to the number. From the day I learnt my lesson, fortunately without injury to myself, I have never approached dangerous ground without satisfying myself that the weapon I am carrying is loaded. If I am carrying a double-barrelled rifle I change the cartridges from one chamber to the other, and if I am carrying a single-barrelled rifle I eject the cartridge, see that the bolt is working smoothly, and then replace the cartridge in the chamber.

chapter ten

KUNWAR SINGH, OF WHOM I wrote in *My India*, had a great aversion to shooting in the jungles near Kaladhungi, which he said were full of ground creepers which made it difficult to run away from zealous forest guards and angry tigers, and for this reason he confined all his poaching activities to the Garuppu jungles. Good woodsman and good shot though he was, and greatly as I admired him, Kunwar Singh was not a super-sportsman and this I attribute to the fact that the jungles in which he did his shooting were teeming with game. Knowing every game-path and every glade and open stretch of ground on which deer were to be found, his method of approach was to stride through the jungles without any attempt at silence, and if he disturbed the deer in one glade he would say it did not matter for there were sure to be more in the next glade. Nevertheless I learnt many things from Kunwar Singh for which I have never ceased to be grateful, and I am also grateful to him for having helped me to overcome some of my fears of the unknown. One of these fears concerned forest fires. Having heard of the danger of forest fires and seen the effect of them in our jungles, I carried the fear in the back of my mind that I would one day be caught by a forest fire and roasted alive, and it was Kunwar Singh who dispelled this fear.

In village areas in the Kumaon foothills every one is interested in his neighbour's affairs or doings, and to people who never see a daily paper and whose lives are, more or less, circumscribed by the forest that surrounds their village or group of villages, every scrap of news is of interest and is eagerly passed on, losing nothing in repetition. It was not surprising, therefore, for Kunwar Singh to have heard about my shooting of the leopard in the Farm Yard almost before the animal had time to cool, and being the sportsman he was he lost no time in coming to congratulate me. He knew about the rifle the Sergeant-Major had lent me, but until I shot the leopard I do not think he had any faith in my ability to use it. Now, however, with this concrete evidence before him he evinced a great interest in me and in the rifle, and before he left me that day I had promised to meet him at 5 o'clock on the following morning at the fourth milestone on the Garuppu road.

It was pitch dark when Maggie brewed a cup of tea for me, and with an hour in hand I set off to keep my appointment with Kunwar Singh. I had walked that lonely forest road on many occasions and the dark held no terror for me, and as I approached the fourth milestone I saw the glimmer of a fire under a tree by the side of the road. Kunwar Singh had arrived before me and as I sat down near his fire to warm my hands he said, 'Oh look, you have come away in such a hurry that you have forgotten to put on your trousers.' I tried, with little success, to convince

Kunwar Singh that I had not forgotten to don my trousers but that I was wearing—for the first time—a new style of nether garment called shorts. For though he confined himself to saying that *jangias* (panties) were not suitable for the jungles, his look implied that I was indecently clothed and that he would be hanged if he would be seen with me in public. After this bad start the atmosphere did not clear until a jungle-cock started crowing in a near-by tree, on hearing which Kunwar Singh got to his feet, put out the fire, and said it was time to be going for we still had a long way to go.

The jungle was awakening as we left our tree and stepped out on the road. The jungle-cock who, awakened by our fire, had crowed his welcome to the coming day had set a sound wave in motion and each bird, big and small, as it roused from slumber added its voice to the growing volume of sound. Though our jungle-cock is the first bird to rub the sleep from his eyes, he is not the first to descend to the ground. The privilege of catching the early worm is claimed by the Himalayan whistling-thrush, better known as the whistling-schoolboy. While walking through the Kumaon jungles in the half-light between day and night, or night and day, a bird will flit by on silent wings pouring out a stream of golden song which once heard will never be forgotten. The songster is the whistling schoolboy bidding the closing day good night, or welcoming the new-born day. Morning and evening he pours out his song

while in flight, and during the day he sits for hours in a leafy
tree whistling in a soft sweet minor key a song that has no
beginning and no end. Next to greet the coming light is the
racket-tailed drongo and a minute later he is followed by the
peafowl. No one may sleep after the peafowl has given his
piercing call from the topmost branch of the giant *samal* tree
and now, as night dies and daylight comes, a thousand throbbing
throats in nature's orchestra fill the jungle with an ever-growing
volume of melody.

And not only the birds, but the animals also, are on the
move. A small herd of *cheetal* has crossed the road in front of
us, and two hundred yards farther on a *sambhar* hind and her
young one are cropping the short grass by the side of the road.
A tiger now calls to the east and all the peafowl within hearing
distance scream in unison. Kunwar Singh is of opinion that the
tiger is the flight of four bullets from us, and that it is in the
sandy *nullah* in which he and Har Singh met with their experience
which so nearly had a fatal ending. The tiger quite evidently is
returning home from a kill and is indifferent as to who sees
him. First a *kakar*, then two *sambhar*, and now a herd of *cheetal*,
are warning the jungle folk of his presence. We reach Garuppu
as the sun is touching the treetops, and crossing the wooden
bridge and disturbing fifty or more jungle-fowl that are feeding
on the open ground near the ruined
staging buildings we take a footpath
which leads us through a narrow
belt of scrub jungle to the bed of
the dry watercourse spanned by
the bridge we have just
crossed. This watercourse,
which is dry except in the
heavy monsoon rains, is a

highway for all the animals that quench their thirst at the crystal clear spring which rises in its bed three miles farther down. In later years the watercourse became one of my favourite hunting grounds for rifle and camera, for it ran through country which abounded with game, and a human track on its sandy bed was as much a matter for speculation as Friday's footprint on Crusoe's island.

For half a mile the watercourse runs through scrub jungle before entering a strip of *nal* grass a quarter of a mile wide and many miles long. *Nal* grass is hollow, jointed like bamboo, grows to a height of fourteen feet, and when accessible to villages is extensively used for hut building. When the jungles round Garuppu are burnt by our villagers, to get grazing for their cattle, all the game in the vicinity take shelter in the *nal* grass which, because it grows on damp ground, remains green all the year round. During exceptionally dry years, however, the *nal* grass occasionally catches fire, and when this happens a terrifying conflagration results, for the grass is matted together with creepers and each joint of the *nal*, as it heats up bursts with a report resembling a pistol shot, and when millions of joints are exploding at the same time the resulting noise is deafening and can be heard for a mile or more.

As Kunwar Singh and I walked down the watercourse that morning I could see a black cloud of smoke rising high into the sky, and presently the distant roar and crackle of a great fire came to my ears. The watercourse here ran due south and the fire, which was on the eastern or left bank, was being driven towards it by a strong wind. Kunwar Singh was leading and, remarking over his shoulder that the *nal* was burning for the first time in ten years, he kept straight on, and on turning a corner we came in sight of the fire, which was about a hundred yards from the watercourse. Great sheets of flame were curling up into the cloud of black smoke on the edge of which hundreds of starlings, minas, rollers, and drongos were feeding on the winged insects that were being caught up by the hot current of air and whirled high into the sky. Many of the insects that escaped capture by the birds in the air were landing on the sandy bed of the watercourse where they were being pounced on by peafowl, jungle-fowl, and black partridge. Among these game-birds a herd of some twenty *cheetal* were picking up the big red fleshy flowers the high wind was dislodging from a giant *samal* tree.

This was the first forest fire I had ever seen, and I attribute the fear it engendered in me to the fact that most human beings are frightened of the unknown. And then, on rounding the corner and coming in sight of the birds and the animals that were unconcernedly feeding in the vicinity of the fire, I realized that I alone was terrified and that there was no reason, other than ignorance, for my being so. Coming down the watercourse in the wake of Kunwar Singh I had been tempted to turn and run away, and had only been restrained from doing so by the fear of being thought a coward by Kunwar Singh. Now, standing on the sandy bed of the fifty-yard-wide watercourse with the roar of the approaching fire growing louder and louder while black clouds of smoke billowed overhead—waiting for a shootable animal to be driven out of the narrowing belt of *nal* grass—my terror left me, never to return. The heat from the fire could now be felt in the watercourse, and as the deer, peafowl, jungle-fowl, and black partridge climbed the right bank and disappeared into the jungle, we turned and retraced our steps to Garuppu and made for home.

In later years grass-fires provided me with many exciting experiences. Before relating one of these it is necessary for me to state that we who cultivate land at the foot of the Himalayas are permitted, by Government, to burn the grass in unprotected forests to get grazing for our cattle. There are several varieties of grass in these forests and as they do not all dry off at the same time the burning is staggered and, starting in February, ends in June. Throughout this period fires can be seen on the grasslands and anyone passing a patch of grass that he considers is dry enough to burn, is at liberty to put a match to it.

I had been shooting black partridge with Wyndham at Bindukhera in the Tarai, and early one morning Bahadur—an old friend who for thirty years has been headman of our village— and I set out on our twenty-five-mile walk to our home at Kaladhungi. We had covered about ten miles over ground on which most of the grass had been burnt but where there were still a few isolated patches of unburnt grass when, as we approached one of these patches, an animal came out on the cart track we were on, and for a long minute stood broadside on to us. The morning sun was shining on it and from its colouring and size we took it to be a tiger. When, however, it crossed the cart track and entered the grass we saw from the length of its tail that it was a leopard. 'Sahib,' said Bahadur regretfully, 'it is a pity that the Commissioner Sahib and his elephants are ten miles away, for that is the biggest leopard in the Tarai, and it is worth shooting.' That the leopard was worth shooting there was no question, and even though Wyndham and his elephants were ten miles away, I decided to have a try, for the leopard had come from the direction of a cattle station, and the fact that he was moving about in the open at that hour of the day was proof that he was coming from a kill he had made overnight at this station. When I outlined my plan—to burn the leopard out—to Bahadur, he expressed his willingness to help, but was doubtful of its success. The first thing to do was to find out how big the patch of grass was, so leaving the cart track we circled round it and found it was some ten acres in extent and cone shaped, with the cart track running along the base.

The wind was right for my plan, so going to the farthest point of the grass, which was about two hundred yards from the cart track, I cut two tufts of grass and lighting them sent Bahadur to set fire to the grass on the right, while I set fire to it on the left. It was of the variety known as elephant grass, some twelve feet in height, and as dry as tinder, and within a minute of our setting it alight it was burning fiercely. Running back to the cart track I lay down on it and putting my rifle, a ·275 Rigby, to my shoulder I took a sight along the outer edge of the track at a height that would put my bullet in the leopard's body when he tried to dash across it. I was lying ten yards from the grass, and the point where the leopard had entered it was fifty yards from me. The track was ten feet wide and my only hope of hitting the leopard was to press the trigger the moment I caught sight of him, for I was convinced he would cross the track at the last moment, and cross it at speed. There was no possibility of injury to Bahadur for I had instructed him to climb a tree, well clear of the track, after he had set a short stretch of the grass on fire.

Half the grass had been burnt and the roar from the fire was like an express train going over a trestle bridge, when I saw a bare human foot near my right shoulder. On looking up I found a man standing near me who, from his appearance and dress, I knew was a Mahommedan cartman probably out looking for a lost bullock. Reaching up I pulled the man down and yelled into his ear to lie still beside me, and to ensure his doing so I threw a leg across him. On came the fire and when only some twenty-five yards of grass remained to be burnt the leopard streaked across the track and as I pressed the trigger I saw its tail go up. The grass on the left-hand side of the track had been burnt some days previously, and the forest of burnt stalks into which the leopard had disappeared made it impossible for me to see what the result of my shot had been. Reassured, however, by the way the leopard's tail had gone up that he was fatally wounded, I sprang up, took a firm grip of the man's hand, jerked him to his feet, and ran with him down the cart track through a dense cloud of smoke with the flames of the oncoming fire curling dangerously over our heads. Not until we were right over him did we see the leopard, and without losing a moment—for the heat here was terrific—I stooped down and putting the man's hand on the leopard's tail closed my hand over his and as we pulled the leopard round to drag it away from the fire the animal, to my horror, opened its mouth and snarled at us. Fortunately for us my bullet had gone through its neck and paralysed it, and by the time we had dragged it fifty yards to safety it was dead. As I released my hold on the man's hand he sprang away from me as though I had bitten him, and grabbing the *pugree* off his head ran with it trailing behind him as no cartman had ever run before.

I regret I was not present when my friend arrived at whatever destination he was making for. Indians are past masters at recounting tales, and my friend's tale of his escape from the clutches of a mad Englishman would have been worth listening to. Bahadur had witnessed the whole occurrence from his perch on the tree and when he rejoined me he said, 'That man will be very popular at camp-fires for many years to come, but no one will believe his story.'

When conditions are not favourable for walking up so-called dangerous animals and shooting them on foot, the method most generally employed is to beat them out of cover with the help of elephants or men, or a combination of the two. Three of these beats stand out in my memory as being worthy of record, if for no other reason than that two were carried out with the minimum of manpower, while the third provided me with an experience that makes my heart miss a beat or two every time I think of it.

First Beat

Robin—our springer spaniel—and I were out for a walk one morning on the fire track half a mile to the west of the Boar bridge. Robin was leading, and on coming to a spot where there was short grass on the little-used track he stopped, smelt the grass, and then turned his head and looked at me. On going up to him I could see no tracks, so I signalled to him to follow the scent he had found. Very deliberately he turned to the left and, on reaching the edge of the track, ran his nose up and down a blade of grass and then with a quick glance round at me, as if to say, 'It's all right, I was not mistaken', stepped into the grass which here was about eighteen inches high. Foot by foot he followed the scent and a hundred yards farther on, where there was a little depression with damp earth in it, I saw he was trailing a tiger. On the far side of the depression Robin intently examined a blade of grass, and on stooping down I saw he had found a spot of blood. From experiences I have had with animals left wounded in the jungles by others I am very suspicious of any blood I find on a tiger track. However, on this occasion it was all right for the blood was quite fresh, and no shots had been fired in this direction that morning, so I concluded the tiger was carrying a kill, possibly a *cheetal*, or maybe a big pig. A few yards farther on there was a dense patch of clerodendron some fifty yards square, on reaching which Robin stopped and looked round at me for further instructions.

I recognized the tiger from his pug marks on the damp earth.

He was a big tiger who had taken up his residence in the heavy scrub jungle on the far side of the Boar river and who, since our descent from the hills three months previously, had given me a lot of anxiety. The two roads and the fire track on which Maggie and I were accustomed to take our morning and evening walks ran through this jungle, and on several occasions when I was away from home Maggie and Robin had encountered the tiger while out for a walk. On each succeeding occasion the tiger had shown less inclination to give way to them and the stage had been reached when Robin no longer considered it was safe for Maggie to walk on these roads, and flatly refused to accompany her beyond the bridge. Fearing that some day there might be an accident I had decided to take the first opportunity that offered to shoot the tiger, and now—provided the tiger was lying up with his kill in the patch of clerodendron—the opportunity I had been waiting for had come. Robin had trailed the tiger down wind, so making a wide detour I approached the clerodendron from the opposite side. When we were thirty yards away Robin halted, raised his head into the wind, jerked his muzzle up and down a few times, and then looked round at me. Good enough. The tiger was there all right, so we regained the fire track and made for home.

After breakfast I sent for Bahadur, told him about the tiger, and asked him to fetch two of our tenants, Dhanban and Dharmanand, both of whom could be relied on to carry out instructions, and both of whom were as expert at tree climbing as Bahadur and myself. By midday the three men had eaten their food and forgathered at our cottage, and after seeing that they had nothing in their pockets that would rattle I made them remove their shoes and arming myself with a 450/400 rifle, we set off. On the way I outlined my plans for the beat I intended the three men to carry out. The men knew the jungle as well as I did and when I told them where the tiger was lying up, and what I wanted them to do, they were full of enthusiasm. My plan was to put the men up on trees on three sides of the patch of clerodendron, to stir the tiger up while I guarded the fourth side. Bahadur was to be on the central tree and on receiving a signal from me, which would be the call of a leopard, he was to tap a branch and if the tiger tried to break out on either side the man nearest to it was to clap his hands. The essence of the whole enterprise was silence, for the three men would be within thirty or forty yards of the tiger and the slightest sound while approaching their trees, climbing them, or while waiting for my signal, would ruin the plan.

On reaching the spot where Robin had picked up the tiger's scent I made Dhanban and Dharmanand sit down, while I took Bahadur and put him up a tree twenty yards from the clerodendron, and opposite where I intended taking my stand. Then one by one I took the other two men and put them up in trees to Bahadur's right and left. All three men were in sight of each other, and all three overlooked the patch of clerodendron and would, therefore, be able to see any movement the tiger made, but they would be screened from me by a belt of trees. After the last man was safely on his tree, without a sound having been made, I went back to the fire track and going a hundred yards up it met—at right angles—another fire track that skirted the foot of a long low hill. This second fire track bordered the patch of clerodendron on its fourth side. Opposite the tree on which Bahadur was sitting, a narrow and shallow ravine ran up the side of the hill. The ravine was much used by game and I felt sure the tiger on being disturbed would make for it. On the right-hand side of the ravine, and ten yards up the hill, there was a big *jamun* tree. When planning the beat I had intended sitting on this tree and shooting the tiger as he went up the ravine past me. But now, on reaching the tree, I found I could not climb it with the heavy rifle in my hands and as there were no other trees nearby I decided to sit on the ground.

So, clearing the dry leaves from the root, I sat down with my back to the tree.

I had two reasons for giving the call of a leopard. One, a signal to Bahadur to start tapping a branch with the dry stick I had left with him: the other, to reassure the tiger that it was safe for him to cross the fire track, and to disarm any suspicion he may have had that he was being driven towards danger. When I was comfortably seated on the ground I pushed up the safety catch and putting the rifle to my shoulder, gave the call of a leopard. A few seconds later Bahadur started tapping with his stick and he had only tapped a few times when the bushes parted and a magnificent tiger stepped out on the fire track and came to a stand. For ten years I had been trying to get a cine-photograph of a tiger, and though I had seen tigers on many occasions I had not succeeded in getting one satisfactory picture. And now out in the open, twenty yards from me with not a leaf nor a blade of grass between us, and the sun shining on his beautifully marked winter coat, was a tiger that I would have gone anywhere and given anything to photograph. I have on occasions stalked an animal, maybe for hours or maybe for days, and on getting up to it raised my rifle and after taking careful aim lowered it, and then attracting the animal's attention flourished my hat, giving myself the pleasure of seeing it bound away unhurt. I would very gladly have treated this tiger in the same way, but I did not feel that I would be justified in doing so. Apart from consideration of Maggie, Sher Singh and other small boys grazed their cattle in this jungle, and the women and children of the village collected dry sticks in it, and though the tiger had not harmed man or beast his method of demonstrating was very terrifying and might easily result in an accident.

After stepping out on the fire track the tiger stood for a minute or two looking to his right and to his left, and over his

shoulder in the direction of Bahadur. Then very leisurely he crossed the track and started up the hill on the left-hand side of the ravine. My sights had been on him from the time his head parted the clerodendron bushes, and when he was level with me I pressed the trigger. I do not think he so much as heard my shot, and as his legs folded up under him he slid backwards and came to rest near my feet.

Beat No. 2

When His Highness the Maharaja of Jind died—full of years and loved by all who knew him—India lost one of her finest sportsmen. Ruler of a territory of 1,299 square miles with a population of 324,700 and a princely rent-roll, the Maharaja was one of the most unassuming men it has been my good fortune to meet. His hobbies were training gun-dogs and tiger shooting, and at both these sports he had few equals. When I first knew him he had four hundred dogs in his kennels and to see him schooling young dogs, and later handling them in the field, was a lesson in patience and gentleness that I never tired of watching. Only once did I ever hear the Maharaja raise his voice, or use a whip, to a dog. At dinner that night when the Maharani asked if the dogs had behaved themselves the Maharaja said, 'No, Sandy was very disobedient and I had to give him a good thrashing.'

The Maharaja and I had been out bird shooting that day. A long strip of grass and bush jungle was being beaten towards us by a line of elephants and men. At the end of the strip was an open stretch of ground some fifty yards wide. The Maharaja and I were standing a few yards apart at the farther edge of the open ground, with short grass behind us. Sitting in a row to the Maharaja's left were three young Labradors, Sandy golden coloured, the other two black. The line put up a black partridge and the Maharaja dropped it on the open ground and sent one of the black dogs to retrieve it. Next a jungle-fowl came low over my head and I dropped it in the grass behind me. The second black dog retrieved this bird. Some peafowl now got up, but having heard the shots in front, broke away to the left and passed out of range. A hare then broke cover and checking at the Maharaja, who had turned round to speak to a servant behind him, turned at right angles and passed in front of me. Waiting until it was at extreme range—for it is not advisable to break game more than can be helped when young dogs are in the field—I fired, and the hare turned about and passing in front of both of us collapsed thirty yards to the right of the Maharaja. As it went over Sandy shot forward. 'Sandy, *Sandy*,' shouted the Maharaja, but Sandy was listening to no one. His two companions had retrieved their birds and it was his turn now and nothing was going to stop him. In his stride he picked up the hare and racing back handed it to me. Returning to his

master Sandy sat down in his allotted place, and was ordered
to fetch the hare. Picking it up from where I had laid it down
he trotted towards the Maharaja with it held high, and was
waved away, farther, farther, to the right, still farther, until he
reached the spot from where he had originally retrieved it. Here
he was told to drop it and signalled to return. With drooping
tail and hanging ears Sandy returned to his master a second
time, and one of the other dogs was sent out to bring in the
hare. When this had been done the Maharaja handed his gun
to his servant, and taking a whip from him, caught Sandy by
the scruff of his neck and gave him 'a good thrashing'. And a
good thrashing it was but not for Sandy, for he was not touched,
but for the ground on either side of him. When the Maharaja
told his wife of Sandy's delinquency and the chastisement he
had administered, I took a tablet from an attendant behind
me—for the Maharaja was afflicted with total deafness—and
wrote on it, 'Though Sandy Bahadur disobeyed you today he is
the best dog in India, and will win the championship at the
next gun-dog trials.' Later that year I received a telegram from
the Maharaja which read, 'You were quite right. Sandy has won
the Open Championship.'

The days were lengthening and the sun was getting hot, so
making a very early start one morning I walked ten miles and
arrived at the Maharaja's camp at Mohan as the family were
sitting down to breakfast. 'You have come at a very opportune
time,' said the Maharaja as I took a seat at his table, 'for today
we are going to beat for the old tiger that has eluded us for
three years.' I had heard this tiger discussed on many occasions
and knew how keen the Maharaja was to outwit and shoot it.
When, therefore, he offered me the best of the three machans
that had been put up for the beat, and the loan of a rifle, I
declined his offer and said I would prefer to be a spectator. At

ten o'clock the Maharaja and Maharani, their two daughters and a girl friend and I motored down the road up which I had walked earlier that morning, to where the beat was waiting for us.

The ground to be beaten was a valley running deep into the foothills, with a small stream winding through it, and flanked on either side by hills three hundred feet high. At its lower end, where the road crossed it, the valley was about fifty yards wide, and half a mile farther up it again narrowed to fifty yards. Between these two points the valley widened out to three or four hundred yards and here, where there was a dense patch of cover several hundred acres in extent, the tiger was thought to be lying up with the buffalo he had killed the previous night. At the upper end of the valley a small spur ran down from the hill on the right, and on a tree on this spur, a machan had been built which commanded the valley and the lower slopes of the hills on either side. Beyond the spur and on the far side of the stream, which here turned at right angles, two other machans had been put up on trees thirty yards apart.

Leaving our cars on the road we proceeded up the valley on foot, and guided by the head shikari and the secretary in charge of the beat, skirted to the left of the cover in which the tiger was said to be lying. When the Maharaja and his gun-bearer had taken their seats on the machan on the spur, the four ladies and I crossed the stream and occupied the two machans on the far side of it. The head *shikari* and the secretary then left us, and returned to the road to start the beat.

The *machan* I was on, with the two princesses, was a solidly-built affair laid with a thick carpet, with silk cushions to sit on. Accustomed only to sitting on hard branches, the luxury of the *machan*—following on an early rise and a long walk—made me drowsy and I was on the point of falling asleep when I was roused to full wakefulness by the distant sound of a bugle; the beat had started. Taking part in the beat were ten elephants, the Secretaries, A.D.C.s, household staff of the Maharaja, the head *shikari* and his assistants, and two hundred men collected from the surrounding villages. The heavy cover on the floor of the valley was to be beaten by the elephants on which the Secretaries and others were mounted, while the two hundred men beat the slopes on either side. Some of these beaters were to form a line on the two ridges and walk ahead of the beat to prevent the tiger from breaking out.

All the arrangements for the beat, and the beat itself, were intensely interesting for me for I was witnessing as a spectator an event in which I had hitherto always been an actor. There was nothing in the arrangements or in the conduct of the beat that could be found fault with. The time of day had been well chosen; we had been led to our *machans* in perfect silence; and that the cover was being well beaten was evident from the number of birds, including *kalege* pheasants, jungle-fowl, and peafowl, that the line was putting up. Beats are always exciting, for from the moment the distant shouting of the men is heard, the tiger can be expected to be on the move. The Maharaja was handicapped by deafness but he had a good man with him, and presently I saw this man pointing to the right. After looking in this direction for a moment or two the Maharaja shook his head, and a little later a *sambhar* stag crossed the stream and on winding the Maharaja dashed past us up the valley.

The line of men on the ridge on the left was now visible, and the time had come for the tiger to appear. On came the beat with every man taking part in it shouting and clapping his hands, and every yard they advanced my hopes of the Maharaja shooting the tiger on which he had set his heart diminished, for no bird or animal had given an alarm-call. My young companions on the *machan* were keyed up, and the Maharaja was holding his rifle ready, for if the tiger appeared now he would have to take a quick shot. But rifles were of no use today, for the tiger was not in the beat. Ladders were produced and a very dejected party climbed down from the *machans* and joined an even more dejected staff on the ground. No one engaged in the beat had seen anything of the tiger, and no one knew what had gone wrong. But that something had gone wrong was evident, for shortly before our arrival in the cars the tiger had been heard calling in the valley. I had a suspicion

that I knew why the beat had miscarried but, as I was only a spectator, I said nothing. After a picnic lunch we returned to camp, and while the others rested I went off and had a grand evening's fishing on the Kosi, for it was the latter end of April and the fishing was at its best.

During and after dinner that night, the abortive beat of the day and five previous unsuccessful beats for the same tiger were discussed in minute detail and a reason sought for their failure. On the first occasion on which a beat had been organized in the valley for this particular tiger, he had come out on the right of the machan and the Maharaja, taking an awkward shot from a fixed seat, had missed him. In the succeeding beats, carried out over a period of three years, the tiger had not again been seen, though he was known to have been in the valley before the beats started. While the others had been talking and writing on tablets for the Maharaja's benefit, I had been thinking. The Maharaja was a good sportsman, and if I could help him to shoot the tiger on which he had set his heart it was up to me to try. A mistake had been made that day in taking the Maharaja's party to the machans, past the spot where the tiger was thought to be lying up, but this mistake was not responsible for the failure of the beat, for the tiger had left the valley at about the time the Maharaja's party had entered it. The single alarm-call of a kakar, heard shortly after we had left our cars, was all the foundation I had for my suspicion that the tiger walked out of the valley as we walked into it. Later when it became evident that an empty jungle had been beaten, I looked round to see if there was any other way for the tiger to leave the valley without passing the machans. Starting on the ridge behind the machans a landslide extended right down into the valley. The kakar had called at the upper end of this landslide and if there was a game track here running down to the cover in which the tiger had his kill, then it was quite possible that he left the valley by this track every time he heard preparations being made for a beat.

The plan that had been forming in my mind while the others talked was to put the Maharaja on the ridge, where the *kakar* had called, and beat the tiger up to him. Beating a second time for the tiger on the following day had been vetoed by every one, on the ground that as the tiger had not been found on a fresh kill there was no hope of finding him on a stale one. So even if my plan failed no harm would be done, for no arrangements had been made for the following day. Taking a tablet from one of the secretaries I wrote on it, 'If you can be ready at 5 a.m. tomorrow, I should like to do a one-man beat for the tiger we failed to get today', and handed the paper to the Maharaja. After reading what I had written the Maharaja passed the paper to his secretary, and from hand to hand it went round the room. I expected opposition from the staff, and it came now. However, as the Maharaja was willing to fall in with my plans, the staff reluctantly agreed to all conventions being set aside, and to the Maharaja going out with me next morning accompanied only by two gun-bearers.

Punctually at 5 a.m. the Maharaja, his two gun-bearers, and I, left the camp by car and motored three miles down the road to where an elephant, carrying a small *machan*, was waiting for us. Transferring the Maharaja and his two men to the elephant I set out on foot to guide the elephant through several miles of forest in which I had never been before. Fortunately I have a sense of direction, and though it was dark when we started I was able to steer a more or less straight course, and as the sun was rising we arrived on the ridge where the landslide started. Here I was delighted to find a well-used game-track leading up from the valley, and on a tree near the track I put up the *machan*. When the Maharaja and one gun-bearer had taken their seats on the *machan* I sent the elephant away, and taking the other gun-bearer with me, put him up on a tree farther along the ridge. These preparations completed, I set off to do a one-man beat.

The way down into the valley was terribly steep and rough, but as I was not hampered with a rifle, I accomplished the descent safely. Passing the *machans* we had sat on the previous day, I went down the valley on silent feet, and two hundred yards beyond the heavy cover in which I suspected the tiger was lying, I turned and retraced my steps, talking to myself in a low voice as I did so. Where the tiger dragged the buffalo into the heavy cover there was a fallen tree. Lighting a cigarette I sat down on this tree, to listen if the jungle had anything to tell me. All remained quiet, so after coughing a few times and drumming my heels against the hollow tree I set out to find the kill and see if the tiger had returned to it. I found the kill tucked away under some thick bushes and was delighted to see that the tiger had eaten a meal only a few minutes previously, and that the ground on which he had been lying was still warm. Running back to the hollow tree I hammered on it with a stone and shouted at the top of my voice, to let the man with the Maharaja know that the tiger was coming. A minute or two later a rifle shot rang out above me, and when I got to the ridge I found the Maharaja standing on the game track, looking at the fine tiger he had shot.

In the palace at Jind, now occupied by the Maharaja's eldest son, there is a skin with a label which reads, 'Jim's Tiger'. And in the late Maharaja's game-book there is an entry giving the date and place, and the circumstances in which the old tiger was shot.

Beat No. 3

It was the last day of a memorable shoot. Memorable not only for us who had been privileged to take part in it, but also for the administrators of the country, for a Viceroy had for the first time in the history of India left the beaten track to spend a few days in the Kaladhungi jungles.

No individual's movements were more strictly ruled by precedents than the movements of the Viceroy of India, and any deviation from the beaten track was a contingency that had never been contemplated, and for which no provision had been made. When, therefore, Lord Linlithgow, shortly after assuming the Viceroyalty of India, decided to leave the track his predecessors had followed and blaze a track for himself, it was only natural that his decision should have caused consternation throughout the land. Custom decreed that the ruler of India should tour the southern provinces of his domain during the ten days hiatus between the closing of his Legislative Offices in Delhi and their reopening in Simla, and it was Lord Linlithgow's decision not to conform with this age-old custom that caused the long to be remembered flutter in the government dovecotes.

I, a mere man in the street without any connexion with Government, was happily ignorant of the working of wheels within wheels of the administration when one day, towards the end of March, as I was setting out from our cottage at Kaladhungi to catch a fish for our dinner, Ram Singh, whose duty it was to fetch our daily post from the Post Office two miles away, came running back with a telegram which he said the Postmaster had informed him was very urgent. The telegram, which had been redirected from Naini Tal, was from Hugh Stable, Military Secretary to the Viceroy. It informed me that the Viceroy's visit to South India had been cancelled, and asked if I could suggest any place where the Viceroy could spend ten days, with the possibility of getting a little shooting before proceeding to Simla for the summer. The telegram concluded with a request for an early reply, as time was short, and the matter urgent. Ram Singh does not speak English but having served us for thirty years he can understand it, and having stood round finding odd jobs to do while I read the telegram to Maggie, he now said he would hurry up and have his food and be ready in a few minutes to take my reply to Haldwani. Haldwani—our nearest telegraph and telephone office—is fourteen miles from Kaladhungi and by sending my reply by Ram Singh, instead of by the regular dak runner, I would save a matter of some twenty-four hours. After Ram Singh had left with my reply to Hugh Stable which read, 'Please call me on Haldwani telephone at eleven hours tomorrow', I picked up my rod for the second time, for one can do a lot of thinking while fishing and I had much to think about, and, further, I still had our dinner to catch. Hugh Stable's telegram was quite clearly in the nature of an SOS, and the question I had to decide was, what could I do help him?

Going up the Kota road for two miles I cut across the lower end of the Farm Yard—where when a small boy I shot my first leopard—and made for a pool in the river in which a three-pound *mahseer* with whom I was acquainted lived. As I approached the pool I saw in the sand the pug marks of a tiger that had crossed the river early that morning. At the head of the pool, where the water runs fast and deep, there are three big rocks a foot above water which are continually wet with spray and in consequence as slippery as ice. Leopards use these rocks as stepping stones and one day I saw the tiger, whose pug marks were now on the sand, trying to do the same. I had chased the tiger that day for a mile without his knowing I was after him and twice I got to within shooting range, and on both occasions held my fire as I was not sure of killing him outright. And then as I saw he was making for the river I just kept him in sight for I knew I would get the shot I wanted when he was fording the river. As he approached the river it became evident that he intended crossing it dryshod by way of the stepping stones, and not wading it as I at first thought he intended doing. This suited me admirably for there was a twenty-foot drop on our side down which the tiger would have to go before reaching the river, and as he went over the edge to climb down I ran forward and lay down on the top of the bank above him.

The three rocks were at a distance apart that an Olympian athlete could, if he had a good run, have taken in a hop, skip, and jump, and which I had seen leopards do in three graceful bounds. The tiger had just accomplished the first jump safely as I poked my head over the edge, but he bungled the second jump, and as his feet shot off the slippery rock he went heels over head into the deep and broken water. The noise from the water prevented my hearing what he said, but I could guess what it was for I had myself slipped on that self-same rock while trying to cross the river dryshod. On the far side of the broken water there is a short beach of dry sand. Floundering out on to this beach the tiger shook himself and then lay

down and rolled over and over, drying his beautiful rich winter coat in the hot sand. Then getting to his feet he shook himself for a second time and walked quietly away to whatever place he was making for, without let or hindrance from me, for in the jungle it is not considered cricket to molest an animal that has provided entertainment. And now the pug marks of the tiger were showing on the sand again, but this time he had essayed the stepping stones safely for his feet when he crossed the sand had been dry.

Below the stepping stones a rock jutted out from the far bank making a backwater which was my friend the three-pounder's favourite hunting ground. Twice before a Jock Scott cast on the sloping rock and gently drawn off, had brought the *mahseer* out with a rush. The throw was a long and a difficult one, for the branch of a tree hung low over the backwater and the rod had to be used from a crouching position, for *mahseer* who have enemies on land, in the air, and in the water, are keen of sight and need a careful approach. Leaving the sandy beach, with the pug marks on it, I went upstream for a short distance, and while the ten-foot tapered cast I made that morning from carefully selected lengths of gut was soaking under a stone, put my rod together and had a smoke. When all was ready I pulled what I considered to be the exact length of line off the reel, and holding it carefully looped in my left hand crept down to the one spot from where it was possible to make a sideways cast on to the rock, for the bank behind did not permit of an orthodox cast. The new No. 8 Jock Scott put on in honour of the three-pounder landed exactly where I wanted it to, and as the drag of the line drew it off the rock into deep water, there was a swirl and a splash and for the third time my friend was well and truly hooked. It is not possible, when using light tackle, to stop the first mad rush of a *mahseer*, but by using just the right amount of strain he can be guided away from any snag he is making for, provided the snag is not on the same side of the river as the angler. I was fishing from the right bank and thirty yards below where I had hooked the fish a curved root jutted out into the water. On the two previous occasions the fish had broken me on this root, but I managed to steer him clear of it now with only a few inches to spare. Once he was in the pool, he was safe, and after letting him play himself out I drew him to the sandy beach and landed him by hand, for I had brought no landing net with me. My estimate of three pounds was half a pound out, on the right side, so not only would he furnish us with a dinner, but he would also provide a meal for a sick boy Maggie was nursing in the village, who loved fish above all other things.

Having followed the advice given me on the rifle range when I was a boy, by sending Hugh Stable a non-committal telegram, I had given myself ample time to think, and to what extent my seeing the pug marks of the tiger and my success with the *mahseer* influenced my decision I cannot say; anyway, by the time I got home I had decided to tell Hugh Stable that Kaladhungi was the only place I could suggest for the Viceroy's holiday. Maggie had tea ready on the veranda and while we were talking over the decision I had come to, Bahadur arrived. Bahadur can keep his mouth shut when there is any necessity to do so, so I told him about the telegram I had received from Delhi. Bahadur's eyes literally dance when he is excited, and I have never seen them dance as they did that day. A possibility of the Viceroy coming to Kaladhungi! Why, such a thing had never before been heard of. A great *bandobast* would have to be made and fortunately it was just the right time of the year to make it, for the crops had been harvested and every man in the village would be available. Later, when it became known that the Viceroy was coming to our jungles, not only our own tenants but every man in Kaladhungi was as excited and as pleased as Bahadur had been when he heard the news. Not because of any profit or preferment they hoped to derive from the visit, but simply and solely because of their desire to help in their own humble way to make the visit a success.

It was dark when I started on my fourteen-mile walk to Haldwani next morning, for I wanted to see Geoff Hopkins, who was camped at Fatehpur, before my conversation with Hugh Stable. The road runs through jungle for the first seven miles and at that hour of the morning the jungle folk and I had it to ourselves. A mile beyond the Kaladhungi bazaar it started to get light and in the dust of the road I saw the fresh pug marks of a male leopard, going in the same direction as I was. Presently, on rounding a bend in the road, I saw the leopard two hundred yards ahead of me. He seemed to sense my presence for I had hardly rounded the bend when he turned his head and looked at me. However, he kept to the road, occasionally looking over his shoulder, and when I had reduced the distance between us to fifty yards, he stepped off the road into a light patch of grass. Keeping steadily on and looking straight ahead, out of the corner of my eye I saw him crouched down in the grass a few feet from the road. A hundred yards along when I looked over my shoulder

I saw he was back on the road. To him I was just a wayfarer for whom he had made way, and a few hundred yards farther on he left the road and entered a deep ravine. For a mile I had the road to myself, and then out of the jungle on the right trotted five red dogs. Fleet of foot, and fearless; flitting through the forests as silent and free as a butterfly, and when hungry, eating only of the best. Of all the animals I know none has a better life, than the Indian red dog.

Geoff and Zillah Hopkins were sitting down to an early breakfast when I reached the forest bungalow, and were as pleased and excited as they could be when I told them of the errand on which I was going to Haldwani. Geoff was at that time Special Forest Officer, Tarai and Bhabar Government Estates, and without his help and co-operation I could make no concrete suggestions to Hugh Stable. Geoff rose nobly to the occasion. For the success of the shoot it was essential for me to have two shooting blocks in his forests. Both the blocks I wanted were fortunately available at the time, and Geoff said he would reserve them for me. He also very kindly offered me the Dachauri block in the adjoining government forest, which he had reserved for himself. Everything, from seeing the pug marks of the tiger in the sand, the catching of the *mahseer*, and now my successful visit to Geoff, was going splendidly, and I never felt the miles as they passed under my feet as I completed my journey to Haldwani.

Hugh Stable was on the telephone punctually at eleven o'clock and for the next hour we carried on an uninterrupted conversation, over the three-hundred-mile-long line. In that hour Hugh learnt that there was a small village at the foothills of the Himalayas called Kaladhungi; that this village was surrounded by jungles in which there was a variety of game; and that I knew of no place in India where a more pleasant holiday could be spent. From Hugh I learnt that the Viceregal party would consist of Their Excellencies Lord and Lady Linlithgow, and their three daughters, the Ladies Anne, Joan, and Doreen (Bunty) Hope. With the party would come H.E.'s personal staff, for even when on holiday the Viceroy of India does a full day's work. Finally I learnt I had only fifteen days in which to make all my preparations for the shoot. Mouse Maxwell, the Controller of the Viceroy's Household, motored from Delhi to Kaladhungi the following day, and he was followed by the head of the Police, the head of the C.I.D., the head of the Civil Administration, the head of the Forest Department, and by many other heads. But most terrifying of all by a Guardsman who informed me he was bringing a company of soldiers to Kaladhungi to guard the person of the Viceroy.

Bahadur had been right when he said a great *bandobast* would have to be made, but how great that *bandobast* would have to be neither he nor I had dreamed. However, with the whole-hearted help and co-operation of all concerned everything had progressed smoothly and well, without a single hitch or set-back. Four beats had been successfully carried out and four tigers had been cleanly shot, with the minimum expenditure of ammunition, by people who had never before seen tigers in the wilds. Only those who have taken part in tiger beats will know how great an achievement this had been. And now the last day of that memorable shoot had come with only one, the youngest, member of the party left to shoot a tiger. The beat that day was to take place on a semi-circular bit of ground which in bygone years had been the bed of the Boar river, but which now is clothed with dense tree and scrub jungle interspersed with small patches of *nal* grass, and thickets of wild oranges. Five *machans* had been built in trees on what at one time had been the bank of the river, and the tiger was to be beaten off the low ground towards these *machans*.

Making a wide detour, for many beats are ruined by taking the guns to their *machans* past the cover in which the tiger is assumed to be lying up, I brought the party up from behind the *machans* and while the stops, who had accompanied us, fanned out to right and left to take up position on the trees I had previously marked for them, Peter Borwick (one of H.E.'s A.D.C.s), Bahadur, and I, started to put the guns in position. On No. 1 *machan* I put Anne, and on No. 2 *machan* I put H.E. No. 3 *machan* had been built in the only tree available at this spot, a stunted *kart bair* (wood plum) tree. It had been my intention to put Bahadur on this *machan* to act as a stop. On being stopped I expected the tiger to turn to the left, and for this reason I had selected No. 4 *machan* for Bunty, the only member of the party who had not shot a tiger.

Coming from the direction of the cover, in which I knew the tiger was lying up, a game-track ran up the bank and passed right under No. 3 *machan*. I was certain the tiger would come along this track and as the *machan* was only six feet above ground I had decided that, though it would be quite safe to put an experienced stop on it, it would be too dangerous for a gun. Now, however, as the two girls, Peter, Bahadur, and I, reached the *machan* and Bahadur started to climb on to it, on the spur of the moment I changed my plans. Putting my hand on the *machan*, which was on a level with my head, I whispered to Bunty that I wanted her to sit on it with Peter to keep her company. This—after I had pointed out the danger—she consented to do without a moment's hesitation. I then begged her not to shoot at the tiger until it reached a spot on the track that I would mark, and to take very careful aim at its throat. Bunty promised to do both of these things, so Peter and I lifted her on to the *machan*. After I had given Peter a leg up I handed him my 450/400 D.B. rifle, a similar weapon to the one Bunty was armed with. (Peter was unarmed, for he was to have accompanied me in the beat.) Then going down the bank I walked up the game-track, and when within twenty feet of the *machan*, laid a dry stick across the track and as I did so I looked up at Bunty and she nodded her head.

Lady Joan, Bahadur, and I, now went to the tree on which No. 4 *machan* had been built. This *machan* was twenty feet above ground and from it to No. 3 *machan*—thirty yards away—there was a clear and uninterrupted view. When I climbed the ladder after Joan to hand her rifle, I begged her not to allow the tiger to reach No. 3 *machan* if Bunty and Peter failed to stop it. 'I will do my best,' she said, adding, 'don't you worry.' There were no bushes and only a few scattered trees on this part of the bank, and the tiger would be in full view of these two *machans* from the time it left the cover sixty yards away until it was, I hoped, shot dead by Bunty. Putting Bahadur on No. 5 *machan*, to act as a stop if necessary, I circled outside the beat and came out on to the Boar river.

The sixteen elephants that were to do the beating were collected a quarter of a mile down the river, near the pool in which I caught the *mahseer*. They were in charge of old Mohan, a friend of many years standing, who for thirty years had been Wyndham's head *shikari*, and who knew more about tigers than any man in India. Mohan was on the look-out for me, and on seeing me come out of the jungle and wave my hat he started the elephants up the bed of the river. Sixteen elephants walking in line over boulder-strewn ground take some time to cover a quarter of a mile, and while I sat on a rock and smoked I had ample time to think, and the more I thought the more uneasy I became. For the first time in my life I was endangering the life of one, and quite possibly two, human beings, and the fact that it was the first time gave me little comfort. Before his arrival in Kaladhungi Lord Linlithgow asked me to draw up a set of rules. These rules had been scrupulously obeyed, and with over three hundred people in camp, and daily excursions to near and distant shooting and fishing grounds, no one had received so much as a scratch. And now on this last day I, whom everyone trusted, had done a thing that I was bitterly regretting. On a frail *machan*, only six feet above ground, and on which I would not have trusted any man of my acquaintance, I had put a young girl little more than sixteen years of age to shoot a tiger as it came straight towards her, the most dangerous shot that one can take at a tiger. Both Bunty and Peter were as brave as tigers, as was abundantly evident by the fact that after I had pointed out the danger to them they had unhesitatingly taken their seats on the *machan*. But bravery alone without accuracy of aim would not be sufficient, and of their ability to hold a rifle straight I had no knowledge. Mohan arrived with the elephants while I was still undecided whether to call off the beat or go on with it, and when I told him what I had done he drew in his breath—the Indian equivalent to the Western whistle—closed his eyes tight and on reopening them said, 'Don't *ghabrao* (worry) Sahib. Everything will be all right.'

Calling the mahouts together I told them it was very essential for us to move the tiger without frightening it, and that after lining-out on the river bank they would take their signal from me. When they saw me take my hat off and wave it they would give one shout, after which they would clap their hands and continue to clap them until I replaced the hat on my head. This procedure would be repeated at short intervals and if it failed to move the tiger I would give the signal to advance, and the advance would be made in silence and dead slow. Our initial shout would serve a double purpose, it would rouse the tiger from his sleep, and it would alert the guns.

A strip of jungle three hundred yards wide and five hundred yards long was to be beaten, and when the elephants had lined-out on either side of me I took off my hat and waved it. After giving one lusty shout the men started clapping their hands and after they had clapped for three or four minutes, I replaced my hat. There were *sambhar*, *cheetal*, *kakar*, peafowl, and jungle-fowl in that area, and I listened anxiously for an alarm-call, but heard none. Five minutes later I again took off my hat and waved it and a minute, or it may have been two, later, a rifle shot rang out and I started to count the seconds, for much can be learnt by the spacing of shots in a tiger beat. One, two, three, four, five, I counted and I was beginning to breathe again when two shots rang out in quick succession. Again one, two, three, four, and a fourth shot rang out. The first and the fourth shot had been fired when the muzzle of the rifle was facing in my direction. When the other two shots were fired the muzzle had been facing away from me. This could mean only one thing, that there had been trouble and that Joan had had to help, for the *machan*. H.E. was on was not within sight of Bunty's *machan*.

With my heart racing and fears assailing me that I was too frightened to give expression to, I handed over the line to Mohan to bring up and told Ajmat, the mahout of the elephant I was on, to go as fast as he could straight to where the shots had been fired. Ajmat, who has been trained by Wyndham, is absolutely fearless and the best man on an elephant I have ever known. And his elephant is as well trained and as fearless as he is. Straight through thorn bushes, over big rocks and broken ground, and under overhanging branches we went, my uneasy thoughts racing ahead of us. And then as we crashed into a

patch of twelve-foot-high *nal* grass the elephant hesitated before
going on again, and Ajmat leant back and whispered, 'She can
smell the tiger, so hold tight Sahib, for you are unarmed.' Only
another hundred yards to go now, and as yet no signal had
come from the guns, each of whom had been provided with a
railwayman's whistle with instructions to blow it if help was
needed. But the fact that no whistle had sounded gave me no
comfort for I knew from past experience that in times of
excitement even bigger things than whistles can be dropped
from a *machan*. And then through the trees I caught sight of
Joan and could have shouted with joy and relief, for she was
unconcernedly sitting on her *machan* with her rifle across her
knees. On seeing me she spread her arms wide—which I rightly
interpreted as meaning a big tiger—and then pointed down in
front of Bunty's *machan*.

The rest of the story, which makes my heart miss a beat as I
relate it even after this lapse of fifteen years, is soon told; a story
which, but for the courage of three young people and superlative
marksmanship, would have ended in a terrible tragedy.

Our shout when I started the beat was clearly heard by the
guns, also the faint clapping of our hands. Then in the interval
the tiger broke cover sixty yards in front of *machan* No. 3, and
came slowly along the game-track. It reached the foot of the
bank as we on the elephants shouted the second time. On
hearing this shout the tiger stopped and looked over its shoulder.
Satisfied that there was no need to hurry, it stood listening for
a minute or so, and then started up the bank. When it reached
the spot where I had laid a dry stick across the track, Bunty
fired, but she fired at its chest, for the tiger was holding its head
low and she could not see its throat. On receiving the shot,
which was well placed, and before either Bunty or Peter was
able to get in a second shot, the tiger sprang forward with a

roar and attacked the *machan* from underneath. While the frail *machan* was rocking on the stunted tree and threatening to disintegrate under the onslaught of the tiger, and while Bunty and Peter were trying desperately to push the muzzles of their rifles through the floor of the *machan*, Joan, from her *machan* thirty yards away, knocked the tiger down with her first shot and as it fell to the ground put a second bullet into it. On receiving Joan's second bullet the tiger started to go down the bank, evidently with the intention of regaining the thick cover it had just left, and Bunty then put a bullet through the back of its head.

That was our Viceroy's first visit to Kaladhungi, but it was not his last, and during the many subsequent occasions on which he honoured our small foothill village with his presence I never had one moment's anxiety for his safety, or for the safety of those who accompanied him. For I never again took risks such as I took on the last day of that memorable shoot.

chapter eleven

FROM NOVEMBER TO MARCH THE climate of the Himalayan foothills has no equal, and the best of these five months is February. In February the air is crisp and invigorating and the wealth of bird life that migrated down from the high mountains in November, in search of food and of warmth, is still with us. The deciduous trees that have stood gaunt and naked throughout the autumn and winter are bursting into bloom, or are putting on a mantle of tender leaf buds of varying shades of green or pink. In February spring is in the very air, in the sap of all trees, and in the blood of all wild life. Whether it be on the mountains in the north, or the plains in the south, or in the shelter of the foothills, spring comes in a night. It is winter when you go to bed one night and when you awaken next morning it is spring, and round you all nature is rejoicing in anticipation of the pleasures that lie ahead, plentiful food, warmth, and the reproduction of life. The migrant birds are packing into small groups, these groups will join others, and on the appointed day and at the command of the leaders the pigeons, paroquets, thrushes, and other fruit-eaters will fly up the valleys to their selected nesting grounds while insect-eaters flitting from tree to tree in the same direction and on the same quest will cover at most a few miles a day. While the migrants are preparing for departure and the regular inhabitants of the foothills are selecting each his own mate and looking for a building site, the combined population of the jungle are vying with each other in a vocal contest which starts at daylight and continues non-stop until dark. In this contest all take part even to the predatory birds whose most vocal member, the serpent eagle, while showing as a mere speck against the blue sky sends his piercing cry back to earth.

While instructing troops in jungle warfare I was in a forest one day in Central India with a party of men among whom were several bird enthusiasts. High in the heavens above us a serpent eagle was circling and screaming. The party was a new draft from different parts of the United Kingdom, destined for Burma, none of whom had ever seen a serpent eagle. Waiting until we came to an open glade I pointed to a speck in the sky. Field-glasses were produced and disappointment was expressed at the bird being too far away to identify or to see clearly. Telling my companions to stand quite still I took a three-inch-long reed from my pocket, and sounded a note on it. This reed, split at one end and blocked up at the other, reproduced with great exactitude the piercing call of a young deer in distress and was used in my training for signalling, for it is the only natural sound to be heard—both by day and by night—in jungles in which there are deer, and it was, therefore, a sound least likely to attract the attention of an enemy. On hearing the sound the eagle stopped screaming, for though a serpent eagle, living principally on snakes, he does not despise other flesh. Closing his wings he dropped a few hundred feet and then again started soaring in circles. At each call he came nearer, until finally he was circling just above tree-top level where the party with me had a close and clear view of him. Do those who were in that party of fifty, and who survived the Burma campaign, remember that day in the Chindwara jungles and your disappointment at my not being able to make the eagle perch on a branch close enough to photograph? Never mind. Accompany me now on this spring morning and we will see many things just as interesting as that serpent eagle.

You have travelled far on the road of knowledge since that distant Chindwara day. Self-preservation has taught you that the human eye has a field of vision of 180 degrees. Pin-pointing sound which at first you found so difficult is now second nature to you. And having learnt when a boy the difference between the smell of a rose and of a violet you can now identify each tree and plant by the smell of its flower even when that flower is at tree-top level, or hidden deep in the jungle. But much as you have learnt and greatly as the knowledge has added to your confidence, safety, and pleasure, much still remains to learn and on this beautiful spring morning we will add a little to our store of knowledge.

The canal that forms the northern boundary of our estate, and in which the girls used to bathe, is conveyed across the watercourse I have previously referred to by an aqueduct. This aqueduct is known as *Bijli Dant*, which means, 'lightning water channel'. The original aqueduct built by Sir Henry Ramsay was destroyed by lightning many years ago, and because of a local superstition that lightning is attracted to a given spot by an evil spirit, usually in the form of a snake, the old foundations were not used and a parallel aqueduct was built that has been functioning now for half a century. Wild animals that visit the village at night from the jungles to the north, and who do not like wading or jumping the ten-foot-wide canal, pass under the aqueduct. So on this spring morning we will start our walk from this point.

On the sand in the passage-way under the arch of the aqueduct are the tracks of hare, *kakar*, pig, porcupine, hyaena, and jackal. Of these the only tracks we will look closely at are the tracks of the porcupine, for, having been made after the night wind had died down, they are free of drift sand. Five toes and a pad and each footprint is distinct, for a porcupine has no need to stalk and does not superimpose one foot upon another. In front of each print is a small hole in the sand made by the porcupine's strong nails, on which he depends to a great extent for his food. The hind pads of porcupines are elongated. This projection, or heel, is not as marked as it is in the case of bear. It is, however, sufficiently marked to distinguish the track of a porcupine from the tracks of all other animals. If you want further confirmation, look closely at the track and you will see a number of finely-drawn lines running between, or parallel to, the track. These finely drawn lines are made by the long drooping quills of the porcupine when they make contact with the ground. A porcupine cannot cast or project its quills, which are barbed, and its method of defence or attack is to raise its quills on end

and run backwards. At the end of a porcupine's tail are a number of hollow quills, not unlike long wine glasses on slender stems. These quills are used as a rattle to intimidate enemies, and to convey water to the porcupine's burrow. The quills readily fill with water when submerged, and the porcupine uses this water to keep its burrow cool and free of dust. Porcupines are vegetarians and live on fruit, roots, and field-crops. They also consume the horns shed by deer and the horns of deer killed by leopards, wild dogs, and tigers, possibly to obtain calcium or some other vitamin absent in their normal food. Though a comparatively small animal a porcupine has a big heart, and he will defend himself against great odds.

For a few hundred yards above the aqueduct the bed of the watercourse is stony and, except where a game-track crosses it, we shall find no more tracks until we come to a long stretch of fine silt, washed down from the foothills, on which the tracks of all the animals that use the watercourse as a highway show up clearly. This stretch of ground is flanked on either side by dense *lantana* in which deer, pig, peafowl, and jungle-fowl, shelter during daylight hours and into which only leopards, tigers, and porcupines venture at night. In the *lantana* you can now hear jungle-fowl scratching up the dead leaves, and a hundred yards away on the topmost branch of a leafless *samal* tree is perched their most deadly enemy, a crested eagle. The eagle is not only the enemy of jungle-fowl, he is also the enemy of peafowl. These are his natural prey and the fact that there are as many old birds as young ones in the jungle, is proof that they are able to look after themselves. For this reason I never interfered with crested eagles until one day, on hearing the distressed cry of a young deer, I hurried to the spot and found a crested eagle holding down a month-old *cheetal* fawn and tearing at its head, while the distracted mother ran round in circles striking at the bird with her forefeet. Desperately as the brave mother had tried to rescue her young one—and of this the scratches and blood on her muzzle bore ample proof—the great eagle had been too much for her, and though I was able to dispose of her enemy I was unable to do anything for her young, beyond putting it out of its misery, for even if I had been able to heal its wounds I would not have been able to restore its sight. That incident has cost the lives of many crested eagles in the jungles in which I have hunted, for though it is difficult to approach close enough to shoot them with a shotgun, they offer a good target for an accurate rifle. The bird on the *samal* tree, however, has nothing to fear from us for we have come out to see things, and not to deal with the enemies of young deer. In my catapult days the greatest battle in which a crested eagle has ever been engaged took place on a stretch of sand, in the bed of the river, a little below the Boar bridge. Possibly mistaking a fish cat for a hare the eagle stooped on it and either because he was unable to withdraw his talons, or because he lost his temper, became involved in a life-and-death struggle. Both contestants were equally well armed for the battle; the cat with its teeth and claws, and the eagle with its beak and talons. It is greatly to be regretted that photography at that time was confined to studios and movie cameras were unknown, and that no record was made of that long-drawn-out and desperate battle. If a cat has nine lives an eagle has ten, and it was lives that ultimately proved the deciding factor. With one precarious life still in hand the eagle left his dead opponent on the sand, and trailing a broken wing went down to a pool in the river where, after quenching his thirst, he surrendered his tenth life.

Several game-tracks lead on to the open ground from the *lantana* and while we have been looking at the eagle a young kakar stag has walked out of the *lantana* on to the watercourse, fifty yards away, with the intention of crossing it. If we freeze and remain frozen, he will take no notice of us. Of all the animals in the jungle the *kakar* gives the impression of being most on his toes. Even here on this open ground he is walking on tiptoe with his hind legs tucked well under him and at the first indication of danger, be it conveyed by sight, sound, or smell, he will dash away at top speed. The *kakar* is sometimes described as being a mean and a cowardly little animal, and unreliable as a jungle informant. With this description I do not agree. No animal can be called mean for that is exclusively a human trait, and no animal that lives in the densest jungles with tigers, as the *kakar* does, can be accused of being a coward. As for being an unreliable informant I know of no better friend that a man who shoots on foot can have in a jungle than a *kakar*. He is small and defenceless and his enemies are many, and if in a beat he barks at a python or at a pine-marten, when he is expected to bark only at a tiger, he is more to be pitied than accused of being unreliable. For to him and his kind, these two ruthless enemies are a very real menace and he is only carrying out his function— as a watcher—when he warns the jungle folk of their presence.

The *kakar* has two long canine teeth or tusks on its upper jaw. These tusks are very sharp and are the *kakar's* only means of defence, for the points of his short horns are curved inwards and are of little use as weapons of defence. Some years ago there was a long and inconclusive correspondence in the Indian press about a peculiar sound that *kakar* make on occasions. This sound can best be described as a clicking sound, resembling that made by the bones used by Christy minstrels. It was asserted by some that, as the sound was only heard when *kakar* were running, it was caused by double joints, and by others that it was caused by the tusks being clashed together in some unexplained way. Both these assertions, and others that were advanced, were incorrect. The sound is made by the animal's mouth in exactly the same way as all other vocal sounds are made, and is used on various occasions: as, for instance, when uncertain of a seen object, when disturbed by a gun dog, or when pursuing a mate. The alarm call of the *kakar* is a clear ringing bark, resembling that of a medium-sized dog.

While the *kakar* has been crossing the watercourse a large flight of insect and fruit-eating birds has approached us from our right. In this flight are migrants as well as local inhabitants, and if we stand where we are the birds will fly over our heads and you will have an opportunity of studying them as they perch on the trees and bushes on both sides of the watercourse, and also while they are in flight. Birds, except when they are very close, are difficult to identify by their colours when sitting where they have no background or when seen against the sky, but every species of bird can be identified while in flight by its shape and by its wing beats. In the flight that is approaching us, every member of which is either chirping, twittering, or whistling, are two varieties of minivets, the short-billed scarlet, and the small orange-breasted. Minivets perch on the topmost leaves and twigs of trees and bushes, and from these commanding positions keep darting into the air to catch winged insects disturbed by their own kind or by other members of the flight. With the minivets are:

> *Six varieties of tits.* The grey, yellow-cheeked, blue-winged, red-billed, white-eyed, and the common green.
>
> *Four varieties of flycatchers.* The white-browed fantail, yellow fantail, slaty-headed, and verditer.

Six varieties of woodpeckers. The golden-backed, black-naped green, rufous-bellied pied, pigmy pied, yellow-naped, and the scaly-bellied green.

Four varieties of bulbuls. The golden-fronted green, white-winged green, white-cheeked crested, and the red-whiskered.

Three varieties of sunbirds. The Himalayan red, purple, and the small green.

In addition to these birds, which number between two and three hundred, there are a pair of black-headed golden orioles who are chasing each other from tree to tree, and a lesser racket-tailed drongo who, though not as aggressive as his big brother, has nevertheless acquired several juicy morsels from the flight he is guarding, the last being a fat larva industriously dug out of a dry branch by the pigmy pied woodpecker. The flight of birds has now flown over our heads and disappeared into the jungle on our left, and the only sound to be heard is the scratching of the jungle-fowl in the *lantana*, and the only bird to be seen is the crested eagle, patient and hopeful, on the topmost branch of the *samal* tree.

Beyond the *lantana* on the right is an open stretch of parklike ground, on which grow a number of big plum trees. From this direction now comes the alarm bark of a red monkey, followed a few seconds later by the excited chattering and barking of fifty or more monkeys of varying ages and sizes. A leopard is on the move and as he is on more or less open ground it is unlikely that he is trying to secure a kill, in which case he is possibly making for one or other of the deep ravines in the foothills where leopards are often to be found during the hot hours of the day. Winding through the plum trees is a path used both by human beings and by animals. This path crosses our watercourse two hundred yards farther on and as there is a good chance, I would almost say a certainty, of the leopard coming along the path, let us hurry forward for a hundred and fifty yards and sit down with our backs against the high bank on the left. The watercourse here is fifty yards wide and on the trees on the left-hand side is a large troupe of *langurs*. The warning given by the red monkeys has been heeded, and all the mothers in the troupe have got hold of their young ones, and all eyes are turned in the direction from which the warning came.

There is no need for you to keep your eyes on the path, for the young *langur* who is sitting out on the extreme end of a branch on the tree nearest the path will give us warning of the leopard's approach. *Langurs* act differently from red monkeys on seeing a leopard. This may be due to better organization, or to their being less courageous than their red cousins. All the red monkeys in a troupe will chatter and bark at the same time on seeing a leopard, and where the jungle is suitable they will follow it over the tree-tops for considerable distances. The *langurs* act differently. When the young look-out sees the leopard he will give the alarm call of, 'khok, khok, khok', and when the leader of the troupe, taking direction from the young one, sees the leopard and takes up the call the young one will stop. Thereafter only the leader and the oldest female will give the alarm call—the female call resembles a sneeze—and no attempt will be made to follow the leopard. And now the young look-out stands up on all fours, pokes his head forward and jerks it from side to side. Yes, he is convinced he can see the leopard, so he barks, and one or two hysterical companions behind him follow suit. The leader of the troupe now catches sight of the dread enemy and barks, and a second later is followed by the old female whose alarm call, 'tch', resmebles a sneeze. The young ones are now silent and confine themsleves to bobbing their heads up and down, and making faces. The troupe appear to know instinctively that they have nothing to fear from the leopard on this spring morning, for if he had been hungry and out to kill he would not have walked out on to the open watercourse as he has done, but would have crossed either higher up or lower down, and approached them unseen. Being as agile, and little heavier, the leopard experiences no difficulty in catching *langurs*. But it is different with red monkeys, for they retire to the extremities of thin branches, where the leopard is afraid to trust his weight.

With head held high, and the morning sun shining on his beautifully marked coat, the leopard is now crossing the fifty yards of open ground, paying not the slightest attention to the *langurs* clustered on the trees he is approaching. Once he stops, and after looking up and down the watercourse without noticing us as we sit motionless with our backs to the bank, he continues unhurriedly on his way. Climbing the steep bank he disappears from our view, but as long as he is in sight of the leader and of the old female they will continue to send their warning call into the jungle.

Let us now examine the tracks of the leopard. The path where it crosses the watercourse runs over red clay, trodden hard by bare human feet. Over this clay is a coating of fine white dust, so the conditions for our purpose are ideal. We will assume that we did not see the leopard, and that we have come on the tracks by accident. The first thing we note is that the pug marks have every appearance of having been newly made, and therefore that they are fresh. We get this impression from the fact that the pile or nap of the dust where it took the weight of the leopard is laid flat and smooth, and that the walls of the dust surrounding the pads and toes are clear cut and more or less perpendicular.

Presently under the action of the wind and the rays of the hot sun the nap will stand up again and the walls will begin to crumble. Ants and other insects will cross the track; dust will drift into it; bits of grass and dead leaves will be blown on to, or will fall on it; and in time the pug marks will be obliterated. There is no hard-and-fast rule by which you can judge the age of a track, whether it be the pug marks of a leopard or tiger, or the track of a snake or a deer. But by close observation and by taking into consideration the position of the track, whether in an exposed or in a sheltered spot, the time of day and of night when certain insects are on the move, the time at which winds normally blow, and the time at which dew begins to fall or to drip from the trees, you can make a more or less accurate guess when the track was made. In the present case we have satisfied ourselves from the appearance of the track that it is fresh, but this is not the only interesting point about it. We have yet to determine whether the leopard was a male or a female, whether it was old or young, and whether it was a big or a small animal. The round shape of the pug marks show it was a male. The absence of any cracks or creases in the pads, the round toes, and compact appearance of the entire pug marks show that the leopard was young. With regard to size, here again only observation and experience will enable you to judge the size of animals by their pug marks, and when you have gained this experience you can assess the length of either a leopard or a tiger to a possible error of an inch or two. The Koals of Mirzapur, when asked the size of a tiger, measure the pug mark with a blade of grass and then, laying the blade down, measure it with the width of their fingers. How accurate their method is I am not in a position to say. For myself I prefer to guess the size or length of an animal from the general appearance of its pug mark, for whatever method is adopted, it can at best be only a guess.

A little beyond where the path crosses the watercourse there is a narrow strip of firm sand, flanked on one side by rocks and on the other by a high bank. A herd of *cheetal* has gone along this strip of sand. It is always interesting when in a jungle to count the number of animals in a herd, whether *cheetal* or *sambhar*, and to take note of the individual members. This enables you to recognize the herd when you next see it and to assess casualties, and, further, it gives you a friendly feeling towards the herd as being one that you know. If the herd is on open ground it is not difficult to count the stags, note the length and shape of their horns, and count the hinds and young ones. When, however, only one of the herd is visible and the others are in cover, the following method of inducing the hidden animals to come out into the open will, nine times out of ten, be found effective. After stalking to within a reasonable distance of the deer you can see, lie down behind a tree or a bush and give the call of a leopard. All animals can pin-point sound, and when the deer is looking in your direction project your shoulder a little beyond the bole of the tree, and move it slowly up and down once or twice, or shake a few leaves of the bush. On seeing the movement the deer will start calling; and its companions will leave the cover and range themselves on either side of her. I have on occasion got as many as fifty *cheetal* to show themselves in this way to enable me to photograph them at leisure. I would like, however, to add one word of warning. Never try calling like a leopard, or any other animal, unless you are absolutely certain you have the area to yourself, and even then keep a careful look all round. The following is my reason for the warning. I heard a leopard calling repeatedly one night, and from the intonation of the call I concluded it was in distress. Before daylight next morning I set off to try to find out, if I could, what was wrong with the animal. During the night it had changed its position and I now located it on a hill some distance away, where it was still calling. Selecting a spot where a game-track led on to an open glade, and where I would see the leopard before it saw me, I lay down behind a boundary pillar and answered the call. Thereafter, for a matter of half an hour or more, call answered call. The leopard was coming but it was slow about it and was coming very cautiously. Eventually when it was a hundred yards away I stopped calling. I was lying flat down with my elbows resting on the ground and my chin resting in my hands, momentarily expecting the leopard to appear, when I heard the swish of leaves behind me and on turning my head, looked straight into the muzzle of a rifle. Late the previous evening Cassels, Deputy Commissioner of Naini Tal, and Colonel Ward had arrived at the forest bungalow and unknown to me had shot a leopard cub. During the night the mother had been heard calling and at crack of dawn Ward set out on an elephant to try to shoot the mother. Dew was on the ground, and the mahout was well trained, and he brought his elephant up without a sound until only a fringe of trees lay between us. Ward could see me, but he was not as young as he had been and, further, the early morning light was not too good, and he was unable to get the sights of his rifle to bear accurately on my shoulders, so he signalled the elephant to go forward. Mercifully for all of us, when the elephant cleared the fringe of trees and was only ten yards from me, and when the mahout—also an old man—was pointing and Ward was leaning down and aligning his sights for a second time the elephant released a branch it was holding down, and, hearing the sound, I turned my head and looked up into the muzzle of a heavy rifle.

The herd of *cheetal* whose tracks we are looking at and in which we are now interested, went along the strip of sand the previous evening. This you can tell from the night insects that have crossed the tracks, and from the dew drops that have fallen on them from an overhanging tree. The herd may be a mile or five miles away, out on an open glade or hidden in cover; even so, we will count the number of animals in the herd and this I will show you how to do. We will assume that when a *cheetal* is standing, the distance between its hind- and fore-hooves is thirty inches. Take a stick and draw a line across the sand at right angles to the tracks. Measure thirty inches from the line you have drawn, this will be easy for your shoes are ten inches long, and draw a second line across the sand parallel to the first. Now take your stick and count the number of hoof prints between the two lines, marking each print with the point of your stick as you do so. The result of your count is, let us say, thirty. Divide this number by two and you can be *reasonably* sure that there were fifteen *cheetal* in the herd that passed that way the previous evening. This method of counting animals of any species, whether wild or domestic, will give accurate results for small numbers, say up to ten, and approximate results for greater numbers, provided the distance between the hind- and fore-feet is known. In the case of small animals such as wild dogs, pigs, and sheep, the distance will be less than thirty inches, and in the case of large animals such as *sambhar* and domestic cattle it will be more than thirty inches.

For the information of those who were not with me during the years of training for jungle warfare, I should like to assert that it is possible to glean a lot of useful information from the footprints of human beings in a jungle, whether seen on a road, path, or game-track, or in fact anywhere where the footprints of men in motion are to be seen. Let us assume, for the sake of interest, that we are in enemy country and that we have come on a game-track on which there are footprints. From the appearance of the footprints, their size, shape, absence or presence of nails or sprags, iron shod or plain heels, leather soles or rubber, and so on, we conclude that the prints have not been made by members of our own force, but by the enemy. This point being settled we have to determine when the party passed that way, and the number of men in the party. You know how to assess the time. To find out the number of men in the party we will draw a line across the track, and with the toe of one foot on this line take a step of thirty inches, and draw a second line across the track. The number of heel marks between these two lines will give the number of men in the party. There are other interesting things you can learn from the footprints, and one of the most important of these is the speed at which the party was travelling. When a human being is moving at a normal pace his weight is distributed evenly over his footprint and his stride is from thirty to thirty-two inches, according to his height. As the speed is increased less weight falls on the heel and more on the toes, the imprint of the heel gets less and the imprint of the toes greater, and the length of the stride gets longer. This process of less heel and more toes continues to get more apparent until when running at full speed little more than the ball of the foot and the toes come in contact with the ground. If the party was a small one, ten or a dozen in all, it will be possible to see if any were limping, and blood on the track will indicate that one or more were wounded.

If you ever get a flesh wound in the jungles I will show you a small and insignificant little plant that will not only cauterize but also heal your wound better than anything else that I know. The plant, which is found in all jungles, grows to a height of twelve inches, and has a daisylike flower on a long slender stem. The leaves are fleshy and serrated, like the leaf of a chrysanthemum. To use the plant break off a few leaves, rinse them in water to wash off the dust—if water is available—and then squeeze the leaves between finger and thumb, and pour the juice freely into the wound. No further treatment is needed and, if the wound is not a deep one, it will heal in a day or two. The plant is well named, *Brahm Buti*, 'God's flower'.

Many of you were my good comrades in the Indian and Burma jungles during the war years and if I worked you hard, because time was short, you will long since have forgiven me. And I hope you have not forgotten all that we learnt together, as for instance: the fruit and flowers it was safe to eat; where to look for edible roots and tubers; the best substitutes for tea and coffee; what plants, barks, and leaves to use for fever, sores, and sore throats; what barks and creepers to use for stretchers, and for making ropes to sling heavy equipment and guns across streams and ravines; how to avoid getting trench feet and prickly heat; how to create fire; how to obtain dry fuel in a wet forest; how to kill game without resort to fire-arms; how to cook or make a dish of tea without metal utensils; how to procure a substitute for salt; how to treat snake bites, wounds, and stomach disorders. And, finally, how to keep fit and conduct ourselves in the jungles to live at peace with all wildlife. These and many other things you and I, from the mountains and plains of India, from the villages and cities of the United Kingdom, from the United States of America, from Canada, Australia, New Zealand, and from other lands, learned together. Not with the object of spending the rest of our days in the jungles, but to give us confidence in ourselves and in each other, to remove our fears of the unknown, and to show our enemies that you were better men than they. But much as we learned in those days of good comradeship we only touched the fringe of knowledge, for the book of nature has no end as it has no beginning.

We have still much of our spring morning before us, and we have now arrived at the foothills where the vegetation differs from that on the flat ground we have recently traversed. Here there are a number of ficus and plum trees that have attracted a variety of fruit-eating birds, the most interesting of which are the giant hornbills. Hornbills nest in hollow trees and have the unusual habit of sealing the females into the nests. This habit throws a heavy burden on the male, for the female moults and grows enormously fat during the incubation period and when the eggs—usually two—are hatched she is unable to fly, and the male has the strenuous task of providing food for the whole family. By his ungainly appearance, his enormous beak fitted with a sound-box, and his heavy and laboured flight, the hornbill gives the impression of having missed the bus of evolution. And his habit of sealing up the nest and leaving only a small hole through which the female projects the tip of her beak to take the food the male brings her, possibly dates back to prehistoric days when the bird had more powerful enemies than it has today. All birds that nest in hollow trees or that make holes in trees in which to nest, have common enemies. Some of these birds— tits, robins, hoopoes—are quite defenceless and the question therefore arises why the hornbill, who by reason of its powerful beak is best able to defend itself, should be the only one of these many tree-nesting birds to consider it necessary to seal up its nest. Another unusual habit which the hornbill does not share with any other bird that I know of, is its habit of adorning its feathers with pigment. This pigment, which is yellow and can be readily wiped off with a handkerchief, is carried in a small sack above the tail and is laid with the beak on to two broad white bands that extend across the width of the wings. Why the hornbill finds it necessary to paint these white bands yellow with a pigment that washes off every time it rains, I can only attribute to camouflage against an enemy, or enemies, that it suffered from in bygone days. For the only enemy it occasionally suffers from now is a leopard, and against a leopard operating at night camouflage is of little avail.

In addition to the hornbills there are a number of other fruit-eating birds on the ficus and plum trees. Among these are two varieties of green pigeon, the Bengal, and the pintail. Two varieties of barbet, the crimson-breasted, and the common green. Four varieties of *bulbul*, the Himalayan black, common Bengal, red-whiskered, and white-cheeked. Three varieties of paroquets, the rose-ringed, the Alexandrine, and the blossom-headed. Scratching among the dead leaves and eating the ripe fruit dropped by the other birds, are fifty or more white-capped laughing thrushes. These thrushes were the last to migrate from the high nesting-grounds and will be the first to return to them.

Near the ficus trees is a fire-track, and crossing it is a well-worn game-track which runs straight up the hill to a salt-lick near which there is a saucer of water fed by a tiny spring. Between the salt-lick and the water is an old stump. Here a stunted *kusum* tree stood, in the branches of which poachers repeatedly built *machans*. Shooting over salt-licks and over water is prohibited, but poachers are no respecters of game laws, and as dismantling the *machans* had no effect I eventually cut the tree down. I have heard it stated that carnivora do not kill at salt-licks and water holes. However considerate carnivora may be in other parts of the world, in India they certainly have no compunction about killing at salt-licks. In fact it is at these places that they do most of their killing, as you can see from the bones and the horns partly eaten by porcupines that you will find in the vicinity of this salt-lick, and in the vicinity of all salt-licks that are surrounded by forests in which deer and monkeys live.

Let us now climb the hill above the salt-lick to a point from where we can get a bird's eye view of the foothills and the forests that lie at their feet. Before us stretches the forest through which we have just come to our starting-point, the canal. This forest is as nature made it, for it has little timber of commercial value and has, therefore, escaped the devastating hand of man. The light green patches in the foreground are *shisham* saplings which have grown from seeds washed down from the foothills by monsoon floods. Later, when these saplings grow to maturity, they will provide the best timber for cart wheels, and for furniture. The dark-green patches with clusters of red berries are runi trees, which provide the powder known to commerce as *kamala*. When the poor people who migrate in winter from the high hills to the foothills in search of food and warmth——as do the birds——can spare a day from their regular labours, old and young

resort to the jungles to collect *kamala*. *Kamala* is a red powder which adheres to the *runi* berry, and the method of collection is to cut down the branches, strip the berries into big shallow baskets, and then with the hand rub the berries against the sides of the basket. The powder when freed from the berries drifts through the cracks in the basket and is caught on a *cheetal* skin, or square of cloth. A family of five—a man and his wife and three children—working from sunrise to sunset can, when the crop is plentiful, collect four pounds of powder worth from one to two rupees, according to the market price. The powder is used in India and the Middle East for dyeing wool, and until dishonest middlemen started adulterating *kamala* with brick dust, it was extensively used in the United States for colouring butter. The powder is also used for medicinal purposes, and mustard oil in which *runi* berries have been boiled is used for rheumatism.

Interspersed with the *shisham* saplings and *runi* trees, are feathery-leaved *khair* trees. These *khair* trees in addition to providing the foothill villages with plowshares, provide a cottage industry for tens of thousands of poor people in the United Provinces. The industry, which is a winter one and is carried on day and night for a period of four months, produces a commodity known locally as *kach*, and to commerce as catechu. It also produces—as a by-product—the dye known as khaki, used for dyeing cloth and fishing nets. A friend of mine, a man by the name of Mirza, was, I believe, the first to discover khaki dye, and the discovery was accidental. Mirza was one day leaning over an iron pan in which *khair* chips were being boiled, to make *kach*, when a white handkerchief he was carrying fell into the pan. Fishing the handkerchief out with a stick Mirza sent it to the wash. When the handkerchief was brought back Mirza found it had not lost any of its colour, so, reprimanding the washerman, he told him to take it away and clean it. Returning with the handkerchief the washerman said he had tried every method known to his trade of removing stains, but he could not take the colour out of the small square of linen. It was thus that Mirza found he had discovered a fast dye, which is now produced in the flourishing factory he erected at Izattnagar.

Mingled with the many shades of green—for each tree has its own individual colour—are vivid splashes of orange, gold, lilac, pink, and red. The trees with orange coloured flowers are *dhank* (Butea Giondosa) which produces a ruby-coloured gum used for dyeing silk of the finest quality. The trees with the three-foot-long showers of golden bloom are *amaltas* (Cassia Fistula). The two-foot-long cylindrical seedpods of this tree contain a sweet jelly like substance which is used throughout Kumaon as a laxative. The trees with the big lilac coloured flowers are *kachanar* (Bauhinia). The pink are *kusum* trees and the mass of pink shading from delicate shell to deep rose, are not flowers but tender young leaves. The red are *samal* (silk cotton) trees the flowers of which are loved by all birds that drink nectar, and by paroquets and monkeys that eat the fleshy flowers, and by deer and pigs that eat them when they fall to the ground. Later in the year the *samal* flowers will give way to large woody seedpods. When the hot winds blow in April these pods will explode like anti-aircraft shells and a white cloud of silk cotton (kapoc used in life-belts), each section carrying a seed, will drift away in the wind to regenerate nature's garden. All seeds that are not carried from one place to another by birds or animals are provided with buoyant material or with parchment sails or propellers, to enable the winds of heaven to carry them from place to place. There are, of course, exceptions, one of which is the gotail which bears a fruit like a small green apple and which no bird or animal eats. This tree grows on the banks of rivers and the water does for its seeds what birds and animals, and the wind, do for other seeds.

Another is the coconut, which is provided with a husk that enables it to float and be carried by the ocean waves from shore to shore.

Beyond the canal, our starting-point, is our village. The vivid green and gold patches show where the young wheat is sprouting, and where the mustard crop is in full flower. The white line at the foot of the village is the boundary wall, which took ten years to build, and beyond the wall the forest stretches in an unbroken line until it merges into the horizon. To the east and to the west as far as the eye can see is limitless forest, and behind us the hills rise ridge upon ridge to the eternal snows.

Here as we sit in this beautiful and peaceful spot in the shadow of the mighty Himalayas, with the forest round us putting on a new mantle of spring, with every current of wind bringing with it the sweet smell of flowers, and with the air throbbing with the joyful songs of a great multitude of birds, we can forget for a spell the strains and stresses of our world, and savour the world of the jungle folk. For here the law of the jungle prevails. The law that

is older and infinitely better than man-made laws. The law that permits each individual to live his own life, and that anticipates no troubles or sorrows for the mororw. Dangers there are for all, but those dangers only add zest to life, and while keeping every individual alert and on its toes, take nothing from the joy of living. And that there is joy all round you, who can now pin-point sound, recognize every bird and animal from its call, and assign a reason for the call, have ample proof. Away to our left a peacock is screaming his mating call and from that call you know he is dancing, with tail-feathers spread, to impress a bevy of admiring hens. Nearer at hand a jungle-cock is crowing defiance to all and sundry and is being answered by others of his kind who are equally defiant. But of fights there are few, for to fight in the jungle exposes the contestants to danger. Away to our right a *sambhar* stag is warning the jungle folk that the leopard we saw an hour ago is lying out on an exposed spot basking in the sun. The stag will bell until the leopard retires for the day into heavy cover, where he will be screened from the prying eyes of informants. In a thicket below us twenty or more white-eyed tits, white-winged bulbuls, and grey headed flycatchers, have found a spotted owlet dozing in a leafy bower and are calling to companions to come and see what they have found. They know it is safe to approach and scream into the wise one's very ears, for only when he has young will he occasionally kill in daylight. And the owlet on his part knows that no matter how much he is feared and hated by his tormentors, he has nothing to fear from them, and that when they tire of their sport they will leave him to his sleep. In the air all round there is sound, and each sound has a meaning. The liquid notes, the most beautiful of all the songs to be heard in our jungles, is a *shama* wooing a bashful mate. The tap-tap-tapping is a golden-backed woodpecker making a hole in a dead tree for his new home. The harsh braying is a *cheetal* stag challenging a rival to battle. High in the heavens a serpent eagle is screaming, and higher still a flight of vultures are patiently quartering the sky. Yesterday, first a Himalyan blue magpie, and then a pair of crows, showed the vultures where a tiger had hidden his kill in a thicket near where the peacock is now dancing, and today as they circle and soar they are hoping for the same good fortune.

As you sit here, alone or in company with a friend, you can realize to the full what your knowledge of jungle lore means to you, and how greatly that knowledge has added to your confidence and to your pleasure. No longer does the jungle hold any terrors for you, for you know there is nothing for you to be afraid of. If the necessity arose you could live on the jungles, and you could lie down whereever you were and sleep without any feeling of unease. You have learnt to maintain direction, to be conscious at all times of wind direction, and you will never again lose yourself in the jungle no matter whether you move by night or by day. Hard though it was at first to train your eyes, you know now that your field of vision is 180 degrees and that every movement in that field will be seen by you. You can enter into the lives of all the jungle folk, for you have learnt their language; and being able to locate sound, you can follow their every movement. You can now move silently, and shoot accurately, and if the necessity ever arose again for you to face an enemy in the jungles you would not face him with an inferiority complex, but with the full knowledge that no matter what his reputation you are a better-trained man than he is, and have nothing to learn or to fear from him.

It is now time to wend our way home, for we have a long way to go, and Maggie will be waiting breakfast for us. We will return the way we came and as we pass the strip of sand on which we counted the *cheetal* tracks, the path by which the leopard crossed the watercourse, the fine silt washed down from the foothills, and the passage-way under the aqueduct, we will drag a branch behind us. This we will do to obliterate our tracks, and all the tracks we saw this morning so that when we visit the jungle again tomorrow, the next day, or maybe the day after, we will know that all the tracks we see date from the time we last passed that way.

chapter twelve

WHILE ABSORBING JUNGLE LORE IT is possible to develop a sense that has been handed down to us from the days of primitive man and which, for want of a better name, I shall call, Jungle Sensitiveness. This sense, which can be acquired only by living in the jungles in close association with wild life, is the development of the subconscious warning of danger.

Many individuals can testify to having avoided trouble by acting on an impulse that came how they knew not, and that warned their subconscious being against an impending danger. In one case the warning may have been against proceeding along a certain street in which a moment later a bomb exploded; in another, moving just in time from the vicinity of a building wrecked a second later by a shell; or in yet another, stepping away from the shelter of a tree which a moment later was struck by lightning.

Whatever the danger may have been that the impulse enabled
the individual to avoid, it was a *known* and an *anticipated* danger.
In the story of the Chowgarh man-eater I have given two instances
of subconscious warning. At the time the warning was conveyed
to me the whole of my attention was concentrated on avoiding
being killed by the man-eater, and the warning I received that
danger of an attack from a man-eater threatened—in the one
case from a piled-up heap of rocks, and in the other from an
overhanging rock under which I had to pass—was therefore
quite natural and understandable. I should now like to give one
instance of *unconscious* warning of *unsuspected* danger, which I
can only explain as resulting from highly developed jungle
sensitiveness.

It was my custom during the winter months at Kaladhungi
to shoot an occasional *sambhar* or *cheetal* stag for the tenants of
our village. One afternoon a deputation arrived to remind me
that I had shot no meat for some time, and to request me to
shoot a *cheetal* to celebrate a local festival on the morrow. The
jungles were very dry at the time, making stalking difficult, and
the sun had set before I found and shot the stag I was looking
for. Deciding that it was too late to bring in the deer that night
I covered it up to give it a measure of protection against leopard,
bear and pig and made for home, intending to return with a
carrying party early next morning.

My shot had been heard in the village and I found ten or a
dozen men waiting for me on the steps of our cottage, equipped
with ropes and a stout bamboo pole. In reply to their questions
I told them I had shot the deer they wanted, and added that if
they met me at the village gate at sunrise next morning I would
take them to where I had covered it up. The men had come
prepared to bring in the deer that night and they said that if I
would tell them where the deer was they would go out and try

to find it for themselves. On the previous occasions on which I had shot deer for the village, I had laid a trail. The men knew the jungles as well as I did and all the information they needed, when I shot meat for them, was the position of the mark I had made on fire-track, game-path, or cattle-track, and from this mark they would follow the trail I had laid. This system of recovering an animal had never failed, but on the present occasion, having shot the deer late in the evening and there being no moon, I had not laid a trail. The men were anxious to divide up the deer that night in preparation for the feast on the morrow, and as I did not wish to disappoint them I told them to go up the Powalgarh fire-track for two and a half miles and wait for me at the foot of an old *haldu* tree that was a landmark known to all of us. So while the men streamed out of the compound I sat down to a cup of tea Maggie had brewed for me.

A man walking alone can cover the ground much faster than a body of men walking in Indian file, so I did not hurry over my tea, and when I picked up my rifle to follow the men it was quite dark. I had walked a good few miles between sunrise and sunset that day but being as fit as man could be an additional five or six miles meant nothing to me. The men had a good start but they were still some distance from the *haldu* tree when I caught them up. I had no difficulty in finding the deer, and when the men had lashed it to the bamboo pole I took them back by a short cut which reduced the distance by half a mile. It was dinner-time when I got back to our cottage, and telling Maggie I would postpone my bath until bedtime, I asked her to call for dinner while I had a wash.

When undressing to have my bath that night I was very surprised to find that my light rubber-soled shoes were full of red dust, and that my feet were coated with it. I am very careful of my feet and have in consequence never suffered from any form of foot trouble, and I could not understand how I had been so careless as to get my feet all messed up. Small things have a habit of nagging at the memory and the memory in turn nags at the nerves that control the cells in which information is stored, and then, suddenly and without any conscious effort on our part the information we are seeking—be it the name of a person, or of a place, or as in the present case the reason for my messed-up feet—is presented to us.

The old trunk road which carried all the traffic to the hills before the railway to Kathgodam was built, runs in a straight line from our gate to the Boar bridge. Three hundred yards beyond the bridge the road turns to the left. On the right-hand side of this turn the road, at the time I am writing of, was met by the Powalgarh fire-track which for a few hundred yards followed the alignment of the present Powalgarh motor road. Fifty yards from the Boar bridge the trunk road is met on the right by the Kota road coming down from the north. Between the junction of these two roads and the turn, the road runs through a shallow depression. Heavy cart traffic had churned up the red earth in the depression, resulting in the road at this point being six inches deep in dust. To avoid walking in the dust the foot traffic had trodden a narrow path between the dusty road and the jungle on the left. Thirty yards on the near side of the turn, the road and the narrow footpath ran over a small culvert which had parapet walls a foot thick and eighteen inches high, to prevent carts running off the road. The culvert had ceased to function many years previously and at the lower end of it, i.e. the end nearer the narrow footpath, there was a bed of sand eight or ten feet square on a level with the road.

The information concerning my dirty feet that had been brought back to memory was, that when following my men after tea I had left the narrow footpath a few yards on the near side of the culvert; crossed the road from left to right through the six-inch-deep dust; skirted along the right-hand edge of the road and after passing over the culvert, recrossed the road, and continued along the footpath. Why had I done this? From the time I left our cottage, to the time I overtook the men near the *haldu* tree, I had not heard a single sound that had given me even the suspicion of uneasiness, and I had seen nothing, for it was a dark night. Why then had I crossed the road, and after passing over the culvert, recrossed it?

I have stated earlier in this book that from the day I traced the terrifying sound made by Dansay's banshee as the friction of two smooth surfaces, I have made a hobby of finding a reason for every unusual thing I have heard or seen in the jungles. Well, here was something unusual, something that needed an explanation, so before there was any traffic on the road next morning I went out to try to get the explanation.

The men after leaving our gate the previous evening had gone down the road in a bunch and had been joined at the village gate by an additional three men, bringing the number to fourteen. After crossing the Boar bridge the party had proceeded along the footpath in Indian file crossed the culvert, and at the turn crossed from the left to the right of the road, and gone up the fire-track. Shortly thereafter, a tiger came down the Kota road, scratched up the ground near a bush at the junction of the two roads, crossed the trunk road, and proceeded along the footpath. Here the tiger's pug marks were superimposed on the footprints of my men. When the tiger had proceeded along the footpath for about thirty yards, I came over the bridge.

The bridge is an iron one and quite evidently the tiger heard me crossing it, for I was walking fast and making no attempt to

go silently. When the tiger found I was not going up the Kota road, but was coming in his direction, he hurried down the footpath and, leaving it at the culvert, lay down on the patch of sand facing the road and with his head a yard from the footpath. I followed the tiger down the footpath and when I was within five yards of the culvert I turned to the right, crossed the road through the six-inch-deep dust, skirted along the right edge of the road, and after passing over the culvert recrossed the road to the footpath. And this I had done *unconsciously*, to avoid passing within a yard of the tiger.

I believe that if I had continued along the footpath I could have passed the tiger with perfect safety provided (*a*) that I had proceeded steadily on my way, (*b*) that I had made no vocal sound, (*c*) that I had made no violent movement. The tiger had no intention of killing me, but if at the moment of passing him I had stopped to listen to any jungle sound, or had coughed or sneezed or blown my nose, or had thrown the rifle from one shoulder to the other, there was a chance that the tiger would have got nervous and attacked me. My subconscious being was not prepared to take this risk and jungle sensitiveness came to my assistance and guided me away from the potential danger.

On how many occasions jungle sensitiveness has

enabled me to avoid dangers of one kind or another it is not possible for me to say, but from the fact that in all the years I have lived in the jungles I have only once come in actual contact with a wild animal is proof that some sense, call it jungle sensitiveness, or call it my Guardian Angel, has intervened at the critical moment to ensure my safety.

TREE TOPS

INTRODUCTION

JIM CORBETT'S STORY OF THE visit paid by Her Majesty the Queen to Tree Tops in 1952 was written only a short time before his sudden death in Kenya on 19 April 1955. He was then nearing his eightieth year. When he had visited England in 1951 he had shown few signs of his age, but he had in fact never fully recovered from the effects of the severe illness from which he had suffered in Central India, in the course of training British troops in jungle fighting before they took part in the Burma Campaign.

I do not know how far the picture formed of him by his readers differs from that which will live in the memory of his friends. In one respect perhaps the reader who has known him through his books may have some advantage over them. He seldom spoke of the hardships and dangers of those encounters with man-eaters which gave such an incomparable thrill to his record of them. He felt, I think, that these were matters which lay between him and the great beasts whose strength and courage he respected, and whose lapses into ways that were a menace to man he could in due season forget. Many of his acquaintances probably failed to realize that the name and deeds of this quiet and unassuming man were a household word among the hillfolk of the scattered hamlets of Kumaon. I doubt indeed if he would ever have given to the world the earliest of his books, *Man-eaters of Kumaon*, in 1944, had he not hoped that its publication might contribute something to the funds of St. Dunstan's, which had in the previous year opened a training school for blinded Indian soldiers. I remember how modest was his own estimate of what this contribution might be. He did not realize how enthralling were the stories he had to tell, nor how greatly their interest would be enhanced by his manner of telling them. Yet, as the world was soon to acknowledge, he possessed, in fact, that supreme art of narrative which owes nothing to conscious artistry.

Since, however, he is necessarily the centre of his own stories, they have much to reveal of his own history and way of life. Those who have read *My India* and *Jungle Lore* will not need to be told that he was one of a large family and was brought up during the summer months at the Himalayan hill station of Naini Tal, and in the winter on the small property held by his family at Kaladhungi in the foothills below it. Sport was in his blood, and from boyhood he set himself to gain that intimacy with the jungle and its life that he would need if he was to enjoy such sport as his modest means allowed. He never forgot in after life that habit which he then taught himself of noiseless movement in the jungle nor his rare

understanding of its sights and
sounds, and it was then that he
began to acquire that unique
combination of speed and accuracy
in the use of the rifle to which he
was later to owe so much. One
who knew him at that period has
said, however, that even in his youth
he took no special pride in this

achievement. Good shooting was to him an obligation rather
than an accomplishment. If things were to be killed, then this
should be done instantly, and without pain to them.

As soon as he left school at Naini Tal, he found employment
with the Railway Department, at first in small posts but
afterwards in charge of the transport at Mokameh Ghat, where
the Ganges River created a broad gap between the two railway
systems. There is a great bridge over the river now, but at that
time more than half a million tons of traffic were ferried across
it every year, and had to be transhipped from one gauge of rails
to another. The conditions of work were exceptionally arduous,
and that he carried it on for over twenty years was due not
only to his power of physical endurance, but to his friendly
personal contacts with the large force of Indian labour which
he employed as contractor. They gave an unmistakable proof
of their own feelings for him during the First World War. He
helped to raise a Kumaon Labour Corps for service overseas,
and took his section of it to France. It was then that his
Indian subordinates at Mokameh Ghat arranged with the
labourers that they would together carry on the work on his
behalf throughout his absence. In the War he was given the
substantive rank of Major in the Indian Army.

The nature of the work during these years gave him little leisure for sport, but during his holidays in Kumaon he was able on three occasions to answer the calls which were made on him for his help against man-eaters. Between the years 1907 and 1911 he disposed of the Champawat and Muktesar man-eaters and the Panar leopard. The first and last of these marauders were believed to have killed between them no fewer than 836 human beings, and they were perhaps the worst of the man-eaters from which Kumaon suffered in our generation, though others of a later date became more notorious. The leopard of Rudraprayag, for instance, which was officially recorded to have killed 150 human beings, acquired so wide a reputation in India because it preyed on the pilgrims who followed the route to a well-known Hindu shrine.

With his retirement from his work at Mokameh Ghat there began a new chapter in his life. He was now his own master. His requirements were simple; he was unmarried, but he had at Naini Tal and Kaladhungi the devoted companionship of two sisters, one of whom (the Maggie to whom he so often refers) has survived him. It was now that there occurred the majority of the encounters with man-eaters of which he has written in his books. The passing of the years did nothing to diminish the energy or the courage which he devoted to this task. The disposal of the Rudraprayag leopard, with its long tale of hard living and of sleepless nights, when Corbett was almost as often the hunted as the hunter, took place when he was fifty-one. The killing of the Thak tiger occurred when he was sixty-three. There seemed to be no limit to his endurance of fatigue or his ability to meet unruffled what seemed to be misfortune or mishap.

But there was another aspect also in the life which he now led. It seemed that sport, in the sense that the word is commonly used, had ceased to hold first place with him. So far as he was concerned, the tiger and the leopard at all events were immune, unless they were taking human life. Often when he and I were together, we were visited by deputations of the hillfolk asking for help; to be more correct, it was he that they sought out. He it was, as all their world knew, who had so often ventured his own life to save others in Kumaon from a Terror which filled their days and nights with fear. There was indeed here something that passed the ordinary bounds of human fear, for the ways of the ancient gods of the hills are unpredictable, and who could tell that the Terror was not a visitation from them? But the rubric that Corbett applied to the inquisition which was now opened was strict, however friendly and considerate in its terms. It was no use for them to plead their losses in cattle or goats. The tiger was lord of the jungle and must have its dues. Not until he himself was convinced that a tiger had been killing human beings, not by chance or in anger, but because it sought them as food, would he agree to come to their help.

One noticed, too, that the keen observation of jungle life that had once seemed to minister to sport now became of increasing interest for its own sake. There could be nothing more enjoyable than to spend in his company long days on the hillside or in the jungle, where every twisted twig, every call of bird or animal, seemed to carry its own meaning to him; or, if the interpretation was not at once clear, would provide him with matter for most engaging speculation. For him, this was not nature study, it was his world, and these were the things that meant life and death to its inhabitants. Photography became of greater concern than shooting. I recall an occasion when I chanced on him as he emerged in some apparent disorder from a tangled thicket in the jungle near Kaladhungi. He explained that he had been trying to get a picture of a tigress, but she was in a bad temper, and as often as he went into the thicket she drove him out again. He added, however, as one who was ready to make due allowances, that she had her cubs with her. This seemed to be typical of the terms on which he now stood with the animals of Kumaon. There was an understanding which would justify the tigress in demonstrating against the intrusion on her nursery. But the matter need not be carried further.

When during the Second World War he gave the Government his services in training troops in jungle fighting, he received the honorary rank of Lieutenant-Colonel, and in 1946 there was conferred on him the distinction of the Companionship of the Indian Empire. The Government had previously allowed him a privilege which he valued very highly when it gave him the 'freedom of the jungle', or, in other words, the liberty of entry to all its Forest Reserves. I do not need to speak here of the regard in which he came to be held by the people of Kumaon. As kindly and generous as he was fearless, he gave freely of himself, and asked nothing in return. But I think that in the olden days he would have been one of the small band of Europeans whose memory has been worshipped by the Indians as that of men who were in some measures also gods.

When so many of his friends left India in 1947, he and his sister decided to leave also, and made their home at Nyeri in Kenya. It could not have been an easy decision for him to make. He loved his home in Kaladhungi as greatly as he was himself beloved by its villagers. But Kenya could at all events minister to his passion for photographing wild life, and he was able to indulge it to the full. The proximity of Tree Tops to Nyeri made him a frequent visitor there, and it is pleasant to know that we have now his own story of the visit of Her Majesty the Queen to the Tree Tops, for the letters which he wrote at the time to his friends showed how very deeply moved he was by his experiences as a member of her party.

HAILEY

London
September 1955

TREE TOPS

A BRILLIANT SUN WAS SHINING in a deep blue sky and the air was crisp and invigorating, on that fifth day of February 1952.

I was standing on a wooden platform, thirty feet above ground, and before me stretched an oval-shaped clearing in the forest, two hundred yards long and a hundred yards wide. A miniature lake with tall tufts of grass dotted on it occupied two-thirds of this open space, the rest consisted of a salt-lick. On the farther margin of the lake a snow-white heron stood motionless, waiting patiently for the approach of unwary frogs, and in the open water in front of it a pair of dabchicks were taking their young brood of four, which looked no bigger than marbles, on what was evidently their first excursion into a danger-filled world. On the salt-lick a solitary rhino was moving restlessly, occasionally stooping to lick the salt ground and then throwing his head to snuff the wind that was blowing down towards him from the forest.

The lake and the salt-lick were surrounded on three sides by dense tree forests and on the fourth, and farthest from me, by a hundred-yard-wide strip of grass which came right down to the margin of the lake. Beyond the strip of grass, and forming a frame for it, was a belt of Cape Chestnuts. These chestnuts were in full bloom, and sporting among the blue tinged with purple flowers was a troop of colobus monkeys which, with their flowing white tails and long white mantles hanging from their shoulders, looked like giant butterflies as they flitted from tree to tree. A more beautiful and a more peaceful scene it would not have been possible to conceive; and yet not all was peace, for in the dense forest beyond the monkeys was a herd of elephants and in the herd was discord. Every few minutes the air was rent by loud trumpeting mingled with the screaming and deep rumbling of angry elephants. As the sounds of strife drew nearer, the monkeys collected in a group and after barking in alarm flitted away over the tree-tops, led by a mother who had a young babe clinging to her breast. The solitary rhino now decided his need of salt had been met and snorting his defiance he turned in one movement, as only a rhino can turn, and with head held high and tail in the air, trotted into the forest on the left. Only the heron, still patient and unrewarded, and the family of dabchicks, remained unaffected by the approaching herd. Presently out of the dense forest the elephants began to appear, not in Indian file but on a broad front of fifty yards. Silent now, and unhurried, in twos and threes they drifted on to the bush-dotted strip of grass, while my eyes ranged back and forth

until I had counted forty-seven. The last to come into the open were three bulls, one quite evidently the master of the herd and the other two younger brothers, or possibly sons, who were approaching the time when they would wrest the mastery of the herd from their elder, and drive him into exile.

At the far end of the platform on which I was standing a short flight of steps led up into the hut which is known to all the world as 'Tree Tops'. The hut is built in the upper branches of a giant ficus tree and is only accessible by a steep and narrow thirty-foot-long ladder. Time was when, for the safety of the occupants of the hut, the foot of the ladder was cranked by a winch into the upper branches of an adjoining tree, but this safety device had long since been discontinued. The accommodation of the hut consisted of a dining-room, in one corner of which was recessed a wood-burning stove, three bedrooms for visitors, a narrow slip of a room for the White Hunter, and a long open balcony provided with comfortable cushioned seats. From the balcony there was a clear and uninterrupted view of the miniature lake, the salt-lick, and of the forest beyond, with the Aberdare mountains in the background rising to a height of 14,000 feet.

* * *

PRINCESS ELIZABETH and the Duke of Edinburgh had arrived at the Royal Lodge, Sagana, twenty miles from Nyeri, two days before, and on that February morning I had just finished shaving when I received a breathtaking telephone message informing me that Her Royal Highness had been graciously pleased to invite me to accompany her to Tree Tops. The Royal Party were to leave the Lodge at 1 p.m. and, driving slowly, arrive at 2 p.m. at Tree Tops where I was to meet them.

Nyeri has one of the finest polo grounds in Kenya and the previous day a match in which the Duke had taken part had been played there, with the Princess watching. The Polo ground is eight miles from Nyeri and fifteen miles from the Royal Lodge, and is surrounded on three sides by forest and high grass. Neither my sister Maggie nor I feel happy in a crowd, so while the populace from far and wide was collecting at the polo ground for the great event, we motored to a bridge spanning a deep ravine which runs through dense forest towards the ground. Though a state of emergency had not up to that time been declared, security measures were being taken, for the unrest had started and there had been in the neighbourhood a number of cases of arson about which the press, for obvious reasons, had kept silent. I was uneasy about the deep ravine which afforded an easy approach to the polo ground. However, on

examining the stretches of sand in it I was relieved to find
no footprints, so we spent the rest of the evening near the
bridge, keeping watch on the ravine. This accounts for our
absence from the polo match.

*   *   *

AFTER receiving the telephone message I shaved a second
time, had breakfast, and then went to the administrative
headquarters to get a road pass, for I had to use the road
that had been closed for the Royal Party. At midday I motored
eight miles along the main road and, leaving it at the polo
ground, took a rough track which runs for two miles up a
narrow valley to the foot of the Tree Tops hill. Here, where
the track ends and a narrow footpath winds up the hill through
dense cover of six hundred yards to Tree Tops, I removed my
handbag and British warm from the car, and sent it back to
Nyeri. To a number of trees adjoining the path, slats of wood
had been nailed to form ladders as a means of escape in the
event of attack by elephants, rhino, or buffaloes. It is a
sobering fact that two days after the path had been traversed
by the Princess and her party, four of the biggest trees to
which ladders were nailed were uprooted by elephants.

*   *   *

It was now 1.30 p.m. on that fifth day of February, and 2 p.m. was zero hour. The elephants, still silent and peaceful, were quietly browsing on the grass and bushes while slowly drifting down towards the lake, and it was possible to observe them more closely. They were of all sizes and of all ages, and five of the cows were accompanied by calves only a few weeks old. These five cows, and the three bulls, who were in that seasonal condition known as 'must', were a potential danger. However, if the herd remained on the far side of the lake for another thirty minutes, all would be well. The minutes dragged by, as they do in times of strain, and when only fifteen remained the elephants started to edge down towards the salt-lick. This salt-lick extended to within a few yards of the ficus tree, and from the projecting balcony it was possible to drop a handkerchief on to any animal on the lick below. Between the lick and the tree a few small branches had been laid, to form a screen for people approaching the ladder leading to the hut above. These branches had been crushed down by elephants and other animals and, at the time I am writing of, the screen was a screen only in name.

On the platform, with the passing of every moment, my anxiety was growing. The herd of forty-seven elephants was crowded together on the salt-lick. It was zero hour and the Royal Party, if it was up to time, would now be on the path, and at the moment the big bull elephant, annoyed by the attention the two young bulls were paying to one of the cows, charged them and all three enraged animals dashed into the forest on the left, trumpeting and screaming with rage, and started to circle round at the back of Tree Tops, *and in the direction of the path*. Would the escort with the Royal Party, on hearing the elephants, decide that it was too dangerous to go forward and so return to the comparative safety of the open ground where they had alighted from their cars, or would they take the risk of trying to reach the ladder leading up to the hut? Crossing the platform, I peered into the forest. From the foot of the ladder the path ran for forty yards in a straight line, and then curved out of sight to the left. Terrifying sounds were to be heard in plenty but nothing was to be seen on the path, and there was nothing that could be done. Presently I caught sight of a man carrying a rifle at the ready, followed closely by a small trim figure. The party had arrived, and on reaching the bend in the path, from where the elephants on the salt-lick were in full view, came to a halt. No time was to be lost, so, slipping down the ladder, I approached the small figure which, from her photographs, I recognized as Princess Elizabeth. Smiling her greeting, and without a moment's hesitation, the Princess walked unhurriedly straight towards the elephants which were now crowded at the end of the salt-lick, and within ten yards of the foot of the ladder. Handing her handbag and camera to me, the Princess climbed

the steep ladder, followed by Lady Pamela Mountbatten, the Duke, and Commander Parker. The escort, led by Edward Windley, then turned and retraced their steps down the footpath.

In the course of a long lifetime I have seen some courageous acts, but few to compare with what I witnessed on that fifth day of February. The Princess and her companions, who had never previously been on foot in an African forest, had set out that glorious day to go peacefully to Tree Tops and, from the moment they left, their ears had been assailed—as they told me later—by the rampaging of angry elephants. In single file, and through dense bush where visibility in places was limited to a yard or two, they went towards those sounds, which grew more awe-inspiring the nearer they approached them. And then, when they came to the bend in the path and within sight of the elephants, they found that they would have to approach within ten yards of them to reach the safety of the ladder. A minute after climbing the ladder the Princess was sitting on the balcony and, with steady hands, was filming the elephants.

It was not usual for elephants to be seen at Tree Tops at that time of the day and, while they were being filmed, they did all that elephants could be expected to do. The old bull returned to the herd, followed at a respectful distance by the two young bulls, and he again chased them away, to the accompaniment of loud trumpeting and angry screaming. A flock of doves alighted on an open patch of ground, and on seeing them one of the elephants filled its trunk with dust and, cautiously approaching, discharged the dust at them, for all the world like a man discharging a gun loaded with black powder. The doves were doing no harm and it was out of sheer mischief that the elephant frightened them away, for after doing so it flicked its trunk up and down as if laughing and

flapped its ears with delight. The Duke witnessed this
side-play with great amusement and when the doves
returned and the same elephant, or it may have
been another, again sucked dust into its trunk
and approached the birds he drew the Princess's
attention to the scene, which she filmed. A cow
elephant now came towards us with the
smallest of the calves close to her side.
Stopping a few yards in front of the balcony
the mother pressed the damp tip of her trunk

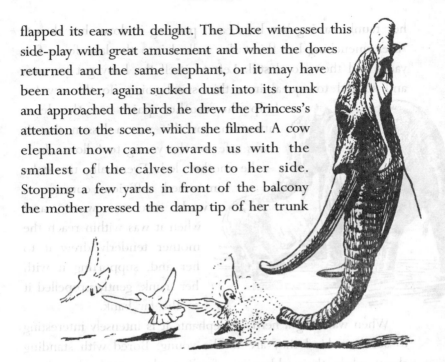

on to the salt-impregnated dust, and then conveyed it to her
mouth. The calf, taking advantage of its mother's
preoccupation, inserted its head under her left foreleg and
started to suckle. Greatly interested in this filial scene the
Princess, who had her eye to her cine-camera, exclaimed, 'Oh,
look. It is going to drive the baby away!' This was said as a
small elephant, three or four years of age, trotted up to the
mother and inserting its head under her right foreleg, also
started to feed. The mother stood perfectly still while the meal
was in progress and when the baby and its sister had had
enough, or possibly when there was no more to be had, the
mother disengaged herself and passing under the balcony,
accompanied by the baby, went out on to a spit of land jutting
into the lake. Here she had a drink, sucking the water into

her trunk, raising her head, and pouring it down her throat.
After quenching her thirst she walked into the lake for a few
yards and then stood still. Left to itself the baby got nervous
and started to squeal in a thin small voice. To the cry for
help the mother paid not the least
attention, for this was a lesson that it
was safe for the young to follow where
the mother led. Eventually the baby
summoned sufficient courage to
wade into the water, and
when it was within reach the
mother tenderly drew it to
her and, supporting it with
her trunk, gently propelled it
to the far bank.

When watching a herd of elephants it is intensely interesting
to see how kind they are to the young. Bored with standing
about while their elders are feeding, the young play about
and get in the way. When this happens, even with great
terrifying-looking bulls, the young are gently put aside, and
are never struck or trodden on. Of all the animals in the
wild, elephants have the most real family or herd life. When
a female retires for maternity reasons the elders
of her own sex are always on hand to keep
her company and to protect the young, and
until the new arrival is able to walk the herd
remains in the vicinity. If young or old get into
difficulties or are threatened with danger, real
or imaginary, the others rally round to give
what help they can. It is for this reason that herds in
which there are young are avoided, and it was for the
same reason that the approach to the ladder was dangerous,

for if the wind had changed, or if a nervous cow with a very young calf had seen the party, there would have been grave risk of an attack. Fortunately the wind did not change and by approaching the elephants unhurriedly and noiselessly the Princess and her companions avoided detection.

Karra, a big male baboon who had recently lost a part of his upper lip in a fight, which gave him a very sinister look, now led his family of eleven down a forest track to the edge of the salt-lick. Here they halted, for elephants dislike baboons and I have seen them chase such a family into trees and then shake the trees in an attempt to dislodge them. Karra was taking no risks on this occasion. After surveying the scene he led his family back into the forest and, circling round the salt-lick, approached the ficus tree from the left. A bold young female now left the family and, climbing one of the wooden supports of the hut, arrived on the balcony. Running along the railing, and avoiding dislodging the cameras and field-glasses placed on it, she gained a branch of the ficus tree jutting out from the hut. Here she was rewarded with a sweet potato nearly as big as her head and while she sat contentedly peeling it with her teeth was filmed and photographed at a range of a few feet.

* * *

TIME slipped by unnoticed, and when the Princess was told that tea was ready in the dinning room, she said, 'Oh, please may I have it here? I don't want to miss one moment of this.' While tea was being taken, the elephants drifted off the salt-lick, some going into the forest on the left, and others passing under the balcony and going along the shore of the lake to the right.

The Princess had laid her tea-cup aside and was looking at a sheaf of photographs, when I saw two male waterbuck racing at full speed down a forest glade towards the salt-lick. On my drawing the Princess's attention to the two animals, she reached for her camera, and the photographs slipped from her lap to the floor. Saying a word or two, amply justified in the circumstances, the Princess got her camera to her eye just as the two bucks, with only a length between them, dashed with a great splash into the lake. When the leading one had covered about forty yards it stumbled over a sunken tree-stump, and without a moment's hesitation the one behind plunged its horns into it. One horn entered the unfortunate animal's left buttock, while the other went between its legs and into its stomach. So firmly fixed were the horns that their owner was dragged forward for a short distance before it could free itself. The wounded animal plunged on until it reached the shelter of a big tuft of grass. Here where the water was up to the neck it halted, while the aggressor circled round through shallow water and after shaking its head in defiance walked off into the forest. This incident, which was evidently the final act in a battle that had started in the forest, had been filmed by the Princess and now, laying her camera aside, she picked up her field-glasses. Presently passing the glasses to me, she asked, 'Is that blood? Do you think it will die?' Yes, it was blood. The water all round was red with it and, judging by the laboured way in which the stricken animal was breathing, I said I thought it would die.

Karra and his family, who had been joined at the salt-lick by five warthogs and a dainty young doe bushbuck, were now causing a diversion.

Two teenage females were competing for the affection of a boy friend, whom both of them claimed, and this was causing

angry scenes and a lot of screaming. Karra would have settled
the dispute by chastising all three of the young ones if he
had not at the time been contentedly lying in the sun—being
filmed—while one of his wives ran her fingers through his
thick fur, looking for the things that were irritating his skin
and which it was her wifely duty to find and remove. While
this was going on, the five warthogs were down on their knees
cropping the short grass on the edge of the salt-lick, and the
youngest of Karra's children was industriously trying to climb
up the young doe's hindlegs in order to catch its tail. Every
time an attempt was made the doe skipped aside, enjoying
the game as much as the onlookers.

Neither the Princess nor the Duke smokes, so, as I am
addicted to this pernicious habit, I left my seat near the
Princess and went to the end of the balcony,
where I was presently joined by the Duke.
In the course of our conversation I told
him that I knew Eric Shipton, that I
had read the articles in *The Times* relating
to the Abominable Snowman, and that
I had seen the photographs taken by
Shipton of the footprints in the snow.
Asked if I had any theories about the
Abominable Snowman, I told the Duke,
much to his amusement, that I did
not believe that the tracks in the
snow photographed by Shipton
had been made by a four-legged
creature, and that while I would
not dream of accusing Shipton
of a leg-pull, I had a
suspicion that his own

leg had been pulled. I went on to say that knowing the great interest that was being taken in the snowman I was disappointed that Shipton had not followed the tracks back to see where they had come from, and forward to see where they led to. This, the Duke said, was a question he himself had put to Shipton, and that Shipton had told him the tracks had come from the direction of windswept rocks which had no snow on them, and that they led to other rocks devoid of snow where it was not possible to follow them.

* * *

WITH the passage of time, the shadows were beginning to lengthen. More animals, more in fact than had ever before been seen at Tree Tops, were coming out of the forest on to the open ground. In the slanting rays of the sun these animals, together with the massed bloom of the Cape Chestnuts, reflected in the still water of the lake, presented a picture of peace and of beauty which only an inspired artist could have painted, and to which no words of mine could do justice.

On rejoining the Princess she again handed me her field-glasses, and said, 'I think the poor thing is dead.' The stricken waterbuck did indeed look dead, but presently it raised its head from the tuft of grass on which it was resting and, struggling to the bank, lay with its neck stretched out and its chin resting on the ground. After it had been lying without movement in this position for a few minutes, three elephants went up and, stretching out their trunks, smelt it from head to tail. Not liking what they smelt they shook their heads in disapproval and quietly walked away. From the fact that the buck had not reacted in any way to the presence of the elephants we concluded that it was now dead, so Commander Parker and I

air of the forest had given everyone a keen appetite. While coffee was being made on the table, the spirit lamp caught fire, and was swept off the table on to the grass-matted floor. As frantic efforts were being made to stamp out the blaze the African boy who had served dinner unhurriedly came forward, extinguished the flames with a wet cloth, retired to his cubbyhole behind the stove, and a minute later replaced the lamp refilled and relit on the table. Not long after, Tree Tops was raided and that very efficient boy was carried off, together with all the bedding, provisions, cooking utensils, and other movable articles in the hut, and it is left to conjecture whether the boy's bones are bleaching in the African sun, or whether he became a terrorist.

After dinner the Princess and her party returned to the balcony. In the dim light of the moon nine rhino could be seen on the salt-lick. The heron and the family of dabchicks, the elephants, and the other animals, had all retired and the frogs that had been so vocal earlier were now silent.

Leaving the Royal Party on the balcony, where they stayed until the moon set, and taking my old British warm which had served me well during the war years, I went down and made myself comfortable on the top step of the thirty-foot ladder. I had spent so many long nights on the branches of trees that a few hours on the step of a ladder was no hardship; in fact it was on this occasion a pleasure. A pleasure to feel that I would have the honour of guarding for one night the life of a very gracious lady who, in God's good time, would sit on the throne of England. And after that day of days I needed to be left in quietness with my thoughts.

The moon set and in the heart of the forest the night was intensely dark. Visibility was nil but that did not matter, for with the exception of a snake nothing could climb the ladder without my feeling the vibration. Within a few inches of my face, and visible against the sky through a break in the foliage of the ficus tree, was hanging a manila rope which went over a pulley and was used for hauling up baggage and provisions from the ground to the room above. Presently, and without my having heard a sound, this rope was agitated. Something moving on soft feet had laid a hand on it, or had brushed against it. A few tense moments passed, but there was no vibration on the ladder, and then the rope was agitated again for the second time. Possibly one of the leopards whose pug marks I had seen on the path had come to the ladder and on finding it occupied had gone away. The ladder, though steep, would have offered no obstacle to an animal with the climbing ability of a leopard, and for all I knew to the contrary the platform above me may have been used by leopards as an observation post, or as a place on which to sleep at night. In contrast with an Indian jungle the African forest is disappointingly silent at night and, except for an occasional quarrel among the rhinos, all I heard throughout the night was the mournful call of a hyena, the bark of a bushbuck, and the cry of a tree hyrax.

At the first glimmer of dawn I washed and shaved, and on going up to the hut found the Princess sitting on the balcony with a meter in her hand, testing the light before making a film record of an old rhino that was on the salt-lick. Daylight comes rapidly in Africa, and when the first rays of the sun lit up the scene before her, the Princess started to take the picture she had been waiting for. While she was filming the rhino the Duke drew her attention to a second rhino that was coming down to the salt-lick. The two animals were evidently old enemies, for they ran at each other in a very aggressive manner and for a time it appeared that a great fight would be staged for the benefit of the Royal onlookers. Advancing and retreating like experienced boxers manoeuvring for position, the two rhinos sparred round each other until the newcomer decided 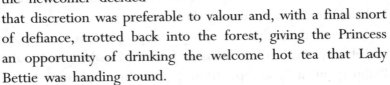 that discretion was preferable to valour and, with a final snort of defiance, trotted back into the forest, giving the Princess an opportunity of drinking the welcome hot tea that Lady Bettie was handing round.

Though she had spent so few hours in sleep the Princess had started that second day with eyes sparkling and a face as fresh as a flower. No artificial aids were needed or used to enhance the bloom on her cheeks. Many years previously I had stood one winter's day on the banks of the Ganges with the Princess's grandfather, and looking at her now it was easy to see from whom she had inherited her beautiful colouring.

With the rhinos gone and only the white heron standing motionless on the margin of the lake and the family of dabchicks cutting furrows across its smooth surface, cameras and field-glasses were put away and we went to the dining-room for breakfast, which consisted of scrambled eggs and bacon, toast, marmalade, and coffee made this time without mishap, and the choicest and most luscious fruit that Africa could provide. There was no need now to talk in hushed voices, and as we finished breakfast I remarked that the Princess was the only member of her family who had ever slept in a tree, or eaten a dinner and a breakfast prepared in one.

The escort that was to conduct the Royal Party through the forest to the waiting cars now arrived, led by Edward Windley, and as the radiantly happy Princess drove away she waved her hand and called out, 'I will come again.' Soon after her return to the Royal Lodge the Princess was told that her father, of whom she had spoken with such affection and pride, had died in his sleep during the previous night.

I do not think that any two young people have ever spent such happy and carefree hours as Princess Elizabeth and Duke Philip spent at Tree Tops, from 2 p.m. on 5 February to 10 a.m. on 6 February. For myself, those hours that I was honoured and privileged to spend in their company will remain with me while memory lasts.

A register is kept of visitors to Tree Tops, and of the animals seen. The day after the Princess Visited Tree Tops the register was brought to me to write up. After recording the names of the Royal Party, the animals seen, and the incidents connected with them, I wrote;

For the first time in the history of the world a young girl climbed into a tree one day a Princess, and after having what she described as her most thrilling experience she climbed down from the tree the next day a Queen—God bless her.

* * *

ALL that now remains of the ficus tree and the hut honoured by Princess Elizabeth and the Duke of Edinburgh, and visited for a quarter of a century by thousands of people from all parts of the world, is a dead and blackened stump standing in a bed of ashes. From those ashes a new Tree Tops will one day arise, and from another balcony a new generation will view other birds and animals. But for those of us who knew the grand old tree and the friendly hut, Tree Tops has gone for ever.

NYERI
6 April 1955

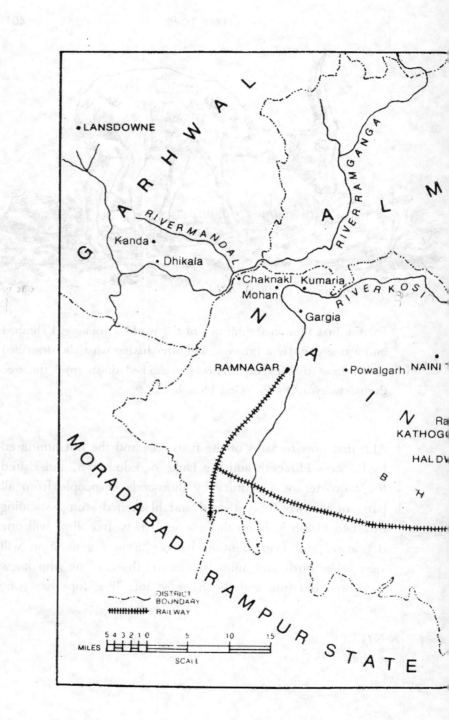

GARHWAL

• LANSDOWNE

RIVER MANDAL

Kanda •

• Dhikala

• Chaknaki   Kumaria

Mohan •

• Gargia

RAMNAGAR •

N A I N I

RIVER RAMGANGA

A L M

RIVER KOSI

• Powalgarh   NAINI

N   Ra

KATHGO

HALDW

B

H

MORADABAD   RAMPUR STATE

DISTRICT
BOUNDARY
RAILWAY

5 4 3 2 1 0   5   10   15
MILES
SCALE

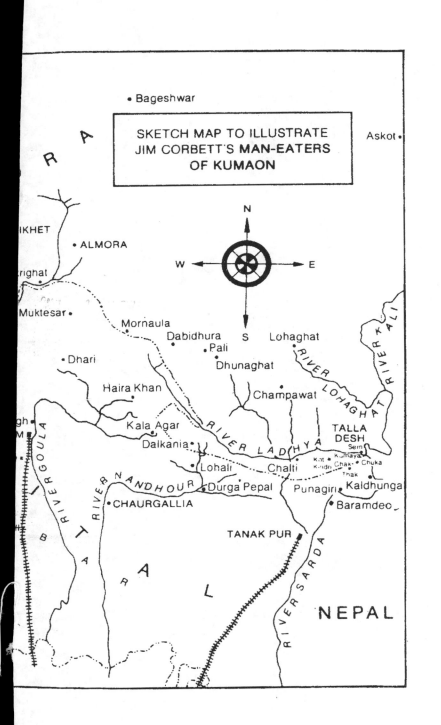

• Bageshwar

SKETCH MAP TO ILLUSTRATE
JIM CORBETT'S **MAN-EATERS**
OF KUMAON

Askot •

R A

R

IKHET

• ALMORA

rīghat

Muktesar •

N

W ← → E

S

Mornaula

Dabidhura

• Pali

Lohaghat

Dhunaghat

RIVER LOHAGHAT

RIVER KALI

• Dhari

Haira Khan

Champawat

gh •
M

Kala Agar

Dalkania •

RIVER LADHYA

TALLA
DESH

Sem

Kumaya
Kot • Chak- • Chuka
Kindo Chak
Thak

RIVER GOULA

RIVER NANDHOUR

• Lohali

Chalti

• Durga Pepal

Punagiri

Kaldhunga

• CHAURGALLIA

B

T

A

R

A

L

TANAK PUR

• Baramdeo

RIVER SARDA

NEPAL